MW00512594

KARL RAHNER'S
THEOLOGICAL AESTHETICS

KARL RAHNER'S
THEOLOGICAL AESTHETICS

PETER JOSEPH FRITZ

THE CATHOLIC UNIVERSITY OF AMERICA PRESS
WASHINGTON, D.C.

Library of Congress Cataloging-in-Publication Data

Fritz, Peter Joseph.

Karl Rahner's theological aesthetics / Peter Joseph Fritz.

pages cm

Includes bibliographical references and index.

ISBN 978-0-8132-2593-7 (cloth : alk. paper)

1. Rahner, Karl, 1904–1984.   2. Aesthetics — Religious
aspects — Christianity.   I. Title.

BX4705.R287F75 2014

230'.2092 — dc23   2013041582

FOR ROCHELLE AND ZEPHANIAH

The Lord, your God, is in your midst,
a mighty savior;
He will rejoice over you with gladness,
and renew you in his love,
He will sing joyfully because of you,
as one sings at festivals.

(Zep 3:17–18)

CONTENTS

ACKNOWLEDGMENTS

Very little else in this book will be understated, but given the prodigious debts of gratitude I owe, even this lengthy set of acknowledgments can be nothing other than an understatement.

To my teachers: Cyril O'Regan directed the dissertation that became a preliminary step on the way to this book. His prodding me during my doctoral candidacy exams to rethink Rahner in terms of theological aesthetics and his relationship to Heidegger opened a world of thought for me. Cyril's careful guidance helped me to navigate this world sensibly and, I hope, effectively. His generosity and friendship, which have manifested itself in numerous other forms over the past several years, have made me forever grateful. Lawrence Cunningham's encouragement and, on occasion, forthright criticism kept me enthusiastic yet careful as I researched and wrote this book. Matthew Ashley's praise of my reading of Rahner heartened me, but his challenges to it made all the difference. Chapter 3 of this book could not have been written without our detailed conversations in March and April of 2010. His gracious invitation to lead a session of his doctoral seminar on Rahner in April 2011 afforded me the invaluable opportunity of presenting Rahner's theological aesthetics to graduate students. Mary Catherine Hilkert and Robert Krieg also made distinctive marks on my interpretation of Rahner. Robert Imbelli at Boston College deserves prominent mention. He introduced me to Rahner—particularly how to think critically about him.

To my classmates from Notre Dame, especially John Thiede, Steven Battin, and Joél Schmidt: thank you for accompanying me along the way, from our first doctoral seminars to the opening years of our professorial careers. Your patient listening, careful consideration, demanding questions, and devoted friendship have indelibly marked my thinking in this book.

To my colleagues at the College of the Holy Cross, especially Alice Laffey, William Reiser, Alan Avery-Peck, Joanne Pierce, Matthew Eggemeier, John Gavin, Robert Green, John Manoussakis, Joseph Lawrence, and the other members of the Religious Studies and Philosophy Departments: you have welcomed me into a wonderful community of scholars. For this, I feel profound gratitude. I shall foreground Matthew Eggemeier here, since he has been both classmate (at Notre Dame) and colleague (at Holy Cross) to me, and since he so kindly endured reading the entire manuscript before I sent it to press. Matt's exacting reading, probing queries, and insightful suggestions strengthened this book immeasurably. At many of its key junctures, Matt's influence is substantially present. For your friendship and collegiality, Matt, thank you.

To my colleagues in the Karl Rahner Society (KRS): I owe special thanks to Leo O'Donovan, Richard Lennan, Ann Riggs, Robert Masson, and Thomas O'Meara, all of whom have directly and positively affected my research and writing on Rahner. Of particular mention here is Leo O'Donovan, whose intensive mentorship while I was preparing a manuscript for *Theological Studies* in the fall of 2011 I shall always consider a turning point in my career as a writer. My fellow members on the steering committee of the KRS, Heidi Russell, Paulette Skiba, Mark Fischer, Melvin Michalski, and Richard Penaskovic, have been warm and welcoming colleagues. I look forward to many years of collaboration with them. I shall add here the name of Philip Endean, a fellow Rahnerian whom I met first via email and then at Holy Cross, where we had a delightful conversation about our mutual interest in Rahner and our shared concern to carry his legacy forward.

Writing this book allowed me to work with engaging and professional editors, who made this arduous process surprisingly smooth. Before I thank the editors, the board, and my readers at the Catholic University of America (CUA) Press, I would like to mention John Jones, who until he passed away in October 2012 was editorial director at Crossroad/Herder & Herder Publishing. He and I never met in person, but our two-year correspondence greatly strengthened my resolve to publish this book. A well-respected editor of Catholic theology, he kindly read an early draft, and expressed great faith in this book's promise. May he rest in peace.

I am very pleased that the acquisitions editor, James Kruggel, and the Editorial Board at CUA Press shared John's confidence in my project. Jim has been absolutely fantastic to work with. I have come to know him as a man of faith, compassion, and kindness, who relishes the intellectual life and keenly perceives its merit for the mission of our Church. Thank you, Jim, for your assistance and care along the way. Thank you as well to Theresa Walker, who kindly and ably guided me through my final preparations of the manuscript, and to Philip Holthaus for his meticulous and generous copyediting. Thank you, finally, to the anonymous referees and to the referee who revealed his identity, Harvey Egan. Your affirmations, criticisms, and even, at times, reproaches, prompted me to discover what this book needed to be.

To my family: my brothers, grandparents, aunts, uncles, cousins, in-laws, thank you for your love and support. But to my parents most of all, Paula and Matthew Fritz, my first teachers in life and in faith, I hope that the words you read here fill you with pride. I am proud to be your son.

To Rochelle and Zephaniah: I will never forget the summer of 2012, during which the bulk of this book's final draft was written.

Rochelle: my beautiful wife, my love, as you and I worked together through the challenges of being parents to our first child, you kept me sane while I labored through the writing of my first book. Zeph: my firstborn son, my joy, long will you hear the stories of Daddy holding you in one arm while holding Rahner's *Geist in Welt* in the other. Our new life as a family I take to be a foretaste of the heavenly joy we are promised in Christ and the Spirit, and to which Rahner so wonderfully witnesses. To you both, with deep and abiding love, I dedicate this work.

ABBREVIATIONS

The following is a list of abbreviations for the main works I consult in the book. I have foregone two conventions of scholarship in developing this list of abbreviations. First, I have based almost all of the abbreviations on the titles of English translations (ETs) of foreign-language works. Second, for works in Rahner's *Sämtliche Werke* and Heidegger's *Gesamtausgabe,* I have developed the abbreviation out of the work's title, instead of the SW or GA volume. For example, Heidegger's *Hölderlins Hymnen "Germanien" und "Der Rhein,"* which is usually abbreviated GA 39, is in this book HGR. I hope that the English-speaking reader will find my method of abbreviation more reader-friendly than the standard practice.

I have, in keeping with the best scholarship, cross-checked all ETs with the original language. Again, though, to keep the text reader-friendly, I have cross-referenced the original language with the ET only in two cases: (1) where my point bears significantly on a linguistic difference between the original and the translation, and (2) where I have modified the existing ET. The exception to these rules is Rahner's *Geist in Welt,* which I cross-reference throughout. I do this because this text is the central one at issue in the book. This merits extra care.

WORKS BY KARL RAHNER

AMDG "Being Open to God as Ever Greater"

CH "Christian Humanism"

CM "The Concept of Mystery in Catholic Theology"

DJCR "The Death of Jesus Christ and the Closure of Revelation"

HW *Hearer of the Word / Hörer des Wortes*

HWSH "The History of the World and Salvation History"

IM "The Ignatian Mysticism of Joy in the World"

ISD "Ignatian Spirituality and Devotion to the Heart of Jesus"

LED "The Logic of Existential Decision in Ignatius Loyola"

PP "Priest and Poet"

RM "Reflections on Methodology in Theology"

SW *Spirit in the World/Geist in Welt*

TI *Theological Investigations*

VIP "*Virginitas in partu*: A Contribution to the Problem of the Development of Dogma and of Tradition"

WORKS BY MARTIN HEIDEGGER

BT *Being and Time*

CP *Contributions to Philosophy: From the Event*

EHP *Elucidations of Hölderlin's Poetry*

EM *Introduction to Metaphysics*

G *Discourse on Thinking/Gelassenheit*

HGR *Hölderlin's Hymnen "Germanien" und "Der Rhein"*

KPM *Kant and the Problem of Metaphysics/Kant und das Problem der Metaphysik*

LH "Letter on Humanism"

OWA "The Origin of the Work of Art"

OWL "On the Way to Language"

PLT *Poetry, Language, Thought*

WPF   "What Are Poets For?"

ST   *Schelling's Treatise on the Essence of Human Freedom*

T   "The Thing"

WORKS BY OTHERS

DE   Rainer Maria Rilke, *Duino Elegies*

KRIS   Philip Endean, *Karl Rahner and Ignatian Spirituality*

KRTP   Karen Kilby, *Karl Rahner: Theology and Philosophy*

RR   Patrick Burke, *Reinterpreting Rahner: A Critical Study of His Major Themes*

ST   Thomas Aquinas, *Summa theologiae*

A NOTE ON INCLUSIVE LANGUAGE

Rahner and Heidegger, though they lived not long ago, were educated and worked in a culture very different from ours today. Not until the end of their lives did the question of inclusive language really, palpably emerge as widely asked. Since I do not want to rewrite history to make it seem as if these two men would have used inclusive language if given the chance (this we cannot know), I shall leave all quotes from them untouched when they use gender-exclusive terms and formulations (e.g., Rahner's essay "The Man of Today").

When I am explicating quotations from Rahner and Heidegger, I often keep some gender-exclusive language when I feel that introducing gender-inclusive language would distort the sense of what they were saying. I have, though, when using my own voice, tried to employ gender-inclusive language. Where I deemed that impossible or unwieldy, I have alternated between masculine and feminine pronouns.

INTRODUCTION

PEOPLE know Karl Rahner as a Catholic theologian who once studied with Martin Heidegger. They may be aware that the period of study was the summer of 1934 through the summer of 1936. Then they may think that Rahner developed an "existentialist" theology out of his encounter with the Heidegger of *Being and Time* (1927). For almost all readers of Rahner, the story stops there. I am writing this book because if the story stops here, it has already gone horribly wrong.

Philip Endean once wrote, "It is not that Rahner's theology has been tried and found wanting; it has been found difficult and therefore not really tried."[1] This statement is somewhat of an exaggeration. It expresses a partial truth, though, in the case of the Rahner-Heidegger relation. Attempts have been made to account for some sort of Heideggerian influence on Rahner, but they remain limited, due to an almost exclusive focus on *Being and Time*.[2] Also, it has be-

1. Philip Endean, "Has Rahnerian Theology a Future?" in *The Cambridge Companion to Karl Rahner*, ed. Declan Marmion and Mary E. Hines (New York: Cambridge University Press, 2005), 281–96, here 282.

2. The classical texts are Robert Masson, "Rahner and Heidegger: Being, Hearing, and God," in *The Thomist* 37, no. 3 (1973) 455–88; and Thomas Sheehan, *Karl Rahner: The Philosophical Foundations* (Athens: Ohio University Press, 1987). Another work on Rahner and Heidegger, published in the same year as Sheehan's book, mainly follows his line of interpretation, by focusing on the so-called early Heidegger: Jack Arthur Bonsor, *Rah-*

1

come unfashionable to delve into the philosophical—especially the Heideggerian—resonances of Rahner's theology, making it less likely that this side of him will ever be tried.[3] In part, this tendency in Rahner scholarship goes back to the man himself. He once stated in an interview that he really doubted that Heidegger had much influence on his theology.[4]

Nevertheless, recently commentators who knew Rahner well have intimated that a reexamination of the Rahner-Heidegger relation demands another try. Thomas O'Meara, a former student of Rahner, insists that one can detect a broad Heideggerian impression on Rahner's theology.[5] Likewise, Albert Raffelt, another former student of Rahner's and coeditor of his *Sämtliche Werke,* maintains that the Rahner-Heidegger conversation still needs further examination, lest Rahner's works be misunderstood.[6]

In order for Rahner really to be tried, we must return to Heidegger's lecture hall and seminar room at Freiburg im Breisgau in the mid-1930s, and then trace the effects of what happened there through Rahner's later career. The years 1934 to 1936 were a watershed period for Heidegger that had deep implications for his thinking. These same years were also crucially important for Rahner. They set in motion forces that would coalesce into Rahner's major theological achievement: a presentation and performance of the ethos of Catholicism. In dialogue with Heidegger, Rahner learned how to disclose Catholicism's heart.

---

ner, *Heidegger, and Truth: Karl Rahner's Notion of Christian Truth, the Influence of Heidegger* (Lanham, Md.: University Press of America, 1987).

3. This is due mainly to the thesis of Karen Kilby that Rahner is a nonfoundationalist whose philosophical works do not mean much for his theology. See Karen Kilby, *Karl Rahner: Theology and Philosophy* (New York: Routledge, 2004).

4. See Paul Imhof and Harvey Egan, *Karl Rahner in Dialogue: Conversations and Interviews, 1965–1982* (New York: Crossroad, 1986), 13.

5. Thomas O'Meara, *God in the World: A Guide to Karl Rahner's Theology* (Collegeville, Minn.: Liturgical Press, 2007), 26.

6. See Albert Raffelt, "*Geist in Welt*: Einige Anmerkungen zur Interpretation," in *Die philosophische Quellen der Theologie Karl Rahners,* ed. Harald Schöndorf (Freiburg: Herder, 2005).

This leads to two questions: (1) What is Catholicism's ethos? and (2) How does Heidegger, an atheist *former* Catholic whose path of thinking explicitly militates against Catholicism,[7] help Rahner discover it? I shall treat each question in order.

When I write of "the ethos of Catholicism," I refer to what I take to be the normative form of Catholic life as Rahner explicates it across his corpus. The ethos of Catholicism is what Catholics should be, are sometimes, but often are not. Catholicism's ethos is this: radical openness to God's self-manifestation through the world. This openness comes to light in the broad range of Catholic doctrines, devotions, prayers, policies, sayings, songs, political actions, social interactions, and any other expressions of faith in the God who saves through Jesus Christ. Catholicism's ethos shines through Rahner's writings because he leaves virtually no Catholic stone unturned. He attempts to treat, in however fragmentary a way, each of the numerous facets of Catholic life, from meditations on the crucified Jesus and the Assumption of Mary to interventions regarding political utopianism and the ethics of war. He aims to find in all these things the shining of God's glory, or how Catholics might help God's light to shine. In this way, he enacts the Catholic ethos as I define it here.

Rahner constructs a theological program that symbolizes Catholicism at its best: when it fearlessly engages with the world, unconcerned that it might sully Christian "purity," but also unwilling to compromise on the good news of salvation through Jesus Christ. Rahner's thinking-through of Catholicism's way of being offers just as much to the church today as it did in his own day, particularly because in our time the fearless openness of Catholicism is often traded for panicked assertions of Catholic "distinctiveness" and boisterous calls for Catholic opposition to evils of "the culture." Such fearful stances toward the world stifle Catholic intellectual, social, politi-

---

7. On Heidegger's former Catholicism, see S. J. McGrath, *The Early Heidegger and Medieval Philosophy: Phenomenology for the Godforsaken* (Washington, D.C.: The Catholic University of America Press, 2006).

cal, artistic, and even—contrary to what their proponents believe—devotional and religious life. How, given this situation, can we recover Rahner's committed openness? This book provides tools for answering this question, while recognizing the difficulty, the height, the sublimity of this task. For this reason and others, I call the Catholic ethos that Rahner presents "the Catholic sublime."

How, then, does Heidegger help Rahner on his path toward unveiling the Catholic ethos? The answer has to do with the fact that Catholicism is a great and vast tradition. The Heidegger that Rahner met in Freiburg was a thinker deeply invested in reexamining, reforming, and refounding a great and vast tradition: Western metaphysics. The 1930s was a decade that Heidegger used to review the history of metaphysics, mainly in lectures like the ones Rahner attended, so as to find openings within this history to a more comprehensive, generous, and thus adequate thinking of being.[8] This Heideggerian habit of thinking—finding the openness in a tradition that seems to have closed itself to its proper task—proved pivotal for Rahner's philosophy and theology. Rahner surpasses his contemporaries and today's theologians in wideness of scope and in finding ways to reopen the Catholic tradition so it might proclaim the glory of God better than it has in centuries. In large part, he learned how to do this from Heidegger.

With these important prolegomena now behind us, the remainder of this introduction is devoted to three things: (1) establishing further why now is an opportune time to revisit the Rahner-Heidegger conversation; (2) elucidating this book's three main contributions; and (3) providing an outline of the chapters to follow.

---

8. See Martin Heidegger, *Contributions to Philosophy (From Enowning)*, trans. Parvis Emead and Kenneth Maly (Bloomington: Indiana University, 1999), 123–24, which explains how the "historical" lectures belong to his task of retelling the history of metaphysics. Heidegger wrote this book, *Beiträge zur Philosophie (Vom Ereignis)*, just after the time Rahner was studying with him. It would not be published, though, until 1989.

RAHNER AND HEIDEGGER: AGAIN?

Over twenty years have elapsed since the release of the last major book on Rahner and Heidegger, Thomas Sheehan's *Karl Rahner: The Philosophical Foundations*. Greater time for reflection brings clarity. This could be considered a sufficient impetus for writing a new book on the subject. However, I am more interested in three other factors that make our time a ripe one for revisiting the Rahner-Heidegger relation.

First, even though Thomas Sheehan catalogues the courses Rahner took from Heidegger, he does not assign them enough significance. He opts instead to focus on the relationship between Rahner's texts and Heidegger's *Being and Time*. But let us reexamine Rahner's class schedule. The courses Rahner took with Heidegger included lectures on Hölderlin and Schelling, an introduction to metaphysics, the foundational questions of metaphysics, and seminars on Hegel's *Phenomenology of Spirit*, Leibniz's *Monadology*, and Kant's *Critique of Judgment*—quite a rich array.[9] Had Rahner stayed another semester at Freiburg he would have been able to attend Heidegger's first course on Nietzsche, *Der Wille zur Macht (als Kunst)*, which was offered in the winter semester of 1936–1937.[10] Really to delve into the Rahner-Heidegger relation would involve more than just a passing mention of such course offerings. More likely, it would behoove one to examine some of the courses and the scholarship surrounding them. I do that here.

Second, a more adequate treatment of Rahner's time with Hei-

9. See Thomas Sheehan, *Karl Rahner: The Philosophical Foundations*, 5, and cf. William J. Richardson, *Heidegger: Through Phenomenology to Thought* (The Hague: M. Nijhoff, 1963), 668. Probably the most interesting article regarding Rahner's time with Heidegger, written by one of Rahner's fellow Jesuits, was recently translated into English: Thomas F. O'Meara, "Johannes B. Lotz, S.J., and Martin Heidegger in Conversation: A Translation of Lotz's *Im Gespräch*," *American Catholic Philosophical Quarterly* 84, no.1 (2010): 125–31.

10. Martin Heidegger, *Nietzsche, Vol. I: The Will to Power as Art*, trans. David Farrell Krell (New York: Harper Collins, 1991).

degger at Freiburg has become possible because of the publication of Rahner's *Sämtliche Werke*. Particularly relevant are its second (1996) and fourth (1997) volumes, which contain the texts of *Geist in Welt* and *Hörer des Wortes*, respectively, and other supporting materials.[11] Included among these materials are lecture notes in which Rahner records many of his thoughts on Heidegger. They also show that Rahner has read and reflected upon Heidegger's *Kant and the Problem of Metaphysics* (1929) and "What Is Metaphysics?" (1929), and that he has some constructive disagreements with Heidegger.[12] From Rahner's side there is an impetus toward reappraising the relation to Heidegger.

Third, within the past two decades, the gathering and publication of numerous volumes of Heidegger's *Gesamtausgabe*, many massively important translations of his works into English, and new, rich reflections on his corpus have yielded fresh perspectives on him. A new wave of Heidegger scholarship is now flourishing. Debates are alive as ever. Since Heidegger's significance is actively in question, it stands to reason that those influenced by him—like Rahner— might justifiably come in for reassessment. Mapping the Rahner-Heidegger relation onto *Being and Time* or "The Origin of the Work of Art" (1935) is merely a preliminary, hardly the final, word on the subject.

Remapping this terrain by taking more texts and ideas into consideration is exigent for contemporary Rahnerian studies, largely because of the postmodern critiques that have been leveled against Rahner's theology. Showing Rahner's proximity to Heidegger, who distances himself from the transcendental philosophy of Immanuel Kant, will clarify Rahner's use of "transcendental" philosophy,

---

11. See Karl Rahner, *Geist in Welt: Philosophischen Schriften, Sämtliche Werke Band 2*, ed. Albert Raffelt (Freiburg: Herder, 1996); and Rahner, *Hörer des Wortes: Schriften zur Religionsphilosophie und zur Grundlegung der Theologie: Sämtliche Werke Band 4*, ed. Albert Raffelt (Freiburg: Herder, 1997).

12. Karl Rahner, "Sechs Vorträge" in *Geist in Welt*, 438–55, at 444; Rahner, "Lektürenotizen zu Martin Heidegger: 'Was ist Metaphysik?'" in *Geist in Welt*, 455–60.

which postmodern critics discount as all-too-modern. It will reveal Rahner's postmodern potential and interest for expanding theology's purview beyond simply modern (i.e., epistemological) concerns.[13] Likewise, placing Rahner in conversation with Heidegger's expansive vision of the future of philosophy, which discounts modern subjectivist discourses of control, will illuminate Rahner's broad Catholic vision of the world, which avoids controlling the things it sees. To be more concrete, Rahner has been criticized for ironing out historical realities in favor of comprehensive vision.[14] This critique of Rahner can be problematized by further examination of Rahner's Catholic vision in light of Heidegger's narrative of the history of being.

Thus we have three reasons for the timeliness of this book. By exploring these three avenues, we shall see with new eyes the complexity of Rahner's appropriation of Heidegger, as opposed to the relative simplicity that prior treatments ascribed to it. Although this is a matter of historiographical import, its constructive significance will be central to this book.

CONTRIBUTIONS

This book's contributions arise from a renewed dialogue between Rahner and Heidegger, which takes into account more evidence than previous works have. The renewal of this conversation

13. Michael Purcell summarizes such critiques, while trying to show a way beyond them. See Purcell, "Rahner amid Modernity and Post-Modernity," in *The Cambridge Companion to Karl Rahner*, 196–98. Paul Crowley has already begun work in this vein. See Crowley, "Encountering the Religious Other: Challenges to Rahner's Transcendental Project," *Theological Studies* 71 (2010): 567–85.

14. Ignacio Ellacuría's critique of Rahner is notable in this respect, especially because of Ellacuría's read on Heidegger's influence on Rahner. Following Xavier Zubiri, Ellacuría focuses on *Dasein* from *Being and Time* as a source for Rahner's view of human transcendence in *Spirit in the World* and in his later theology of the supernatural existential. While this is a viable interpretation of Rahner (and Heidegger), it is a partial one that does not recognize the development of Heidegger's *Dasein* between 1927 and 1936. See an explanation of Ellacuría's appreciative critique of Rahner: Robert LaSalle-Klein, "Rethinking Rahner on Grace and Symbol: New Proposals from the Americas," in *Rahner Beyond Rahner: A Great Theologian Encounters the Pacific Rim,* ed. Paul Crowley (Lanham, Md.: Rowman and Littlefield, 2005), 87–99.

yields a Rahner who looks different from the stock images of him to which we have grown accustomed. While Rahner is usually depicted as the paradigmatic theologian of the "turn to the subject" or the "anthropological turn,"[15] by the end of the book we shall access a Rahner who in fact turns away from the modern subject. Heidegger opens the door for Rahner to this path, and Rahner makes it his own, often in ways resistant to the Heideggerian way of surpassing the subject. Furthermore, this path beyond the subject is an aesthetic one. Heidegger provided Rahner with certain insights that led Rahner to develop his own theological aesthetic. Especially distinctive about this theological aesthetic is the heightened index of the sublime within it. These are the components of this book's contribution. In anticipation of a fuller explication of the argument, let me say more about each contribution: Rahner as countersubjective, a theological aesthetician, and resistant to Heidegger.

A COUNTERSUBJECTIVE RAHNER

For Heidegger, "subjectivity" refers to the constitutive principle of modern thought, human consciousness that relates to anything outside it in terms of representation, or a presentation to self, ordered toward knowledge through conceptual control.[16] In the modern (Western) world, subjectivity becomes the normative framework for understanding the human person. The human person turns into the one who transforms the world into a mass of objects. Having made this subjectivity normative, the human person becomes unable to relate to the world and the things within it. The human person relates only to himself.

15. Peter Eicher, *Die anthropologische Wende: Karl Rahners philosophischer Weg vom Wesen des Menschen zur personalen Existenz* (Freiburg: Universitätsverlag, 1970); Anton Losinger, *The Anthropological Turn: The Human Orientation of the Theology of Karl Rahner,* trans. Daniel O. Dahlstrom (New York: Fordham University Press, 2000).

16. See especially Martin Heidegger, "The Age of the World Picture," in *Off the Beaten Track,* trans. Julian Young and Kenneth Haynes (New York: Cambridge University Press, 2002), 67–68.

We shall concern ourselves with modern subjectivism because Rahner is so often called a theologian who turns to the subject.[17] We shall see that this is hardly the case. I shall suggest that Rahner's avoidance of a world dominated by the subject is, in part, an effect of his time studying with Heidegger.

For Heidegger, the problem of modern subjectivism is largely a philosophical problem, but it is also a problem of life. Modern subjectivism makes the world unlivable. A consideration of Rahner will add a theological dimension to this, while the dimensions of philosophy and life will be always before us. Modern subjectivism obscures the revelation of God. A norm for humanity predicated upon control allows no room for God as absolutely incomprehensible — *unbegreifliche,* ungraspable. As his career progressed, Rahner increasingly emphasized the incomprehensibility of God. This was largely in response to his supporters, many of whom happily yet erroneously read Rahner's theology as a carte blanche to determine theology subjectively, via the category of "experience," which is a euphemism for making God into whatever one wants God to be.

This book will show that Rahner calls for nothing of the sort. His devotion to the ungraspable God, and furthermore to the dignity of all creation, which derives from its Creator a measure of ungraspability and uncontrollability, leads him to reject modern subjectivity. In this way, Rahner takes Heidegger's influence in a direction his atheist teacher would not have. Rejection of subjectivism becomes a defense of the Mystery of God and the opening of the human person by the grace of Jesus Christ.

To read Rahner as a countersubjective theologian is, at this

17. In addition to Eicher's and Losinger's classic studies of Rahner, Anne Carr's influential essay "Starting with the Human" presupposes this "subjective" reading of Rahner. Though the contribution of these works to prior Rahnerian studies is undeniable, today's world situation calls for a reframing of the Rahnerian conversation. See Carr, "Starting with the Human," in *A World of Grace: An Introduction to the Themes and Foundations of Karl Rahner's Theology,* ed. Leo O'Donovan (Washington, D.C.: Georgetown University Press, 1995), 17–30.

point in time, an unconventional approach.[18] Indeed, to attempt such a reading would seem to cut against the very texts it aims to interpret. The best counterexample to the proposal of a countersubjective Rahner is the opening chapters of *Foundations of Christian Faith,* which reflect at length on the human person as a subject, thus seemingly setting a subjectivist tone for the rest of the book.[19] But is it not possible that simply using the word "subject" does not mean that one succumbs to modern subjectivism? Do not words—particularly technical terms—have multiple meanings? Have we really understood what Rahner means by "subject" and "subjectivity"? I am writing this book because we have not.

Whereas in the past Rahner's "turn to the subject" was touted as a positive theological development, today it is more likely to be viewed with disdain.[20] In both cases, the nuance of Rahner's account of subjectivity goes largely ignored. Such nuance appears in statements such as this: "Whenever man in his transcendence experiences himself as questioning, as disquieted by the appearance of being, as open to something ineffable, he cannot understand himself as subject in the sense of an *absolute* subject, but only in the sense of one who receives being, ultimately only in the sense of grace."[21] The subject as receiver is vastly different from the subject as controller. If Rahner turns to the subject, he turns toward the former—the re-

---

18. That said, other Rahnerians have begun swimming against the tide, also. See, for example, Ethna Regan, "Not Merely the Cognitive Subject: Rahner's Theological Anthropology," in *Karl Rahner: Theologian for the Twenty-First Century,* ed. Pádraic Conway and Fáinche Ryan (New York: Peter Lang, 2010), 121–40.

19. Karl Rahner, *Foundations of Christian Faith,* trans. William Dych (New York: Crossroad, 1978), see especially 17–21 and 26–31.

20. In addition to the critiques of Rahner's transcendentalism already cited above, one could add those of Hans Urs von Balthasar and John Milbank, among others, who hold that Rahner's "modern" theology is inhospitable to a robust articulation of the Catholic view of reality and ultimately capitulates to modern secularism. See Balthasar, *The Moment of Christian Witness,* trans. Richard Beckley (San Francisco: Ignatius Press, 1994), passim; Milbank, *Theology and Social Theory* (Malden, Mass.: Blackwell, 2006), 222–25, 230–49.

21. Rahner, *Foundations,* 34, emphasis in original.

ceiver. He turns away from the latter—the grasper, the objectifier—the modern subject.

AN AESTHETIC RAHNER

I accomplish the book's first contribution, bringing to light a countersubjective Rahner, in tandem with a second: discovering a Rahnerian theological aesthetic. Before we delve into what this might mean, I should define "aesthetics" as I use it below. Although "aesthetics" refers quite rightly in some contexts to a theory of art, beauty, or human perception of art and beauty, it denotes something slightly different here. The difference lies in the increased breadth of my definition. "Aesthetics" means an account of the manifestation of being. I shall occasionally use the word "ontophany" (the appearance of being) to designate this manifestation of being. Aesthetics thus closely relates to ontology. If ontology asks what being is, aesthetics asks how being manifests itself.

"An aesthetic Rahner" indicates that Rahner interests himself in the manifestation of being. Since, for him, God is absolute being, his interest in ontophany focuses on how God reveals Godself. In this way, Rahner comes off as quite proximate to Hans Urs von Balthasar, whose theological aesthetic theory intertwines a "theory of vision" and a "theory of rapture." Whereas the former denotes the "perception" of God's self-showing, "subjective evidence," the latter indicates God's drawing of the perceiver into communion with God's glory, so "objective evidence."[22] Though Balthasar gives dual emphasis to both forms of evidence, the latter outweighs the former. God's self-manifestation in glory outstrips and elevates the human perception of this glory. Something similar obtains for Rahner's theological aesthetics.

This book argues that Rahner's major theological achievement consists in his account of God's self-revelation, which implies a way

22. Hans Urs von Balthasar, *The Glory of the Lord 1: Seeing the Form*, trans. Erasmo Leiva-Merikakis (San Francisco: Ignatius Press, 1982), 125–26.

of being—a Catholic way of being—that seeks, receives, and responds to divine revelation with radical openness. The Catholic way of being I call the Catholic sublime.

It has become a commonplace in the study of Heidegger that the aesthetic index of his thought increases from the early 1930s onward. This means that Rahner studied under Heidegger during the period when this aesthetic ferment waxed. Careful readers of Heidegger will know that he has rather negative things to say about "aesthetics" as an area of inquiry. In "The Age of the World Picture," for example, he laments that "aesthetics" has cornered the market on the study of art.[23] The aesthetics of which Heidegger speaks, though, is aesthetics narrowly defined—as the "scientific" study of art: modern aesthetics, where art's power of manifestation is subsumed to the human subject's power of perception. If one gives aesthetic a different definition, then Heidegger would approve. After all, his famous lecture "The Origin of the Work of Art" argues for something very similar to my definition of "aesthetics." The study of art must be seen under a broader rubric, the thinking of being's manifestation.[24] For Heidegger, modern subjectivity obscures the manifestation of being in art. Thus his view of aesthetics involves resistance toward and overcoming of modern subjectivism.

Rahner likely attended the "Origin" lecture at Freiburg, and even if he did not, we know that he heard similar ideas on art and the manifestation of being in a course on Hölderlin.[25] I shall argue below that Heidegger's aesthetic, which he develops in earnest in the mid-1930s, plants a countersubjective, aesthetic seed in Rah-

23. Heidegger, "Age of the World Picture," 57.
24. Martin Heidegger, "The Origin of the Work of Art," in *Poetry, Language, Thought,* trans. Albert Hofstadter (New York: Harper Perennial Modern Classics, 2001), 17–86; hereafter cited as OWA. Heidegger writes, amid his description of his alternative way of viewing the work of art, "The nature of art would then be this: the truth of beings setting itself to work" (35).
25. See Martin Heidegger, *Hölderlins Hymnen 'Germanien' und 'Der Rhein': Gesamtausgabe 39* (Frankfurt am Main: Vittorio Klostermann, 1999); hereafter cited as HGR.

ner's mind that bears immediate fruit in *Geist in Welt* and that offers a continuing harvest throughout Rahner's career.

This book keeps in mind and builds off of prior explorations of the possibility of a Rahnerian theological aesthetic, with their work on Rahner's anthropology and his writings on art and poetry.[26] This is, though, the first comprehensive statement on Rahner's theological aesthetics. In this way it continues on a trajectory of thought set by Stephen Fields, who writes of the symbolic metaphysics that suffuses Rahner's theology.[27] The present book's advance on Fields and others is this: it shows how Rahner's theology can and should be read as aesthetic all the way down. A concern for aesthetics does not lie in isolated pockets like the essays on poetry or "The Theology of the Symbol" (nevertheless, we shall examine these along the way).[28] A theological aesthetic, a specific view of how being manifests itself, how the Spirit of God makes Godself at once perceptible and beyond all perception, inflects every part of Rahner's thinking.

RAHNER AND THE SUBLIME   I would be remiss if I did not define "the sublime" and preliminarily indicate how this word, which

---

26. Richard Viladesau, *Theological Aesthetics God in Imagination, Beauty, and Art* (New York: Oxford University Press, 1999), and Viladesau, *Theology and the Arts: Encountering God through Music, Art and Rhetoric* (Mahwah, N.J.: Paulist Press, 2000); Gesa Elsbeth Thiessen, "Karl Rahner: Toward a Theological Aesthetics," in *The Cambridge Companion to Karl Rahner*, 225–34; James Voiss, "Rahner, von Balthasar and the Question of Theological Aesthetics," in *Finding God in All Things: Celebrating Bernard Lonergan, John Courtney Murray, and Karl Rahner*, ed. Mark Bosco and David Stagaman (New York: Fordham University Press, 2007), 167–81; Brent Little, "Anthropology and Art in the Theology of Karl Rahner," *Heythrop Journal* 52 (November 2011), 939–51.

27. Stephen Fields, "Balthasar and Rahner on the Spiritual Senses," *Theological Studies* 57 (1996): 224–41, and Fields, *Being as Symbol: On the Origins and Development of Karl Rahner's Metaphysics* (Washington, D.C.: Georgetown University Press, 2000).

28. Karl Rahner, "Priest and Poet," in *The Theology of the Spiritual Life: Theological Investigations 3*, trans. Karl H. Kruger and Boniface Kruger (New York: Crossroad, 1982), 294–317. Since there are twenty-three volumes in the English translation of the *Theological Investigations*, I shall provide a blanket citation here: Rahner, *Theological Investigations*, 23 vols., various translators (London, Baltimore, and New York: Darton, Longman and Todd, Seabury, Crossroad, 1961–1992), hereafter cited as TI. See also Rahner, "Poetry and the Christian," in TI 4.357–67, and Rahner, "The Theology of the Symbol," in TI 4.221–52.

Rahner uses only sporadically and hardly ever technically, might illuminate his thought.

Since the eighteenth century, the term "sublime" has been used in philosophy to refer to something pleasurable because apprehension of it outstrips the limits of human perception. In Kant's *Critique of Judgment* (1790), "sublime" means a feeling of negative pleasure that arises in a subject who encounters immeasurably large or small things, or incomparable power.[29] Post-Kantian philosophies distinguish the sublime from the aesthetic. The latter refers to the human subject's apprehension and judgment of beauty. For Kant and others, the judgment of beauty is important because it gives a sense of an orderly world that fits well with human subjective faculties. The sublime suggests that disorder underlies the order of the world. Thus, in a way, it undermines the integrity of human subjectivity by uncovering its inadequacy for representing nature.[30] Kant recognizes this, and demotes the sublime to the status of an appendix of aesthetic theory.[31]

While the sublime did not fit Kant's purposes—developing a philosophical system built from the subject outward—the Romantics, German Idealists, and many French postmoderns would later deem the sublime vitally important for thinking about the disclosive power of reality. Heidegger and Rahner in his wake stand in this line of thinkers who positively appropriate what Kant left aside: the sublime.

My definition of the sublime still demands clarification. The sublime relates to aesthetics. It specifies aesthetics, by foregrounding the fact that being's manifestation is broader than the human capacity

29. See Immanuel Kant, *The Critique of the Power of Judgment*, trans. Paul Guyer and Eric Matthews (New York: Cambridge University Press), §§23–29, 128–60: "Analytic of the Sublime."

30. For a book-length exegesis of Kant's *Critique of Judgment* that argues that the sublime destroys human subjectivity, see Jean-François Lyotard, *Lessons on the Analytic of the Sublime*, trans. Elizabeth Rottenberg (Stanford, Calif.: Stanford University Press, 1994).

31. See Kant, *Critique of Judgment*, 130.

to receive and to contain it. Being is, then, beyond our grasp. On this point, Rahner and Heidegger agree. Just as the Kantian sublime has been identified as bearing countersubjective potential, so too shall we see how Rahner's sublime, which resembles but revises Heidegger's, turns away from modern subjectivity. In addition to using the sublime to specify Rahner's theological aesthetics, then, I shall utilize this term to identify the countersubjective thrust of Rahner's thought.

Theologically speaking, "sublime" refers primarily to the incomprehensible Mystery of God, and secondarily to how creation, particularly the human person, reflects this incomprehensibility. I shall follow a roughly chronological presentation of Rahner's works, starting with *Geist in Welt* (1939), which focuses on the metaphysics of finite, human knowledge. Thus Rahner's version of the sublime will appear first through its referring of human imagination and intellection toward God's infinity. Later in the book, particularly in chapters 4 and 5, which treat later theological texts, it will become clear that Rahner's thought is sustained through and through by reflection on Mystery as the positive, abiding, constitutive attribute of God. God's incomprehensibility breaks all human attempts at mastery, whether of God or of the creation that comes from God. Rahner's deployment of God's incomprehensibility throughout his thinking works against modern subjectivism's pretensions to all-encompassing mastery. Furthermore, Rahner's view of the divine incomprehensibility results in a presentation of a form of life that attempts to reflect this incomprehensilbity: the Catholic sublime.

It may be objected that I could achieve the same or even a better reading of Rahner without the term "sublime." I am aware that theologians like John Milbank, Phillip Blond, Frederick Bauerschmidt, John Betz, and David Bentley Hart have diagnosed the sublime as the symbol of modernity's (and postmodernity's) fallenness.[32] In fact, I am taking these latter views of the sublime into

---

32. See, for example, John Milbank, "The Sublime in Kierkegaard," *Heythrop Journal* 37, no. 3 (1996): 298–321, and Milbank, "Sublimity: The Modern Transcendent,"

account. I have elected "the Catholic sublime" as this book's anchor idea to signify two things: (1) Rahner's active and sophisticated resistance of modern subjectivism; and (2) the fact that Catholic theology need not cede terms like "subjectivity" and "sublime" to modernity — we can develop our own versions of them. Rahner did with respect to "subjectivity," and to great effect. I shall do so with the "sublime." I do so in keeping with the ancient Christian tradition of "taking every thought captive in obedience to Christ" (2 Cor 10:5). "The sublime" is a modern "thought" that I turn toward Christ by applying it to the achievement of Rahner's thinking.

A RAHNER RESISTANT TO HEIDEGGER

The final major contribution of this book revolves around the influence of Heidegger and post-Heideggerians on contemporary theology, which is vast and well known. I argue that Rahner's thought has much to contribute to contemporary theological discourse because his thought constructively resists Heidegger and, by implication, post-Heideggerian thought. Prior treatments of the Rahner-Heidegger relation have focused on what Rahner gained from his study with Heidegger. They ignore, or at least downplay, what Rahner brought to the conversation.

Exemplary in this respect is Laurence Paul Hemming, who avers that "Rahner . . . never problematizes the thought of Heidegger in relation to theology as such." Instead, Rahner is a merely "conventional" interpreter of Heidegger, who praises him for his virtuosity in reopening the question of being, but worries vaguely about his

---

in *Transcendence: Philosophy, Literature, and Theology Approach the Beyond,* ed. Regina Schwartz (New York: Routledge, 2004), 207–29; Phillip Blond, "Introduction: Theology Before Philosophy," in *Post-Secular Philosophy: Between Philosophy and Theology,* ed. Phillip Blond (New York: Routledge, 1998), 1–33; Frederick Bauerschmidt, "Aesthetics: The Theological Sublime," in *Radical Orthodoxy: A New Theology,* ed. John Milbank, Catherine Pickstock, and Graham Ward (New York: Routledge, 1999), 201–19; John Betz, "Beyond the Sublime: The Aesthetics of the Analogy of Being" (two parts), *Modern Theology* 21, no. 3 (2005): 367–411, and 22, no. 1 (2006): 1–50; David Bentley Hart, *The Beauty of the Infinite: The Aesthetics of Christian Truth* (Grand Rapids, Mich.: Eerdmans, 2003), 43–93.

possible atheism.[33] The implication is that Rahner either does not have the intellectual heft or never takes care to contend with Heidegger in a serious fashion.

This book presupposes that Rahner brings sufficient intellectual gravitas to the table to contest Heidegger's views on theology, finitude, language, history, and several other topics. Likewise, it locates in Rahner various examples of such contestation. I argue that Rahner's study with Heidegger led him to carve out philosophical and theological positions that actively (if often silently) resist Heideggerian thinking.

I have already noted that the second volume of Rahner's *Sämtliche Werke* contains unpublished manuscripts and lecture notes in which Rahner shows both his interest in and his reservations about Heidegger's philosophy.[34] Let us cull a few details from them. The lecture notes, in addition to being determined structurally by Heidegger's thought, are peppered with several details that vividly illustrate Rahner's wrestling with the still developing Heideggerian corpus, as he attempts to adjudicate its philosophical coherence and theological utility. Three points stand out as pertinent for us.

First, Rahner's attempts at articulating lessons on metaphysical anthropology from the perspective of the "foundational structure" (*Grundstruktur*) of the human person show his appreciation for Heidegger's work. Rahner voices his agreement with Heidegger's "realistic" opposition to Idealism.[35] Rahner breaks ranks with Heidegger, though, when the latter's opposition to Idealism comes to include an a priori preference for considering finitude that leads to a proscrip-

33. Laurence Paul Hemming, *Heidegger's Atheism: The Refusal of a Theological Voice* (Notre Dame, Ind.: University of Notre Dame Press, 2002), 27, 19.

34. See Rahner, *Geist in Welt*, "Teil C: Unveröffentliche Manuskripte," especially 407–26 ("Protokolle aus Seminaren Martin Heideggers"), 438–61 ("Begleittext zu 'Geist in Welt,'" "Vortragsskizzen und Materiellen—Zwischen Existentialphilosophie und Fundamentaltheologie," and "Lektürenotizen zu Martin Heidegger: 'Was ist Metaphysik?'").

35. Rahner, "Unveröffentliche Manuskripte," 444.

tion of the infinite. Since, for Rahner, God is infinite spirit, he cannot accept a philosophy that bars the infinite's entry.

Second, Rahner asks whether Heidegger's thought is an atheistic philosophy.[36] This question flows from the fact that "the Absolute does not present itself" (*das Absolute tritt nicht auf*) in Heidegger's philosophy. This is a "de facto" condition in Heidegger, but Rahner's next question seems to suggest that Rahner sees it as a Heideggerian de jure prescription: "Is this a methodological failure? (*Ist das ein methodisches Ausfallen?*)." Rahner goes on to imply that Heidegger has taken his cues vis-à-vis the nonappearance of the absolute from Nietzsche.[37] Rahner differs from Heidegger on this point. The philosophical possibility that the absolute, or the infinite, could appear within the metaphysical field need not be foreclosed. As far as Rahner is concerned, the infinite finds its way into metaphysics, by way of an unthematic anticipation (*Vorgriff*) of being, "prior" to a specific encounter with a being.[38]

Third, among his notes on metaphysical anthropology, Rahner brings up the topic of negative theology. He calls Heidegger's philosophy a "secularist negative theology" (*säkularistische theol[ogia] negativa*). Certainly, as Heidegger knows, *theologia negativa* is the suppression (through language) of that after which one grasps. The question is how negation, or the nothing (*das Nichts*), appears to thought. For Rahner, following Thomas Aquinas, a negation follows some affirmation. Apophatic theology must predicate itself upon prior divine revelation. Heidegger's own thought on negation, which he famously expounds in "What Is Metaphysics?" looks vapidly "secular" by comparison.

The above three points from Rahner's lecture-sketches aim to show that, from the mid-1930s on, Rahner resists Heidegger's think-

---

36. Cf. Karl Rahner, "The Concept of Existential Philosophy in Heidegger," in *Philosophy Today* 13, no. 2 (Summer 1969): 126–37.
37. Rahner, "Unveröffentliche Manuskript," 441.
38. Rahner, "Unveröffentliche Manuskripte," 446.

ing with some sophistication. This book will elaborate that point, by guiding the reader through Rahner and Heidegger's respective careers, underscoring their similarities and differences as it goes.

CHAPTER OUTLINES

I develop the theses and arguments introduced above in five chapters, with four sections each. The following chapter outlines should give the reader a solid orientation to the book's form and content.

Chapter 1, "Rahner's Aesthetics," has a three-part thesis: (1) Rahner's encounter with Heidegger's writings and teaching bred in him an affinity for aesthetics; (2) *Geist in Welt* lays the groundwork for a theological aesthetic, even if Rahner does not call it this; (3) this incipient aesthetic assimilates the best while resisting the worst elements of Heidegger's thought. The chapter finds that Rahner and Heidegger develop their theories of sensibility out of a strikingly similar view of the imagination. The imagination is vital to Rahner's theological aesthetic. Rahner's chief contribution to theological aesthetics is his teaching that God moves through the imagination. By this divine movement, being manifests itself to and through the human person. This is not an exclusively anthropological claim, as interpreters of Rahner often think. Instead, it leads to a greater insight into how God moves and acts through the world. The chapter ends with a disagreement between Rahner and Heidegger over the issue of finitude. Later chapters will show how this parting of ways between Rahner and Heidegger proves definitive for their later development.

Chapter 2, "Rahner's Sublime," argues that once we apply "the sublime" to Rahner's thought and explain its specific significance, it will shed new light on how his corpus contests modern subjectivism. In order to accomplish this, the chapter reinterprets Rahner on Thomas's view of the agent intellect, which he figures as a "return of the subject to himself." If any aspect of *Geist in Welt* is overtly subjectivist, this would be it. Thus I carefully interpret this motif of the "abstractive return" to discover exactly what sort of subjectivity it describes. The exegesis involved here calls attention to Rahner's time in Heidegger's first lecture course on Hölderlin, in which Rahner would have witnessed Heidegger developing countersubjective ideas about poetic thinking. The chapter proposes that Rahner's encounter with Heidegger set him on a track toward his own vision of the sublime, which he honed in the two decades after his study with Heidegger, and which he would continue to develop for the rest of his career. The two thinkers differ, though, on the question of ethos, what form of life is a sublime form.

Chapter 3, "Rahner and the Spirit of the Age," continues my argument that Rahner is not a theologian who turns toward the modern subject, but rather away from it. This indicates yet again Heidegger's influence on him. Examinations of Rahner's angelology and his appropriation of Ignatius Loyola, set in tandem with more of Heidegger's writings, lay bare how Rahner comes to see beyond the spirit of modern subjectivity. The chapter concludes by contending that Rahner develops a theological point of view resistant to modern humanism that bears significant resemblance to, though it occupies a different register than, Heidegger's critique of the insufficiencies of modern humanism. Again, their difference comes down to ethos.

Chapter 4, "Rahner's Refounding of Theological Language," explicates Rahner's theory of theological language, which takes shape in his writings on mystery in the 1950s and 1960s. It shows how Rahner's subtle contestation of modern subjectivism's hold on Catholic neo-scholasticism parallels in interesting ways Heidegger's opposition in his later works on language to modern subjectivism's "calculating" language. A comparison of Rahner's Mariology and Heidegger's thinking of "the thing" provides a case study of how these two thinkers converge in their refusal to reduce language to a mechanism by which a subject controls objects. But by the end the chapter argues that despite their similar sensitivity to mystery and language's capacity for bringing it to light, Rahner and Heidegger differ sharply in their estimation of the type of openness to mystery language can allow. The chapter concludes with the idea that Rahner articulates a true idea of sublimity, while both modern subjectivism and Heidegger purvey false sublimities.

Chapter 5, "Rahner's Apocalypse," explores Rahner's theology of history, particularly in his works post-Vatican II. The chapter narrates how Rahner's countersubjective aesthetics (including his version of the sublime) reaches its full expanse in a theological vision of history that—perhaps surprisingly to those who know Rahner—deserves the ascription apocalyptic. Though Rahner is commonly regarded as a modern rejecter of apocalypticism, this chapter claims that the Rahner-Heidegger relation in particular reveals the apocalyptic cast of his theology. A tandem treatment of (1) Rahner's writings on salvation and profane history and on the pivotal significance of the Cross of Christ and (2) Heidegger's thinking of the history of being, especially in *Contributions to Philosophy*, justifies the invocation of the Apocalypse. The culminating conflict between Rahner and Heidegger concerns history. In fact, this chapter concludes with the provocative suggestion that Rahner's apocalyptic theology of history exemplifies the way that Catholic theology should contest Heidegger's entire philosophical project.

The outcome of the Rahner-Heidegger relation remains to be seen. At the end of this book, after following Rahner and Heidegger through their respective careers, we will be faced with one question: how their interaction should live on in today's theology.

FINAL NOTE: THE CATHOLIC SUBLIME

I have written this book because a quality of Rahner's writings has captivated me. The sheer scope of Rahner's purview led me to a fundamental insight into Rahner's mind, which in turn is an insight about Catholicism. His writings are a performance of the in-principle-unlimited concern of Catholicism. The Catholic way of life is named for its holism (*kata-holon*). Rahner's writings bring this holism to light. And the argument of this text is that Rahner's study with Heidegger contributed significantly to his capacity for elucidating Catholicism's holism.

As we delve deeper into Rahner's writings, I shall call Catholicism's holism the Catholic sublime. For now, let us give an example of Rahner's articulation of the Catholic sublime. One year before his death (1983), Rahner extols the

wonderful fact that in its religiosity Christianity does not omit a single human dimension, that it is not afraid of points of contact, that it does not consider the loftiness of its relation to God through grace to be endangered when Christian existence becomes earthly, carnal, full-blooded, willing to assume whatever is human.[39]

This sentence appears in an essay on devotion to Mary. Rahner mentions the holistic humanity of Catholic Christianity, its admission of contact with worldly things and its elevation by grace so it may surpass the world. Catholic Christianity in principle and in fact (though not often enough) opens itself to an incomprehensible width of scope. Herein lies its sublimity, as Rahner discloses it.

39. Rahner, "Courage for Devotion to Mary," in TI 23.129–39, here 130.

1 RAHNER'S AESTHETICS

BEFORE we can consider the proposal that Rahner presents the
Catholic sublime, we must establish that his corpus relates somehow to aesthetics and to the sublime. Chapters 1 and 2 accomplish
this task. The first exposes Rahner's aesthetics, and the second the
beginnings of Rahner's view of the sublime. The present chapter argues three points: (1) Rahner's encounter with Heidegger's writings
and teaching bred in him an affinity for aesthetics; (2) *Geist in Welt*
lays the philosophical groundwork for theological aesthetics, even
if Rahner does not say this; and (3) Rahner's incipient aesthetics assimilates the best while resisting the worst elements of Heidegger's
thought.[1]

The chapter proceeds in four parts. The first discusses the parameters and implications of Rahner's view of sensibility in *Geist
in Welt*. The second compares the account of the imagination that
Rahner folds into his view of sensibility with Heidegger's approach
to the imagination in *Kant and the Problem of Metaphysics*. The third
outlines Rahner's chief contribution to philosophical and theological aesthetics: his description of the Spirit of God moving through
created being. The fourth contrasts how Rahner and Heidegger

---

1. From now on, I shall leave the title untranslated as *Geist in Welt*, largely because
the English translation, *Spirit in the World* (with the added definite article) is misleading.

23

think about finitude and infinitude. Heidegger's barring of infinitude from philosophy is a breaking point between him and Rahner that will prove very significant for this book.

By the end of this chapter, the case will be made that Rahner's interaction with Heidegger produced a unique, if inchoate, aesthetic, centering on the imagination. The stage will have been set for showing how Rahner's aesthetics can incorporate a key aesthetic concept—the sublime—although the possibility for this will not become clear until chapter 2. We shall arrive at the sublime in due course, and then at Rahner's particular version of it: the Catholic sublime.

THE RAHNERIAN THOMAS

Rahner enrolled in a doctoral program in philosophy at the University of Freiburg in the summer semester of 1934. Although his official selection for a *Doktorvater* was the Thomist philosopher Martin Honecker, Rahner (along with fellow Jesuit Johann Baptist Lotz) took greater interest in and more courses from Martin Heidegger. This state of affairs remained constant up to the time that Honecker failed Rahner's doctoral thesis in the summer of 1936. This thesis, of course, would be published three years later as *Geist in Welt*.

The following pages will lay out several aspects of Rahner's reading of Thomas Aquinas in *Geist in Welt* that, we shall find in the next part, resonate with Heidegger's thinking, particularly his interpretation of Immanuel Kant. As promised, I shall uncover in the Rahnerian Thomas some ingredients for theological aesthetics. It will take the remainder of the book to acquire the rest of the ingredients, but we shall at this early stage make substantial headway. Our focus for now will be on the issue of sensibility in the Rahnerian Thomas. In *Geist in Welt*, sense experience of the world functions as an important entrée into a wider apprehension of being.

One note before we proceed: against Karen Kilby, who treats *Geist in Welt* as disjoined from Rahner's later theology, and Patrick

Burke, who views *Geist in Welt* as sowing the seeds of Rahner's eventual theological downfall,[2] I regard *Geist in Welt* as a monumental step on Rahner's path of thinking. This book introduces a number of themes that bear abundant fruit in his theology. Furthermore, Rahner seems to have held the book in high esteem, since he cites it in articles throughout his later career. Although current Rahner scholarship wishes to marginalize this book, it must be read, understood, and appropriated if we are to discover how Rahner develops a distinctive type of theological aesthetics.

PRELIMINARIES

Geist in Welt centers on a question: How does one give an account of metaphysics without recourse to intellectual intuition?[3] It is true that Rahner derives this question from Kant. For Kant, the metaphysical tradition stipulates a direct access of the understanding to an intelligible world inaccessible to the senses. He deems this "intellectual intuition" to be impossible, a falsehood held by a metaphysics that has reached past its limits. In a sense, but one that is less decisive than commentators commonly recognize, Rahner finds Thomas agreeing with Kant. In Thomas's metaphysics of knowledge, Rahner sees no doctrine of intellectual intuition. In its place is a doctrine of the imagination. That is, knowledge does not come from direct, unmediated access to intelligible ideas. Instead, knowledge results from a process of receiving sense impressions, configuring them imaginatively, acting upon these reconfigured impressions

2. See Kilby, KRTP, 10–11, and Patrick Burke, *Reinterpreting Rahner: A Critical Study of His Major Themes* (New York: Fordham University Press, 2002), viii, hereafter RR. It is notable that Kilby disjoins Rahner's philosophy from his theology because she worries that too many interpretations of Rahner's theology have seen it "determined, even straitjacketed, by his philosophy" (11). Her apologetic motive makes good sense, especially because Burke legitimates her worry. However, an interpretation of Rahner that renders a positive, constructive relationship between his philosophy and theology is not impossible, and here we shall see it as the most illuminating one.

3. Or as Kilby phrases it, "how is metaphysics possible given that all our knowledge is grounded in the world?" (Kilby, KRTP, 17).

with the intellect, and coming to a concrete recognition of the thing sensed.

This has implications for Thomas's rapport with the world, philosophically and theologically: "Even Thomas's theology is not a flight from the earth, but the hearing of the word of God within the narrow confines of this world and within the flitting brevity of an earthly hour."[4] The answer to *Geist in Welt*'s question, then, is this: one must construct a metaphysics starting from the imagination.

Rahner's interest throughout *Geist in Welt* is metaphysics. He approaches general metaphysics through the metaphysics of knowledge. This has given rise to a widespread scholarly reading of *Geist in Welt* as a work of epistemology, and a popular reading of Rahner as an epistemologist or epistemologically oriented theologian.[5] Those who have read Rahner in this way have failed to attend to a decisive distinction he presupposes between the metaphysis of knowledge and epistemology. Had he intended to use the word *Epistemologie* to describe the object of his inquiry in Thomas, he could have. He did not. Rahner writes about Thomas's *Erkenntnismetaphysik,* from the book's first sentence forward.[6]

Why is this distinction so important? The answer lies in the following passage from *Geist in Welt*'s preface:

Let it be said here explicitly that the concern of the book is not the critique of knowledge, but a metaphysics of knowledge, and that, therefore, *as opposed to Kant,* there is always a question of a noetic hylomorphism, to which there corresponds an ontological hylomorphism in the objects, in the sense of a thoroughgoing determination of knowing by being.[7]

---

4. SW 62/58.

5. A helpful recent article rejects this approach, and thus accords with the one taken here; see Ryan Duns, "Recovering Rahner's Concept of Being in *Spirit in the World,*" in *New Blackfriars* 91 (2010): 567–85.

6. SW xlix/12. Patrick Burke, whose critique of Rahner rests on flaws in his "epistemology," misses this distinction—which is not just terminological—and refers throughout his book to Rahner's "epistemological metaphysics" (Burke, RR, 1 and passim).

7. SW liii/14, emphasis added.

Just as soon as Rahner has affirmed a Kantian question as fundamental to *Geist in Welt,* he differentiates himself from Kant. For Rahner, Kant's primary concern is epistemological, a study of knowledge, its processes (*noesis*), and the mental faculties involved. Though Rahner cannot avoid all of these topics entirely, his examination of Thomas has a different emphasis. The metaphysics of knowledge is an ontological enterprise—being is its first question. That is, what does an examination of knowing tell us about how being manifests itself? This contrasts with an epistemological critique of knowledge that treats being as a secondary question, or may discount being as a question altogether (Kant himself is guilty of this). *Geist in Welt,* then, is not a work of epistemology that places limits on being's manifestation. It is a work about the endless span of being's manifestation. And we shall discover as we go why we can and should call it a work of aesthetics.

Before we delve into an explication of the Rahnerian Thomas's account of sensibility, we should orient ourselves in Rahner's text, with a preliminary glimpse of its overall structure. Kilby writes, "The overall plan of *Spirit in the World* . . . is to establish the possibility of our having a world-transcending knowledge by investigating how knowledge of the world itself works."[8] Kilby's language angles toward an epistemological reading of *Geist in Welt,* so let us revise using language of being's manifestation. The plan of *Geist in Welt* explicates the manifestation of being to the senses in order to elucidate the full range of being's manifestation to the human knower, who possesses both senses and intelligence.

The book has three parts. First, Rahner inserts article 84, question 7 of the prima pars of Thomas's *Summa theologiae.* We must not lose sight, as so many Rahner commentators have, of the fact that this article stands within Thomas's treatise on creation. Too little attention has been paid to this fact, since commentary on Rahner

8. Kilby, KRTP, 18.

has remained so anthropologically focused, often for the purpose of criticizing Rahner's alleged anthropocentrism. Also in this first part, Rahner offers a brief running commentary of his chosen text from Thomas, giving a preview of the coming analysis.

Second, Rahner enters into a philosophical exposition of the text. Here, admittedly, Rahner seems to show some influence of German Idealism. As we shall see below, though, he also places himself at a distance from the Idealists, especially G. W. F. Hegel, with whom he has been rather speciously compared.[9] The influence lies in Rahner's tripartite breakdown of Thomas's metaphysics of knowledge, devoting chapters to sensibility (part 2, chapter 2), the intellect (chapter 3), and the Conversion to the Phantasm (chapter 4).

Prior to these chapters, he makes preliminary remarks about metaphysics in general. Here he makes his famous statement that being is the "being-present-to-self of being [*Beisichsein des Seins*], and this being-present-to-self is the being of the existent,"[10] which caused much consternation among the Thomistic community. As with the German Idealists, this general preface on metaphysics is merely a starting point, which is fundamentally altered by the time Rahner reaches part 2's end. In short, the metaphysical doctrine of *Geist in Welt* develops. It is not static, as prior Rahner commentators understood.[11] I shall have more to add on this issue as we go. We shall also see how the development of Rahner's metaphysical teaching both converges with and diverges from Heidegger's view of being in the works of the late 1920s through the mid-1930s. This interaction with Heidegger will account for Rahner's proximity to and distance from German Idealism.

---

9. Denis Bradley popularized this form of argument in the mid-1970s; see Bradley, "Rahner's *Spirit in the World*: Aquinas or Hegel?" See also Thomas Pearl, "Dialectical Panentheism: On the Hegelian Character of Karl Rahner's Key Christological Writings," *Irish Theological Quarterly* 42 (1975): 119–37.

10. SW 69/62.

11. Refreshingly different from the rest is Robert Hurd, "Being is Being-Present-to-Itself: Rahner's Reading of Aquinas' Metaphysics," *The Thomist* 52 (1988): 63–78, which at-

Third, Rahner ends the book with a brief part entitled "Meta-physics on the Basis of the Imagination." This part integrates the material that goes before it. Here—and not before—Rahner's philosophical position on the metaphysics of knowledge comes fully to light. Also, it is here, *not* in the opening phrase to part 2, chapter 1, "Man questions," that the influence of Heidegger becomes most pronounced. I shall unpack this part's title in due course, thus showing how Heidegger makes a deep, not just superficial or terminological, impact on Rahner's Thomas interpretation.

The foregoing makes it possible to declare several starting points for our own exposition of *Geist in Welt*. (1) Rahner keeps Kant's critique of metaphysics in mind, while resisting it. (2) Rahner differentiates himself from Kant by focusing on the metaphysics of knowledge, instead of epistemology. (3) Rahner's ontological, rather than epistemological, viewpoint opens the door to aesthetics. (4) This aesthetics opposes Kant's, which is subjectively driven. (5) If Rahner distances himself from Kant, he does so along the lines of the German Idealists. (6) Rahner's stance vis-à-vis German Idealism is made more complex by his disposition toward Heidegger, and vice versa. (7) Finally, this multilayered conversation with modern philosophies yields a rather simple upshot: Rahner retains a dogged, Catholic commitment to Thomas's *philosophia perennis*. Whatever Rahner resists in his modern interlocutors, Thomas would have. Likewise, anything to which he opens himself, Thomas would have too.

THOMAS AND HUMAN SENSIBILITY

Rahner prepares for his aesthetics with the account of sensibility in *Geist in Welt*. The central component of this aesthetics will not arrive until the chapter on intellection, but no sense could be made of this component without the chapter on sensibility. I had said

---

tempts to defend Rahner's appropriation of Thomas by urging sensitivity to the polyvalence of Rahner's concepts and terminology.

above that the central question of *Geist in Welt* is this: How does one give an account of metaphysics without recourse to intellectual intuition? Revised aesthetically, the question becomes this: How does one account for the manifestation of being without recourse to a direct, intelligible manifestation? That is, what if being, in order to be perceived, manifests itself to the senses? Rahner aims to answer these questions.

Rahner accesses an answer through Thomas's thesis in ST.I.84.7: "I answer that it is impossible for our intellect, in its present state of life, where it is joined with a passive body, to understand anything actually, if not through converting to phantasms."[12] Thomas aims in this thesis to defend at least two positions: (1) the human intellect is passive (cf. ST I.79.2.corpus), but nevertheless (2) actual knowledge is possible (cf. ST I.79.3.corpus). Knowledge is possible, Thomas argues, through a process of gathering sense impressions, producing likenesses (*similitudines*, i.e., *phantasmata*) of them in the imagination, and interpreting these likenesses in the intellect after an intellectual turn "toward" them. Rahner defines "the phantasm" as "the keyword designating sense knowledge as such."[13] This one word summarizes the idea that human knowledge can be had only through the cooperation of sensibility and intellect. "Conversion to the phantasm," then, is the "expression of the fact that sense intuition is the essential and abiding presupposition of all thought."[14]

This all might sound like epistemology, even of an empiricist sort. Rahner digs deeper, though.[15] His concern is, as has been noted, metaphysics—being. A careful reader of *Geist in Welt* will notice

12. "Respondeo dicendum quod impossibile est intellectum nostrum, secundum praesentis vitae statum, quo passibili corpori coniungitur, aliquid intelligere in actu, nisi convertendo se ad phantasmata" (ST I.84.7.corpus, my translation).

13. SW 237/181.

14. SW 310/232.

15. Cf. James Conlon, "Karl Rahner's Theory of Sensation," *The Thomist* 41 (1977): 400–417, which lauds—and with good reason—the superiority of Rahner's transcendental-metaphysical approach to sensibility over an empirical approach.

that for Rahner corporeality and sensibility are conditioned a priori by a way of being he calls "receptivity." Rahner clarifies, "This much we can presume already: we have not grasped the essence of sensibility if we understand the senses as passageways through which things enter into us."[16] The Rahnerian Thomas speaks of sensibility as a human being's loss of self in the other, the entrance into a relationship of undifferentiation with an object received through the senses. This sensible apprehension is made possible because human being is a receptive sort of being. The Rahnerian Thomas has the insight "that the human person has sense organs of a material kind because he can and must know receptively, and not vice versa."[17]

Again, this is a metaphysical statement. I noted above that the context for ST I.84.7 is Thomas's treatise on creation. The prima pars might be divided into two sections: a treatise on God, and one on creation. The second treatise consists of several parts: (1) prefatory words on creation and God as its cause (I.44–49); (2) on the angels, or spiritual creation (I.50–64); (3) on material creation (I.65–74); (4) on the creature that comprises both spirit and matter, or the human being (I.75–102); and (5) on the government of creation by God's providence (I.103–19). The entire treatise ultimately concerns the showing forth of God's power, and the different ways in which this showing forth happens. For the human person, the manifestation—indeed the revelation—of God happens by a mediation of spirit through matter. As material, the human person receives the influence of another, but as spirit, the human person acts. Thomas observes in ST I.93.6 that God shows forth in the human person primarily through the intellect (spirit), which is the image of God, and secondarily, by way of a trace, through the body. Thus the human person stands between an active emulation of God and a passive reception of God.

16. SW 45/45.
17. SW 344/255–56. See also HW 113/202: "[F]or Thomas receptive knowledge and sense knowledge are essentially the same thing."

This is all significant because Rahner has been roundly criticized, most recently by Patrick Burke, following John McDermott, for his idea that the human person is a *schwebende Mitte,* an oscillating middle between spirit and matter.[18] The charge against Rahner is twofold: first, he misreads Thomas, making him a dialectical thinker in the vein of Hegel, *avant la lettre*; second, his dialectical Thomas holds to an epistemology in which the "moment" of the concept is weak, thus robbing epistemology of a hard-and-fast purchase on knowledge.

To the first objection, it seems that Rahner's insight into Thomas and his placement of the human person amid the rest of creation goes much deeper than any commentator, especially Burke and McDermott,[19] has hitherto recognized. Thus, if Rahner's reading of Thomas seems unorthodox, it only *seems* so. Despite vocabulary borrowed from modern dialectical philosophies, Rahner remains remarkably faithful to the original Thomas, and uses his thought to surprisingly powerful effect. To the second objection, Rahner is not interested in epistemology—this cannot be said enough—and if he weakens the concept, it is to avoid a subjectivist overlay on Thomas. The implication of Burke's/McDermott's critique of Rahner is that he produces a subjectivist, relativist Thomas, and that this subjectivist relativism has prevailed in Rahner's later disciples. But the Rahnerian Thomas resists subjectivism, and this begins in his view of sensibility.

18. See Burke, RR, passim; John McDermott, "The Analogy of Knowing in Karl Rahner," *International Philosophical Quarterly* 36 (1996): 201–16, and McDermott, "Dialectical Analogy: The Oscillating Center of Rahner's Thought," *Gregorianum* 75 (1994): 675–703.

19. McDermott's "Analogy of Knowing in Karl Rahner," 215–16, criticizes Rahner for ignoring the human person's placement in Thomas's "hierarchically ordered universe" (216). This criticism is unfounded, and merely derives from McDermott's a priori judgment that "Rahner seems to let the human intellect be the starting point and norm for all metaphysics" (215). The key word here is "seems." It may *seem* that Rahner does this, but he does not. It is true that he focuses on the metaphysics of human knowledge in *Geist in Welt,* but he never pretends to do otherwise. Any general remarks about metaphysics he makes are by extrapolation or for the purpose of regulation and, again, never claim to envision the whole, even if they claim to give access to the whole. This distinction must be made.

For Rahner, then, the human way of being is receptive. Rahner approaches the "essence of sensibility" with a question that lays bare the receptivity (*Empfänglichkeit*) of human being: "How can there be a knowledge of another as such in which this other is the proper object of the knowledge, that is, *in which there is no knowledge antecedent to the other* in which the other is known through the object of this knowledge, which object is identical with the knowing?"[20] Instead of possessing "knowledge antecedent to the other," Rahner tells us that before "any apprehension of a definite other, the knower of itself must have already and always entered into otherness."[21] Receptivity is an attitude toward the other characterized by a "real abandonment" of oneself into the other. Sensibility as the being of materiality consists in moving "out into the exterior of the world."[22]

With such a statement Rahner underscores the inherent spatiality and temporality of human knowing, in particular with respect to metaphysical questioning. As a receptive being endowed inevitably with sensibility, the human person "is located at a definite place whose boundary he does not overstep and which contains in itself an indication of how the question is to be posed, and by that very fact of how it is to be answered also. He asks as one who is already and always in the world . . . through sensibility."[23] By a real, even seemingly total, loss, the human knower becomes inserted into the world. This happens in every act of knowing, and, since the being of the human person is a sensible sort of being, has always already happened.

James Conlon writes of the Rahnerian Thomas, "The medium of sensibility does not mutilate othernesses, but is the means for their perfection."[24] This idea of perfecting the other complements Rahner's idea that sensibility consists in abandoning oneself to the other. The two ideas work together to begin Rahner's resistance to modern subjectivity.

---

20. SW 78/69, emphasis in original.   21. SW 79/70.
22. SW 81/79, 86/75, 80/70, 95/81.   23. SW 116/96.
24. Conlon, "Rahner's Theory of Sensation," 416.

In the introduction to this book, I briefly laid out Heidegger's definition of the modern subject, a definition with which Rahner would have familiarized himself during his study with Heidegger. The subject represents the world to itself, in the interest of controlling it. Already in the Rahnerian Thomas's teachings on sensibility we see that a central feature of the human way of being is its receptivity. This receptive way of being has been specified as abandonment to the other and helping the other to perfection. It is possible that this latter point could be taken as crypto-modern subjectivism, if the implication is that the other would be more perfect if it more closely resembled the subject. We shall have to keep this concern in mind as we go. Does Rahnerian receptivity, which implies a pacific relation to the other, stop when the human knower becomes "the creative ground of this other"?[25] That is, when the Rahnerian Thomas comes to discuss the spiritual side of the human knower, as opposed to the material side, does the knower assume the guise of the modern subject?

METAPHYSICS AND THE IMAGINATION

Thus far we have commented upon some significant aspects of the Rahnerian Thomas's view of sensibility. *Geist in Welt* treats sensibility, though, in order to show how metaphysical knowledge might be accessed through sense experience. Though the intellect must rely on the senses, since human knowing is first and foremost a receptive enterprise, the intellect must get involved. This raises the question of how sensibility, which directs itself toward matter, might communicate and cooperate with intellection, which deals with immaterial ideas. The imagination is this means of communication and cooperation. This is why Rahner entitles the third and final part of *Geist in Welt* "Metaphysics on the Basis of the Imagination."

Rahner says that the "whole thrust" of ST I.84.7 "goes to show

25. SW 75/66–67.

that the imagination's intuition [*imaginatio*] is the only human intuition, and without this the intellect would be blind."[26] The imagination is the "fountain and root of the senses [*fontalis radix omnium sensuum*]," more precisely, the medium "by which spirit itself forms itself into sensibility [*durch die der Geist selbst sich in die Sinnlichkeit einbildet*]."[27] Thus it relates intimately with the senses. But likewise the imagination connects closely with the intellect. From the imagination flows the entire "process" of the conversion to the phantasm, the unique manner of human knowing.

For the Rahnerian Thomas, all transcendence of human intelligence beyond itself to metaphysics is that of the imagination.[28] If the imagination is the means of communication and cooperation between sensibility and the intellect, it is also the primary way that the human person transcends herself. What especially interests Rahner as he pursues metaphysics on the basis of the imagination is the imagination's scope: What, if any, are the bounds of the imagination?

In ST I.84.7.ad3, Thomas responds to the objection that, if knowledge can be had only by turning to the phantasms, then knowledge of incorporeal things is impossible. Within his reply, Thomas states that knowledge of God comes by way of "excess."[29] Rahner interprets this phrase in a manner indebted to (though not identical with) Joseph Maréchal—the "excess" (*excessus*) of which Thomas writes is an active exceeding of a creature's reference to the world. It is a dynamism that reaches out toward being as such, or God.[30] Now, for Thomas, God is, generally speaking, the object of metaphysics. However, more strictly speaking, since God cannot be completely objectified, God is the principle of metaphysics—that which renders metaphysics possible. God opens physics beyond corporeal substances: meta-physics. The *exces-*

---

26. SW 41/42.   27. SW 106/89, 309/231.

28. SW 38/40.

29. Thomas also adds "remotion" and "comparison" as ways to the knowledge of God (ST I.84.7.ad3). Rahner argues that these ways "appear as inner moments within the *excessus* itself," hence I shall not explicitly discuss these ideas here.

30. Cf. Kilby, KRTP, 20.

sus, then, is "the opening of the knower to being as such as the ground of the existent and its knowledge." By way of *excessus,* human intuition shows its purview not to be limited to worldly being.[31] Also, this *excessus* at play in human knowing discloses being (*esse*) itself as more than worldly.

"Excess" becomes for Rahner a marker for the full breadth of the imagination. He takes this full breadth to be a condition of the possibility of "the human imagination, of the human experience of the world itself [*Welterfahrung selbst*]."[32] Within the imagination itself, "a being beyond the realm of the imagination is affirmed."[33] Without exceeding the world, there is no imagination. The fundamental human act occurs in a *Vorgriff* (anticipatory sense) of being as such.[34] While sensibility marks human being's character as receptive, and thus ordered toward "matter," the *Vorgriff* expresses the human being as "spirit."[35] The *Vorgriff* makes manifest the ordering of human knowing toward "that which is absolutely infinite."[36]

Nevertheless, the *Vorgriff* can never be divorced from sensibility, since the *Vorgriff* is an act of the imagination, and the imagination remains rooted—no matter the extent of its scope—in the world. This ambivalence of the human person is what has been so inspiring to Rahner's supporters and so maddening to his critics. For us, it is essential.

With the remark about the imagination's necessary rooting in the world, I have prepared the way into Heidegger's *Kant and the Problem of Metaphysics.* This book's influence on Rahner has been widely recognized.[37] Even with this decades-old recognition of in-

---

31. For the preceding several sentences: SW 390/287–88, 392/289, 394/291, 399/294.

32. SW 53/50.

33. SW 398/294.

34. SW 393/290. From here forward, I shall leave *Vorgriff* untranslated. Any English translation that has been suggested for the term has been misleading in one or more ways.

35. SW 156/125, 186/146, 406–7/299.

36. SW 186/146.

37. Francis Fiorenza, "Karl Rahner and the Kantian Problematic" in SW xix–xlv, at xxi–xxii, xxxviii–xlii; Sheehan, *Karl Rahner,* 177; Kilby, KRTP, 135n17.

fluence, a substantial comparison between *Geist in Welt* and Heidegger's Kant book remains to be done, particularly given the emphasis I have begun to make on the imagination—a topic Heidegger foregrounds in this book as much as in any other.

THE HEIDEGGERIAN KANT

It is only marginally true that the Heidegger under whom Rahner studied was the Heidegger of *Being and Time*. The truth lies in the fact that Heidegger refers continually to *Being and Time* throughout his career. Without a doubt, he looks upon that book as a major philosophical event that keeps paying dividends. The falsehood appears if one recognizes that the once accepted stock reading of *Being and Time* as a founding "existentialist" text is misleading at best and entirely erroneous at worst.[38] The Heidegger that Rahner meets is the one who sees the first part of *Being and Time* as the momentous preface to his diagnostic reading of the history of metaphysics. At the latest, this Heidegger emerged in 1929, with *Kant and the Problem of Metaphysics*.[39]

By the time Rahner meets him, Heidegger has spent the better part of a decade reflecting on *Being and Time* and its implications for the history of metaphysics. For us, the major contention from *Being and Time* is that modern subjectivity's dominance over Western thinking must be overcome. Heidegger's historical inquiries, such as that prosecuted in his 1929 Kant book, seek precedents and tools for

38. Heidegger's "Letter on Humanism," which I shall examine at length in chapter 3, might be read as an extended repudiation of just such a reading, as it was popularized by Jean-Paul Sartre. See Martin Heidegger, "Letter on Humanism," in *Basic Writings,* ed. David Farrell Krell (New York: HarperCollins, 2008), 217–65. Although *Contributions to Philosophy* was not published until 1989, and thus no commentators before then can be held accountable for not attending to it, it is remarkable that this book, written in the 1930s, takes pains to refute an existentialist interpretation of *Being and Time*. For example: *"Being and Time* is the crossing to the leap (asking the grounding question). As long as one accounts for this attempt as 'philosophy of existence,' everything remains uncomprehended" (Heidegger, *Contributions to Philosophy,* 165).

39. Cf. Alison Ross, *The Aesthetic Paths of Philosophy: Presentation in Kant, Heidegger, Lacoue-Labarthe, and Nancy* (Stanford, Calif.: Stanford University Press, 2007), 69.

thinking through the overcoming of modern subjectivity. This part exposes the resources Heidegger finds in Kant for turning against the modern subject. It comments along the way on what Rahner stood to gain from studying under the Heidegger who penned the Kant book.

AGAINST EPISTEMOLOGY

Heidegger constructs *Kant and the Problem of Metaphysics* as a commentary on the *Critique of Pure Reason*. It aims to elucidate Kant's reflections on the metaphysics of knowledge. As with Rahner's *Geist in Welt,* crucial here is the distinction between the metaphysics of knowledge and epistemology. Heidegger openly and at times rather brusquely opposes the prevailing Kant interpretation of his day, which held Kant out to be an epistemologist and theorist for the natural sciences. In a lecture that was part of the famous interchange between Heidegger and Ernst Cassirer,[40] Heidegger declares that the *Critique of Pure Reason* contains "no theory of mathematical, natural-scientific knowledge," and even further no "theory of knowledge at all."[41] Instead, Heidegger argues, the *Critique of Pure Reason* is a book fundamentally preoccupied with the question of being—knowledge is merely a topic that opens this question. Thus we see a similar strategy to that which Rahner will employ in *Geist in Welt.* Human knowledge gives access to deeper questions; it is not the question itself.

The *Critique of Pure Reason* interests Heidegger as an exercise in "laying the ground for metaphysics."[42] For Heidegger, this ground-laying begins with the "humanness of reason, i.e., its finitude."[43] Heidegger calls finite knowledge "non-creative intuition."[44] As finite, human reason does not create objects. Instead, it receives them. Thus,

---

40. For background on this exchange, see Peter E. Gordon, *Continental Divide: Heidegger, Cassirer, Davos* (Cambridge, Mass.: Harvard University Press, 2010).

41. Martin Heidegger, "Davos Lectures: Kant's *Critique of Pure Reason* and the Task of a Laying of the Ground for Metaphysics," Appendix III in KPM, 191–92, here 191.

42. KPM 9–12/13–18.   43. KPM 15/21.

44. KPM 18/ 25–26.

metaphysics begins with a theory of receptivity. Since, as with the Rahnerian Thomas, the human mode of receptivity is sensibility, Kant must develop an ontological concept of sensibility.[45] This concept is incomplete, though, without some principle of determination. Finite, receptive intuition merely receives impressions of objects, but cannot make these indeterminate appearances determinate. Kant ascribes this action of determination to the understanding, which can also be called "productive" intuition.[46]

There are, then, "two basic sources" of knowledge. The groundlaying for metaphysics must examine both. Heidegger argues that these two basic sources, sensibility and the understanding, must not be envisioned as juxtaposed or standing apart. Instead, the essence of finite knowledge comes to light only through the "original unity" of the two sources. Hardly a work of epistemology, which would systematize the faculties of human knowledge, the *Critique of Pure Reason* becomes in Heidegger's hands a book about "unveiling the origin"—disclosing the ground for ontological truth as it manifests itself in human knowing.[47]

In a historical situation in which the epistemological reading of Kant prevailed, even the opening pages of Heidegger's Kant book, which the last paragraph recounted, were enough to disturb Kant scholars. Heidegger takes his metaphysical turning of the text even further, by specifying it. He writes, "What occurs in the Kantian ground-laying? Nothing less than this: the grounding of the inner possibility of ontology is brought about as an unveiling of transcendence, i.e., of the subjectivity of the human subject."[48] The Heideggerian Kant, then, centers his inquiry not merely on the subject, but on the very core of the subject: subjectivity. Heidegger deems such an inquiry important because of the anthropological cast of contemporary philosophy.[49] Despite numerous inquiries into the human

---

45. KPM 19/27.
46. KPM 21/30.
47. KPM 25–27/36–40.
48. KPM 144/205.
49. See KPM 146–50/208–13.

being, the idea of anthropology has become less and less clear. Heidegger attributes this lack of conclusions to a lack of direction. A fundamental question about anthropology remains to be asked in the philosophy of his day.[50]

By contrast with his twentieth-century followers, though, Kant lays bare this fundamental question. In the first edition of the First Critique, he does not proceed forward assuming that he knows what the human person is. Rather, he recognizes that "inquiring into the subjectivity of the subject ... leads us into darkness."[51] The major achievement of Kant's *Critique of Pure Reason,* then, is not its success in laying the ground for metaphysics. It does not consist in developing a philosophical anthropology. It lies in "forcing to light" the "questionableness of the questioning about human beings."[52] Subjectivity, then, does not function as an answer for the Heideggerian Kant, but as a question.

Let us review what we have learned thus far about Heidegger's Kant book, which again is generally agreed to have exerted great influence on Rahner. (1) It foregrounds the character of human knowledge as finite, and thus receptive. (2) Nevertheless it indicates that human knowledge, to be knowledge, must not be simply receptive, but must involve some intellectual determination. (3) This interplay of reception and active determination leads to a question of the origin of this twofold knowing. (4) This question reduces to another—that of ontological truth. (5) This all shows that inquiry into human knowing is not merely an "anthropological task." (6) Instead, questions about human knowledge bring one to question what the subjectivity of the knowing subject is.

For Heidegger, subjectivity is a prior, more original question than the question of human being. And even prior to the question of subjectivity is that of *Dasein.*[53] Everything in Heidegger's Kant book,

---

50. KPM 149/213.
51. KPM 150/214.
52. KPM 150/215.
53. KPM 160/229.

then, feeds into his questioning of finite *Dasein*. In this way, and only in this way, does the Heidegger of *Kant and the Problem of Metaphysics* remain roughly equal to the Heidegger of *Being and Time*. This general overview of Heidegger's reading of Kant has laid bare the questions he brings to Kant, and these are somewhat illustrative for my contention that *Geist in Welt* shows a massive debt to this Heideggerian text. However, more needs to be said about the specific way in which Heidegger appropriates Kant. What, in other words, lies at the center of the Kant book's program? As with Rahner's *Geist in Welt*, which culminates in a part entitled "The Possibility of Metaphysics Based on the Imagination," the Kant book centers on the imagination.

CENTRALITY OF THE IMAGINATION

Heidegger argues that the "central core" of the *Critique of Pure Reason* is Kant's doctrine of the schematism.[54] This is the section of the First Critique in which Kant navigates the interaction between the pure concepts of the understanding and the pure intuition of sensibility. Kant discusses the capacity of the imagination for making sensible images for intelligible concepts. In doing so, the imagination shows itself to be the linchpin of human ontological knowledge, and thus human transcendence. It is the "structural center" of human knowing, an "original unity of receptivity and spontaneity." The schematism is, then, a teaching about the subjectivity of the knower. Subjectivity is the original unity effected by the transcendental imagination. It is the unconscious "root" from which the "stems" of sensibility and understanding spring.[55]

Heidegger claims that, at least in the first edition of the *Critique of Pure Reason*, Kant discovers the need to account for a unity of sen-

---

54. KPM 63/89. See Immanuel Kant, *Critique of Pure Reason*, trans. Paul Guyer and Allen Wood (New York: Cambridge University Press, 1998), 271–77, "On the Schematism of the Pure Concepts of the Understanding."

55. KPM 68/97, 45/64, 107/153, KPM 97/138, 25–26/37.

sibility and understanding, or their ontological underpinnings, pure intuition and pure understanding. The Heideggerian Kant finds in the transcendental imagination, particularly its function of schematism, this principle of unity. In doing so, Heidegger will argue, Kant makes a watershed advance in philosophy. Instead of treating the imagination as merely the synthesis of empirical impressions, and thus a purely receptive faculty, the Heideggerian Kant finds a new role for the imagination. It retains its connection with sensibility, but also acquires an active dimension that will ground the activity of the understanding. The transcendental power of the imagination is—in a hitherto unimaginable way—at once "pure receptivity" and "pure spontaneity."[56] As such, the imagination governs the whole of human knowing.

This governance of sensibility and understanding by the imagination yields a different Kant than the epistemological Kant of the neo-Kantian Marburg school.[57] Instead of a Kant interested in logic and pure thinking, we are confronted with a Kant for whom the aesthetic dimension of thinking is markedly pronounced. By aesthetic dimension I mean the noncognitive, preobjective aspect. For instance, even the side of the imagination that neighbors on the understanding, that is, the "productive" imagination, "never refers to the forming of objects, but refers instead to the pure look of objectivity in general."[58] The Heideggerian Kant is, then, less concerned with establishing objective knowledge than with defining the prior conditions for it. This is, after all, the purpose of transcendental method in the first place. However, Heidegger's construal of a transcendental method with a heightened aesthetic index proves to be quite an innovation on Kant, and one that has provoked widespread derision since the moment he published the Kant book.[59] But this aesthetically read Kant became key to Rahner's reading of Thomas.

---

56. KPM 112/159.   57. See KPM 102/145.
58. KPM 93/131–132.
59. There is some internal warrant for Heidegger's aesthetic reading of Kant. It

At this point we have already begun to advance beyond prior commentaries on *Geist in Welt*. The centrality of imagination for the Rahnerian Thomas is patent—this is still no advance. However, the fact that the centrality of imagination in Kant leads Heidegger to read him aesthetically, and the implications this might hold for *Geist in Welt,* which used the Kant book as a resource, promise significant developments. I shall name two.

First, it is at least plausible that an aesthetically read Kant might inspire Rahner to offer an aesthetically read Thomas who responds to the aesthetic Kant. It should be clear by now that I believe Rahner does this. Second, this Heidegger-inspired Rahnerian embrace of aesthetics places the modern subject in question. In order for this second point to be understood, we must consider more material from the Kant book.

According to Alison Ross, the power of the transcendental imagination, which Kant himself affords great pride of place, "undoes Kant's attempt to ground metaphysics in the operations of a transcendental subject."[60] Kant writes the First Critique as a response to the subjectivist tradition coming out of René Descartes, where the "I think" serves as the bastion of pure reason, and the proper foundation of metaphysics. The Heideggerian Kant's subjectivity is not the subjectivity of the "I think." Subjectivity is prior to thinking.

The Heideggerian Kant's subjectivity does not primarily think. It is confronted directly, prior to conceptuality, with being. In other words, when Kant unveils the transcendental power of the imagination, he "makes manifest the abyss of metaphysics."[61] Kant lays bare the true origin of his attempt to lay the groundwork for metaphysics: finitude. The human subject is "*Dasein* [that] holds itself into the

---

seems that Heidegger read the First Critique through the optic of the third, in which Kant concerns himself directly with matters aesthetic. Since Kant attempts in the Third Critique to complete his critical system, it stands to reason that one could faithfully interpret Kant by looking backward from the end of the critical system toward its beginning.

60. Ross, *Aesthetic Paths,* 70.

61. See KPM 150–51/215.

Nothing"—rather than the answer of pure reason, it is the foundational question.[62]

The Kant book's search into the idea of the imagination preoccupies itself with redefining the modern subject from the standpoint of *Dasein*. One might even say that Heidegger finds in Kant a replacement for the theory-driven modern subject who stands in for being itself: an aesthetically driven knower who receives and approaches being, rather than claiming to grasp it. This is a specification of *Dasein* beyond the analyses of *Being and Time*. This specification and development manifests itself most clearly in the Heideggerian Kant's view of the imagination and time.

Time is the main impetus for the Heideggerian Kant "to determine the essence of subjectivity in a more original way." The question of pure intuition of time, which makes sensibility possible, leads Kant to the question of the imagination. Having asked this question, the Heideggerian Kant finds that the "transcendental power of the imagination is original time." The sustaining action performed by the imagination, by which it lets sensibility and understanding spring from itself, is time. This means that time is the "essential structure of subjectivity." Human receptivity is conditioned by time, but so too is its spontaneity: "our pure thinking always stands before the time which approaches it."[63] The Heideggerian Kant's understanding of the centrality of time reinforces the centrality of the imagination, and strengthens the First Critique's aesthetic upshot.

As Heidegger concludes the Kant book, he insists that Kant's discovery of the imagination "rattles the mastery of reason and the understanding. 'Logic' is deprived of its preeminence in metaphysics."[64] What remains to be done, Heidegger contends, is a thoroughgoing analysis of being in terms of temporality. Likewise, thinkers should contest any thinker who might compromise on the aesthetic

62. KPM 167/238.
63. KPM 36/51, 131/187, 132/189, 44/63.
64. KPM 171/243.

gains of Kant, and return to a logic predicated upon infinitude. This contestation would be tantamount to a resistance of modern subjectivism.

RAHNER AND THE HEIDEGGERIAN KANT

What, then, might Rahner have gained from reading *Kant and the Problem of Metaphysics?* Let us begin with remarks on two passages from the Kant book:

If finitude is placed at the point of departure for transcendence as clearly as it is by Kant, then it is not necessary, in order to escape an alleged "subjective idealism," to invoke a "turn to the object"—a turn which is praised again today all too noisily and with all too little understanding of the problem. In truth, however, the essence of finitude inevitably forces us to the question concerning the conditions for the possibility of a preliminary being-oriented toward the Object, i.e. concerning the necessary turning toward the object in general.[65]

Heidegger responds here to an epistemological, subjectively driven view of Kant's "Transcendental Deduction of the Categories," and thus an epistemological reading of his account of transcendence. On this view, there are two problems: (1) One wants to affirm that a subject is in a sense prior to the object it constitutes, because the categories provide conditions within the subject for the possibility of experiencing an object. (2) One prefers to avoid an Idealism such as Berkeley's that would place in question whether there is an outside object at all. Thus, one posits a "turn to the object" within the subject to affirm and deny what one wishes. Heidegger believes that this solution is a nonstarter. He proposes a different approach.

The finite knower is, first and foremost, a receiver. Even the understanding, which is the active aspect of knowing, depends fully on intuition (i.e., the aspect of the imagination that angles toward sensation). For this reason, positing a "turn to the object" is entirely

---

65. KPM 51/73.

unnecessary—finite knowledge cannot occur without relating itself to another being. Heidegger continues this thought in the next passage, from just a few pages later:

> For a finite creature, beings are accessible only on the grounds of a preliminary letting-stand-against [*Gegenstehenlassens*] which turns-our-attention-toward. In advance, this takes the beings which can possibly be encountered into the unified horizon of a possible belonging-together. In the face of what is encountered, this a priori unifying unity must grasp in advance [*vorgreifen*].[66] What is encountered itself, however, has already been comprehensively grasped [*umgriffen*] in advance through the horizon of time.[67]

The receptivity of the finite knower involves a fair measure of activity: a preliminary grasping of the entire field of receivable objects. Thus Heidegger describes the "unifying unity of pure understanding." In light of this phrase "unifying unity" (*einigende Einheit*) it is notable that the German word for imagination, *Einbildungskraft*, has connotations of forming (*bildung*) into one (*ein*). Heidegger implies that pure understanding centers on the imagination's capacity to unify the horizon of the understandable. Both pure intuition and pure understanding, then, center on the imagination. And the imagination is the a priori possibility for the finite knower's transcendence. To give an account of the imagination is to accomplish a "structural elucidation of [the] essential unity" of sensibility and understanding, and thus to provide a unified vision of finite transcendence.[68]

The character of this transcendence is what influences Rahner, given the evidence of *Geist in Welt*'s aesthetic approach to things, where metaphysics relies on the imagination as a prime source. Following Heidegger's approach to Kant, Rahner recognizes that avoiding modern epistemology and its subjectivist overtones involves fore-

66. Here I have kept the translation of *vorgreifen* as "grasp in advance," but the reader should be advised that the translation of this term in Rahner is a point of controversy. For Rahner (and for Heidegger), the *griff* ("grasp") root of this verb has varied shades of meaning depending on how it is used.

67. KPM 55/77.   68. KPM 55/77.

grounding the imagination. Like Heidegger, or at his prompting, Rahner recognizes that the metaphysics of knowledge—as opposed to epistemology—can evade the problem of how to link the subject and its object ex post facto if he shows that a "subject" is fundamentally openness to the other from the start. The ability to sense "objects" grounds itself in this prior openness, and so too does the capacity for cognizing "objects," and thus achieving metaphysical knowledge. This openness is for Rahner, a *Vorgriff* (see the verb *vorgreifen* in the Heidegger quote above). And the *Vorgriff* lies at the center of the Rahnerian Thomas's imagination.

To summarize and rephrase, Rahner learns from Heidegger's Kant book how to avoid speaking epistemologically, and how to recast human subjectivity into a metaphysics of knowledge based on the imagination. Rahner's account of the Thomistic metaphysics of knowledge centers on its precognitive element. Thus we can say that the Rahnerian Thomas, like the Heideggerian Kant, exemplifies an aesthetically revised subjectivity.

At this point, I can show how far we have come with an example of a critique of Rahner by Thomas Sheehan. He remarks, "Rahner's formulation of the transcendental approach is markedly Kantian, and, to that degree, not well suited to Heidegger."[69] This critique of Rahner epitomizes the scholarly consensus on the Rahner-Heidegger relation: Rahner is, at best, a deviant Heideggerian who strays toward Kant, and at worst, a careless, superficial exegete of Heidegger who gets his teacher wrong despite serious effort to understand him.

The convergence between Heidegger and Rahner we have begun to discover tells a different story. It may be true that Rahner's only explicit, sustained, published exegesis of Heidegger limps a little.[70] However, Rahner's employment and deployment of Heideg-

---

69. Sheehan, *Karl* Rahner, 116.

70. Karl Rahner, "The Concept of Existential Philosophy in Heidegger," *Philosophy Today* 13, no. 2 (Summer 1969): 126–37.

gerian ideas in *Geist in Welt* and his other works evidences a deep, substantial, and sophisticated engagement with Heidegger that amounts to a rejection of Kantian and other subjectivisms. If Rahner's "transcendental approach is markedly Kantian," the marks are those of the Heideggerian Kant.

RAHNER'S AESTHETIC CONTRIBUTION

This part will build off of the work I have already done in order to unearth Rahner's main contribution to theological aesthetics. From this part's end forward, we shall only need to elaborate upon how Rahner makes this contribution and what it means.

Rahner's aesthetic theory begins to emerge in *Geist in Welt,* where he thinks of God as the driving force that moves through the imagination, bringing the world to light. Rahner never claims that this is the only way that God shows up in the world, though he does treat it as exemplary. I have already stated that though *Geist in Welt* is often referred to as Rahner's philosophical anthropology, this is a rather narrow reading of the book. Instead, *Geist in Welt* is a modest yet comprehensive inquiry into the relationship of God and creation, and how this relationship takes on deep aesthetic dimensionality through the movement of God's spirit.

To say it another way, it is a commonplace in Rahnerian studies to remark that the human person is, for Rahner, a spirit in the world. This is true.[71] But what if *Geist in Welt* has another meaning—a theological one? In this book, God is spirit in world (of course not *only* in the world), the Spirit that infuses world, the human person included. This shifting of the sense of *Geist in Welt*'s title brings us to the threshold of Rahner's aesthetic contribution.

---

71. See SW 406–8/298–300. Johann Baptist Metz seems to have been the one who added to this section on "*Der Mensch*" the rider "*als Geist in Welt*" in GW's second edition.

RESPONSE TO AN OBJECTION

Before going forward, I must address a possible objection. I argue that in *Geist in Welt,* God moves through the imagination. God is the imagination's origin and its end, and God runs the gamut between them. This argument hinges upon Rahner's definition of the "whither" (*Worauf*) of the *Vorgriff.*

It seems that Patrick Burke would object that the *Vorgriff* does not have its "whence" in God. In a lengthy footnote, he accuses a few commentators of making a mistake when they refer the *Vorgriff* directly to God.[72] He attempts to substantiate this criticism with reference to the different phrases Rahner uses to describe the "whither" of the *Vorgriff,* noting that "God" is used only once, and that the phrase most synonymous with God, "absolute Being" (*absolute Sein*), is named as the "whither" only once, also. Both Burke's statistics and his interpretation are wrong.

He is in part correct that a clear statement that "the *Vorgriff* goes toward God" appears only once.[73] It lies, however, in the midst of a few sections that aim to specify the "whither" of the *Vorgriff,* one of which includes the following remark: "But in this 'whither' of the *Vorgriff* … an object does manifest itself in a way indicated earlier: the absolute being [*absolute Sein*], God."[74] Rahner says that this initial statement anticipates further specification of the "whither." Just pages later he uses "the absolute" (*das Absolute*) and God interchangeably, and two sections later he affirms that "*excessus*" (a synonym for *Vorgriff*) "toward the absolute [*das Absolute*] [is] constitutive of human spirituality."[75] It is no mistake, then, that previous commentators would refer the *Vorgriff* toward God.

72. Burke, RR 26n72.

73. SW 181/143.

74. SW 180/142. Burke's "one" reference to absolute Being appears on SW 283/213, so clearly there are at least two. One might also count SW 391/289, which refers to the "*Vorgriff auf das* esse *schlechthin*" as "*die implizite Bejahung des absoluten Seins.*"

75. SW 183/144, 186/146.

Anne Carr in particular must be reinstated in this respect.[76] Burke criticizes her for taking the phrase *der Vorgriff geht auf Gott* "out of context in that it is the only place in the whole of *Geist* where the term of the *Vorgriff* is referred to God."[77] The only reason Rahner explicitly refers the *Vorgriff* to God here and not elsewhere is because he believes he has clearly established that this is the case. He evidently sees no need to repeat himself.

But furthermore, there is a wider context within which a commentator like Carr might refer the *Vorgriff* to God. *Geist in Welt*'s final part, "Metaphysics on the Basis of the Imagination," provides this context. There God is treated as the "principle of knowing" that drives human sensibility and intellectual activity. God is the metaphysical ground that drives the science of metaphysics from within the knower. God "shines forth ... in the limitless breadth of the *Vorgriff*," thus rendering metaphysics possible.[78] We must examine this proposal to respond fully to Burke.

THE SUSTAINING GROUND

Rahner's unpublished lectures give us an example of his use of a phrase that crystallizes the thesis that drives his incipient aesthetics in *Geist in Welt*—with respect to the world, God is its "*tragende Grund*," its sustaining ground that is "*innerlich*," interior to it.[79] Rahner clarifies against pantheism that God is the world's "absolute beyond," but God remains the *tragende Grund*.

In traditional, pre-Kantian metaphysics, God would be treated under the rubric of special metaphysics (*metaphysica specialis*), whose three areas were Theology, Cosmology, and Psychology. The metaphysician would presume to know the meanings of God, the world,

---

76. Cf. Anne Carr, *The Theological Method of Karl Rahner* (Missoula, Mont.: Scholars Press, 1977), 76–77.

77. Burke, RR 26n72.

78. SW 406/299.

79. Rahner, "Vortragsskizzen," in *Geist in Welt,* 448.

and the soul, since these metaphysical ideas were innate ideas in each person. This idea of the *tragende Grund,* since it is "interior" to the world and, we shall learn, the imagination, sounds vaguely like an innate metaphysical idea. It is not. In fact, by seeing God as *tragende Grund,* Rahner deviates from the metaphysical tradition along the lines of the Heideggerian Kant.

Heidegger notes that Kant's calling into question of special metaphysics in the *Critique of Pure Reason* is made possible and plausible by his view of transcendence based in the imagination.[80] The Heideggerian Kant interests himself only in human finitude, and seems to have little interest in replacing the God of special metaphysics once this God has been dismissed. Nevertheless, the Heideggerian Kant's demolition of special metaphysics evidently inspires Rahner.

The Rahnerian Thomas denies the validity of *metaphysica specialis*: "For Thomas ... there cannot be a 'special metaphysics' in the sense that in it definite metaphysical objects would be given to it as already known, and then their essence would be investigated and more precisely defined by it in their essence." Special metaphysics constitutes, among other things, a noetic grasp or subjective control of God. Either that, or God is filed away as the end of metaphysics—the final object that caps a long line of metaphysical objects. The Rahnerian Thomas disallows such views of God and God's place in metaphysics. God is not an object. And if God is the end of metaphysics, it is in the sense of final causality—that which draws all disclosure of beings toward their full disclosure. The Rahnerian Thomas argues, "In metaphysics divine things are considered not as the subject of science but as the principle of the subject."[81] In other words, "God is a *principle* for human metaphysics."[82] How does this principle function?

---

80. See KPM 170–72/243–46.

81. "In der Metaphysik considerantur res divinae non tamquam subjectum scientiae sed tamquam principium subjecti" (SW 389/287, my translation).

82. SW 388–389/287.

With respect to the metaphysics of knowledge, the principle functions as that which moves human transcendence. For the Rahnerian Thomas, transcendence occurs in *excessus,* or the *Vorgriff.* At least structurally in *Geist in Welt,* the *Vorgriff* is presented as an aspect of human knowing, proximate to the agent intellect, since it is mostly active. But a careful reading of the massive chapter on abstraction reveals that the *Vorgriff* belongs at the pivot-point of human knowledge. The *Vorgriff* is, then, the activity of the imagination.

In common German, "*Vorgriff*" means "anticipation." Were one to translate it (as I have above), "anticipatory sense" might be apt. Commentators opt instead for more literal translations, playing on the root *griff* (grasp): fore-grasp, pre-grasp, prior grasp.[83] The connotations of a prior grasp of God that many have incorrectly detected in *Geist in Welt* have put them off Rahner's philosophy, thus making it less likely that the root of Rahner's aesthetic contribution might be discovered.[84] A couple of questions can orient us in another direction. What might it mean that the imagination anticipates being? Or, to put it more pointedly, what might it mean that metaphysics is grounded in an anticipation of being?

The answers to these questions lie in the valences of meaning that "to anticipate" incorporates. If "to anticipate" means "to see everything perspicuously in advance," then surely Rahner's thesis of the *Vorgriff* reaching out toward God seems rather distasteful from a theological if not also a philosophical point of view. However, if "to anticipate" means what it often means for human experiences of anticipation — having some sense of what may come, but not being able

---

83. Thomas Sheehan notes this and criticizes such translations, pointing out that *Geist in Welt* "demonstrates that we have no grasp of God at all, either prior or posterior"; see Sheehan, "Rahner's Transcendental Project," in *The Cambridge Companion to Karl Rahner,* 37.

84. This began with Hans Urs von Balthasar's 1939 review of *Geist in Welt,* which, in effect, accused Rahner of positing a human faculty that could grasp God. See Balthasar, "Review of Karl Rahner, *Geist in Welt,* and J. B. Lotz, *Sein und Welt,*" *Zeitschrift für katholische Theologie* 63 (1939): 371–79.

to reckon exactly what it will be—then the theological and philosophical toxicity of this idea decreases sharply, so as not to exist at all. When Rahner says that the imagination anticipates (*vorgreift*) being, even absolute being, even God, he invokes the latter meaning of "to anticipate." Thereby, he makes a tremendously interesting aesthetic point. At metaphysics' most fundamental level stands an anticipatory sense of God, an aesthetic expectation of God, or an "implicit affirmation" of God—a preliminary "yes" to God. Furthermore, this anticipatory sense comes from and is sustained by God, as its *tragende Grund.*

The principle of metaphysics functions, then, by opening human knowing past pure sensibility, lest the human person be a pure receiver with no proper activity. In doing so, the principle does not grant the human knower full clarity, an iron-fisted grip on reality. Instead, the principle introduces the human knower to reality in an anticipatory mode, where some aspects of being can be expected, while others prove rather unexpected. The principle of human knowing, then, is not perspicuous vision, but an introduction into mystery. Rahner's thesis of God as the *tragende Grund* has precisely this upshot: human knowing begins in mystery, and moves toward mystery as its end. Thus, if God moves through the human imagination, this reveals quite a bit about what human life—not just knowing—is like. One could say that this divine movement in the imagination reveals the human ethos.

CONVERGENCE WITH HEIDEGGER—AGAINST KANT

We have sensed already some of Rahner's objections to modern philosophy's overconfidence in human subjectivity, and how Rahner's objections find corroboration in Heidegger's Kant book. Let us reflect more on the convergence between Rahner and Heidegger as they differentiate themselves from Kant, on the way to an aesthetic revision of human knowing.

Despite Kant's efforts to diverge from his predecessors since Descartes and to call human knowers back to their true aesthetic (that is, sensate) manner of knowing, Kant's version of the subject manages to avoid its humanity by constituting the world. The Kantian subject, as it were, blocks receptivity—this is the payoff of the Kantian insistence that we know only representations of objects, and not these objects in themselves.[85] Subjectivity, then, effectively evades both humanity and world, and becomes locked into the mind alone.

Rahner and Heidegger agree, each in his own way, that this purely noetic focus of Kantian subjectivity is a recipe for disaster. Both try to remedy the problem with appeals to the transcendental imagination, and thus by a move toward aesthetics. While Heidegger repudiates the Kant of the second edition of the *Critique of Pure Reason,* he finds a thinking partner in the Kant of the first edition. The latter's reflection on the transcendental power of the imagination "rattles the mastery of reason and the understanding. 'Logic' is deprived of its preeminence in metaphysics, which was built up from ancient times. Its idea has become questionable."[86] Heidegger finds in the first edition an aesthetic turn, or at least the ingredients for it— the "aesthetic" as a question for metaphysics, a grounding question (*Grundfrage*). Heidegger finds inspiration in this. So does Rahner.

Rahner is frequently cited as saying that theology must begin as anthropology and, so the story goes, this idea, which commences with *Geist in Welt,* culminates in the *Grundkurs des Glaubens.*[87] But what we have said so far, while recognizing that it has zeroed in on Rahner's almost exclusive attention to human knowing, is aimed at giving a different inflection to his supposed anthropocentrism.

85. See, e.g., Kant, *Critique of Pure Reason,* "General Remarks on the Transcendental Aesthetic," 94ff.

86. KPM 171/243.

87. Let us consider two examples. First, in the chapter entitled "The Hearer of the Message," Rahner writes, "[T]heology itself implies a philosophical anthropology which enables this message of grace to be accepted in a really philosophical and reasonable way, and which gives an account of it in a humanly responsible way." Second, in the final chapter on eschatology, Rahner observes, "Christian anthropology is Christian futurology and Christian eschatology" (FCF 25, 431).

From the beginning of his career to the end, Rahner was interested in fundamental ontology, in the showing of being from itself. If accessing this ontophany meant "starting with" humanity, Rahner would, just as Heidegger did. Rahner writes about the Heidegger of *Being and Time* and *Kant and the Problem of Metaphysics,* "What Heidegger says about [the human person] is always first and foremost subordinated to the universal question of being."[88] Besides, if one wishes to call into question the ground of modern metaphysics—human subjectivity—the human should be one's starting point.

If Rahner interests himself in fundamental questions, he starts pursuing these questions in earnest in *Geist in Welt*. Furthermore, we discovered above that the ground of Rahnerian aesthetics is his account of God as the principle of human knowing, or more pointedly, the aesthetic awareness of God moving through the human imagination, allowing it to sense and to understand. Just as the Heideggerian Kant breaks open human subjectivity, placing it radically in question so that it might manifest itself for what it truly is, so too does the Rahnerian Thomas inquire deeply enough into the subject as to find grounds for its redefinition. The Rahnerian subject is not in *Geist in Welt* nor will it ever be in his later theology the "I think" of Descartes, Kant, or anyone else. Rahner locates a subjectivity deeper than this thinking, constituting, self-important, controlling subjectivity, which both unmasks modern subjectivity's falsehood and offers an alternative to it.

The development and deployment of aesthetics as a ground on which to defeat the modern subject: Rahner and Heidegger converge in that they both do this. Even further, Rahner's *Geist in Welt* has quite a bit to say about human finitude. The subtitle of the book indicates this: "On the Metaphysics of Finite Knowledge in Thomas Aquinas." Robert Hurd notes Rahner's affinities with Heidegger in his examinations of the "lived contingency of our own tran-

88. Rahner, "The Concept of Existential Philosophy in Heidegger," 129.

scendence."[89] Rahner and Heidegger agree that the questioning of human finitude sheds light on being, and how it openly manifests itself.

Despite these substantial areas of agreement, though, Heidegger and Rahner sharply part ways. As we saw above, Heidegger codes the imagination in terms of time, thus making finitude not just the starting point, but the whole of his aesthetic appropriation of Kant. This also leads to Heidegger proposing that at bottom, subjectivity is a great abyss. Neither of these philosophical decisions satisfies Rahner, particularly because Heidegger directs his thinking of time and of the abyss implicitly, yet no less seriously, against the Christian God.[90] Since Rahner's view of the imagination includes God moving through it as its sustaining ground, Heidegger would find it unacceptable. Though they converge in opposing modern subjectivity in Kant, Rahner and Heidegger diverge with respect to the construction of this opposition.

THE DISAGREEMENT OVER FINITUDE

The present part articulates in greater detail the breaking point between Rahner and his teacher. The difference between them—the disagreement over finitude—will prove crucial for each of this book's ensuing chapters. It comes down to the scope of the human imagination. By extension, it concerns the breadth of Rahner's and Heidegger's respective ontologies.

APRIORISM OF FINITUDE

Rahner remarks in his lecture notes that Heidegger maintains an "apriorism of finitude" (*Apriorismus der Endlichkeit*).[91] Rahner

---

89. Robert Hurd, "Heidegger and Aquinas: A Rahnerian Bridge," *Philosophy Today* 28 (1984): 105–37, here 119.

90. Rejection of the Christian God is not a prominent theme in the Kant book, but it is a subtext, particularly since Heidegger blames the structure of special metaphysics on a Christian conception of the world as created by God. See KPM 5–6/8–9.

91. Rahner, "Vortragsskizzen" in *Geist in Welt,* 444.

insinuates that his teacher makes an illegitimate philosophical selection in banning the infinite from thought. This section explores how that "apriorism" plays out in Heidegger's Kant book, as well as in other works produced immediately before and during Rahner's study with Heidegger. We shall then show how Rahner differs from Heidegger on this count.

Heidegger states that among the First Critique's tasks "the 'critique' of the difference between finite and infinite knowledge must carry special weight."[92] Heidegger carries the torch of this critique by denying the very possibility of infinite knowledge. In doing so, Heidegger envisions himself reversing a trend of a "growing forgetting of what Kant struggled for," which began with German Idealism. Heidegger opposes German Idealism, for it leads to Hegel's pretension to present "God as He is in His eternal essence."[93] Such philosophy, in forgetting its proper limits, likewise forgets its humanity. Kant left the door open for this philosophical disaster by forcing his discovery of the power of the transcendental imagination into an "architectonic" oriented "toward traditional logic." Heidegger wishes to release the imagination, thus finitude — "to hold the investigation open." He asks, "Is it permissible to develop the finitude in *Dasein* only as a problem, without a 'presupposed' infinitude? What in general is the nature of this 'presupposing' in *Dasein*? What does the infinitude which is so 'composed' mean?"[94]

The problem is an overactive imagination, or a concept of the imagination that allows it activity beyond its means. Heidegger wants to avoid what he regards as the "constructed idea" of "absolute knowing,"[95] which guides German Idealism. He concedes that in the Kantian view of imagination something like infinitude emerges. After all, the imagination is powerfully creative and productive.

---

92. KPM 22/32.   93. KPM 171/244.
94. KPM 172/246.
95. Heidegger, "On Odebrecht's and Cassirer's Critiques of the Kantbook," Appendix V in KPM 208/297.

Heidegger concedes a certain claim to infinitude in the finite human creature, for this being can surpass itself indefinitely to understand being. But the limited means through which the human being attains to such understanding, that is, "thrown" engagement with beings, leads to the following conclusion: "This infinitude which breaks out in the power of imagination is precisely the strongest argument for finitude, for ontology is an index of finitude."[96]

Alison Ross enlightens the above paragraphs: "Heidegger's Kant book can be read ... as identifying in the transcendental power of the imagination the priority of presentation to the supposed terms that are to be related through it."[97] Imagination presents infinitude, but cannot create other beings. Thus it shows itself to be finite. The Heideggerian Kant arrives at the "insight that the absolute does not 'precede' or ground 'its' presentation."[98] Ross sees this movement as counter to what Kant intended: "Heidegger in fact reverses Kant's perspective to argue that the ideas of reason," those that point toward the infinite, "do not, as Kant thought, precede the elements and context of material life but are in fact drawn from this context in the first place."[99] Heidegger's view of presentation effects a shift in apriority. Kant blocks the intellectual intuition of the Absolute, but Heidegger amplifies this position in order to make sure that Kant's granting of precedence to logic does not necessarily pave the way for German Idealism. For the Heideggerian Kant, being shows itself to and through the imagination under the conditions of finitude.

Heidegger argues in his disputation at Davos with Ernst Cassirer, "Because philosophy opens out onto the totality and what is highest in man, finitude must appear in philosophy in a completely radical way."[100] Ontology is a form of thinking. Thinking is by na-

---

96. Heidegger, "Davos Disputation between Ernst Cassirer and Martin Heidegger," Appendix IV in KPM 197/280.

97. KPM 172/246.   98. Ross, *Aesthetic Paths*, 78–79.

99. Ross, *Aesthetic Paths*, 81.

100. Heidegger, "Davos Disputation," 207/296.

ture finite.[101] Thus ontology is an index of finitude. Metaphysics obscures its own modus operandi when, à la Hegel, it pretends to infinite knowledge. In order for thought to return to the right track, being must remain a mystery, questionable, a lure.

Much of Heidegger's thought on mystery and questioning Rahner would find admissible, even fructifying for theology. The problem, from a Rahnerian point of view, is a condition that Heidegger places on one specific question—the question of God. In 1928, Heidegger wrote a text called "Phenomenology and Theology." Jean-Luc Marion summarizes its main thrust: "God will never be able to appear within the field of questioning thought except under the mediating conditions first of 'christianness' and then of *Dasein*."[102] The question of God "plays only ontically," meaning that *ontologically* God has no bearing on thinking.[103] Heidegger sticks by his assertion that ontology is "an index of finitude." There is no room for the absolute, the infinite, or the divine in ontology. Thus Heidegger, who advocates for the question everywhere else, refuses the question of God. Rahner cannot settle for this train of thought theologically, but also not philosophically. This we must now understand.

SIDING WITH IDEALISM

The first book Rahner published was not *Geist in Welt.* It was a book of prayers, *Worte ins Schweigen* (1937, *Encounters with Silence* [ET]). He wrote this book near the end of his philosophical studies at Freiburg. One passage in particular proves apropos of Rahner's resistance of Heidegger's apriorism of finitude. Rahner prays to God:

---

101. KPM 17/24–25.

102. Marion, *The Idol and Distance: Five Studies,* trans. Thomas A. Carlson (New York: Fordham University Press, 2001), 209. See Heidegger, "Phenomenology and Theology," in *The Religious,* ed. John D. Caputo (Malden, Mass.: Blackwell, 2002), 49–66.

103. Marion, *Idol and Distance,* 209.

Suppose I tried to be satisfied with what so many today profess to be the purpose of their lives. Suppose I defiantly determined to admit my finiteness, and glory in it alone. I could only begin to recognize this finiteness and accept it as my sole destiny, because I had previously so often stared out into the vast reaches of limitless space, to those hazy horizons where Your Endless Life is just beginning.[104]

Here, at an undeniably theological, even devotional, moment, Rahner takes aim at people like Heidegger who revel in finitude alone. During his prayer Rahner submits that any inquiry into one's own finitude will be incomplete unless one starts from an awareness of the vast reaches of space, which mark the horizon of God's advent. In other words, though the parameters of "thrownness" and "worldliness" may seem broad, only the horizon of God's endless life provides breadth enough for properly situating human finitude. Proscription of the appearance of the infinite is, then, a philosophical hypothesis that comes up empty on exactly what it claims to deliver.

Rahner's remark in his notes about Heidegger's *Apriorismus der Endlichkeit* suggests that even as Heidegger tries to open the field for the manifestation of being, he restricts it. Another note of Rahner's on Heidegger's "What Is Metaphysics?" adds this objection: "For us the concept of being should not be *inherently* finite."[105] This concept, since it is the grounding concept, demands the widest possible scope for thinking.

While Heidegger spends time in the Kant book rejecting German Idealism's interpretation of Kant, Rahner accepts certain Idealist premises. First among these is the idea that being and knowing are not simply finite. In his lecture notes, Rahner acknowledges his nearness to German Idealism and the consequent distance from Heidegger. He writes that Heidegger is "realistic with us against ide-

---

104. Karl Rahner, *Encounters with Silence*, trans. James Demske (Westminster, Md.: Newman Press, 1965), 6.

105. "Bei uns darf der Seinsbegriff nicht *innerlich* endlich sein" (Rahner, "Lektürenotizen," in *Geist in Welt*, 459).

alism ... against us, wherein we are idealistic."[106] Rahner appreciates the realism Heidegger's thinking of finitude can lend to philosophy and theology. Nevertheless, he finds this realism ultimately insufficient if it refuses to account for the fullness of reality's scope. In order to find this wideness of scope, Rahner turns to the German Idealists in a way, but more nearly the point of his breaking with Heidegger brings him back to his dissertation director, Honecker, and to Joseph Maréchal.[107]

In a crucial portion of his argument, "The Ontological Interpretation of the Light-Image,"[108] Rahner sides with Idealism more than perhaps any other place in *Geist in Welt*. He aims to establish intellectual light as the medium for objective knowledge without falling into the precritical doctrine of innate ideas. He argues that light undergirds both the knower and the known, making possible the activity of knowing and the actuality of being known. By virtue of this common milieu of light, the agent intellect exercises wide-ranging spontaneity, even to the point of presenting the "totality of all objects." Thus the agent intellect exhibits something like infinitude — though it is called back to its finitude by the need for sensible determinations, due to the constitutive receptivity of human knowing, which we examined above. The quasi-infinitude of the human intellect leads Rahner back to the topic of *excessus,* and there he makes his most idealistic statements of the book.

Due to the co-affirmation of absolute being in the agent intellect's presentation of the totality of all objects, "Thomas can understand the agent intellect in a special way as a participation in the light of absolute spirit, not merely because, being dependent on this,

106. "realistisch mit uns gegen Idealismus ... gegen uns, worin wir idealistisch" (Rahner, "Vortragskizzen," 444–45).

107. As I mentioned above, attempts to articulate Rahner's debt to Hegel tend to be problematic. I shall try to establish Rahner's proximity to Schelling in future work — this has not yet been tried sufficiently, and should be. See Rahner's references to Honecker's article on the concept of light in Thomas (SW 212/163) and to Maréchal (SW 221/170).

108. SW 211–26/163–73.

it is as a matter of fact similar to it, but because finite spirit is spirit only through the *Vorgriff* of absolute *esse* in which absolute being is already and always apprehended. Rahner then quotes Thomas: "All knowing beings know God implicitly in everything they know."[109] This espousal of Idealism, whether with respect to light or absolute spirit, would be anathema to Heidegger. But Rahner recognizes the philosophical plausibility, utility, and fundamental truthfulness of it. The truth lies in the breadth that a co-affirmation of absolute spirit allows. It lets appear the "horizons where God's endless life is just beginning." In a more theological vein, the truth of Rahner's statements lies in the fact that philosophical reason can accord with the revelation that God has manifested God's self in the world, most palpably in the life, death, and resurrection of Jesus Christ.

Because of Rahner's siding with Idealism, the following assertion from Sheehan proves scandalously wrong: "The stark outcome of *Geist in Welt* is that human knowledge is focused exclusively on the material order, with no direct access to the spiritual realm."[110] He is right that there is no direct access to the spiritual realm. Rahner avoids the metaphysical pitfall of innate ideas. Likewise, Rahner ultimately rejects Idealism, as Fiorenza notes.[111] But nowhere could one find in this text an exclusive focus on the material order. Unless, of course, one notices that for Rahner, focus on the material order is focus on Jesus of Nazareth, who is assuredly not exclusively material.[112]

In a theological essay on Ignatius from 1936, which we shall treat at length in chapter 2, Rahner identifies as the "original sin in the history of philosophy" that the metaphysics of knowledge from the early Greeks through Hegel allowed "God to be only what the world is, [made] God in the image of man," and even conceived of "piety as a consideration for the world."[113] Even though Heidegger

---

109. SW 226/173, ET modified.
110. Thomas Sheehan, "Rahner's Transcendental Project," 31.
111. Fiorenza, "Rahner and the Kantian Problematic," xlii.
112. SW 408/300.
113. Rahner, "The Ignatian Mysticism of Joy in the World," in TI 3, 285.

tries to evade the metaphysical tradition, one gets the sense that Rahner suspects Heidegger of still representing philosophy's historical sin. Rahner's siding with the Idealists over against Heidegger originates in this concern. Rahner believes that when Idealism accords with the Christian insistence that this world is not the only one—that is, when Idealism affirms the "absolute" or the "infinite"—Idealism ought at least in part to be espoused. Though this flirting with Idealism has vexed Thomists of Rahner's day and ours, when one couches it in terms of Rahner's resistance to Heidegger, it ought to seem less threatening than attractive.

SETTING THE STAGE

Thus far this chapter has given us many questions to pursue. I have claimed that Rahner's theological aesthetics *begins* with his account of sensibility in Thomas, and *develops* in his presentation of the imagination and his initial forays into the agent intellect. How, then, will Rahner's theological aesthetics advance beyond this?

We shall see that Rahner elaborates it even in *Geist in Welt*. In chapter 2 we shall proceed more deeply into Rahner's view of the human intellect. I have argued that Heidegger provided a serious impetus for Rahner's aesthetic theorizing in *Geist in Welt*. What, if any, will be Heidegger's role in this elaboration? How might Heideggerian thoughts that Rahner encountered in listening to his teacher's lectures and reading his texts have affected Rahner's account of the human subject? In what other ways than we have already observed do Rahner and Heidegger converge regarding the question of aesthetics?

We have also seen how Rahner and Heidegger diverge on the idea of infinitude. In future chapters, we must ask several questions in this vein. How does Rahner continue to affirm the Christian notion of God's infinity? On Heidegger's side, how does Heidegger further develop his apriorism of finitude? We shall learn that his readings of Friedrich Hölderlin, in which he first engaged in the mid-1930s, prove crucial in this respect.

The above questions, and soon more, will guide us. Starting with the next chapter's later pages, we shall move beyond Rahner's direct encounter with Heidegger from 1934 to 1936. Whereas this first chapter argued that Heidegger had some direct influence on Rahner, and the next chapter will partially continue this line of argument, all subsequent chapters will proceed differently. I shall contend that post-1936, though Heidegger and Rahner have little personal contact, their respective paths of thought evidence remarkable similarities even in their differences.

Our task for the next four chapters will be this: to follow the divergent yet oddly harmonious careers of Rahner and Heidegger. Furthermore, I shall claim that these two careers arise from and give rise to theories of the sublime. The upcoming chapter, then, will introduce how Rahnerian and Heideggerian aesthetics are directed toward the sublime.

2 RAHNER'S SUBLIME

BEFORE HEIDEGGER delivered his famous lecture "The Origin of the Work of Art," he offered his first course on Friedrich Hölderlin. Before Rahner wrote *Geist in Welt,* he attended this course on Hölderlin. The Heidegger of *Kant and the Problem of Metaphysics* opened for Rahner the notion of metaphysics based on the imagination, and thus the possibility for Rahnerian aesthetics. The Heidegger of the Hölderlin lectures introduced Rahner to a way of thinking that would help him to specify his aesthetics. Rahner's aesthetics would disclose a Catholic version of the sublime, which would resist modern subjectivity along the lines of Heidegger's dialogue with poetry, while also resisting his thinking's strict limits.

This chapter's four parts center on Rahner's encounter with Heidegger reading Hölderlin. Before I expose the first Hölderlin course, though, I set up this exposition with a part on what Rahner calls "the subject's return to itself" (*reditio subjecti in se ipsum*),[1] a central theme in Thomas Aquinas's metaphysics of knowledge. The question of Rahner's so-called turn to the subject pivots on this theme. I then read Heidegger's first lectures on Hölderlin, *Hölderlins Hymnen "Germanien" und "Der Rhein,"* asking how Rahner's understanding of the subject is inflected by Heidegger's poetic thinking,

1. SW 117/98 and passim.

65

which is a thinking of the sublime. The third part argues that Rahner's distinctive aesthetics, with its heightened index of the sublime, arises from his convergent-divergent engagement with Heidegger. Rahner's essay "Priest and Poet" (1958) epitomizes this engagement.[2] The chapter's final part describes a broad area of disagreement between Rahner and Heidegger. The two disagree over what the proper "home" is for human existence. The articulation of the "home" in Heidegger's *Being and Time* and Rahner's essay "The Ignatian Mysticism of Joy in the World" (1936) evidence a sharp contrast. At stake between these two thinkers is ethos: the form of life in the world and how this life reveals being.

RAHNER ON THE SUBJECT'S RETURN TO ITSELF

In the last chapter I examined how the Rahnerian Thomas's account of sensibility provides resources for resisting modern subjectivity aesthetically. This case was easier to make than the one to be undertaken in this section. The modern subject—from Descartes through Kant to Hegel, along with its extraphilosophical manifestations—is known for its intellectual, as opposed to sensible, power. Critics have drawn one major implication from Rahner's view in *Geist in Welt* of the agent intellect in Thomas: it coheres nicely with the modern subject's intellectual power. This is particularly true when Rahner calls intellectual activity an abstractive return of the subject to itself.

This part rejects such a reading of Rahner. It argues that when Rahner examines the agent intellect in Thomas, he constructs a very different form of subjectivity than the modern sort. This is largely because the aesthetic receptivity of sensibility always remains operative, even amid intellectual activity. Sensibility and intellect cooperate. By defending this view of the intellect in Rahner, I gather material to be used later to disclose Rahner's version of the sublime.

2. Karl Rahner, "Priest and Poet" in TI 3, 294–317. Hereafter PP. Cf. Rahner, "Priester und Dichter," in *Schriften zur Theologie, Band III: Zur Theologie des Geistlichen Lebens* (Einsiedeln: Benziger Verlag, 1956), 349–75.

THOMAS, RAHNER, AND THE *REDITIO*
COMPLETA IN SEIPSUM

Summa Theologiae I.84.7.corpus discusses the intellect in terms of its capacity for action. This capacity is facilitated by the senses and the imagination. Thomas makes this case in response to objections, particularly objection 1, which contend that the human intellect can know without "turning to the phantasms," that is, without cooperation from the senses and imagination.

Though he emphasizes the importance of this sense-intellect cooperation, Thomas does maintain a distinction between intellectual and sensual apprehension.[3] The intellect knows many things that the senses cannot apprehend.[4] Thomas presupposes that the proper object of the intellect in act is the "universal nature of the individual existent."[5] The intellect's role, as opposed to sensation's, consists in looking at this universal aspect of the particular.

In commenting on these ideas, Rahner augments his view of sensibility in Thomas with a view of the intellect as "abstractive" and "subjective." Rahner writes of the intellect in act as "returning to itself" from its "abandonment" to the sensible other.[6] Rahner uses spatial imagery of inside and outside. The "return" is from the outside of sensibility to a subjective inside. One might ask, then, whether in part two, chapter three of *Geist in Welt* Rahner abandons the aesthetic perspective he sets up in the previous chapter, and in the book's final part. This question has import because it bears on another: Is Rahner a theologian of the turn to the subject, where subjectivity means private interiority sealed off from others by its own noetic power?

Though I submit that Rahner does not succumb to modern subjectivism, it still bears considering how he arrives at his conception

---

3. He first establishes this distinction in ST I.77.1.

4. ST I.77.1.ad4.   5. ST I.84.7.corpus.

6. SW 117/98.

of subjectivity. This will lead us to discover exactly what kind of subjectivity Rahner affirms. We shall begin with his rendering of the subject-object relationship as he sets up the idea of the "abstractive return."

The subject-object relationship is indispensable given the Rahnerian Thomas's definition of knowledge: "The one human knowledge is objective reception of the other, or the world."[7] Sensibility consists in the undifferentiated unity of subject and object. For this reason, the subject must "return to itself" in order that it might stand over against the object. Without the "return" the other cannot appear as other. Two conditions must be met for human knowledge to be truly human—there must be sense reception *and* intellectual activity.

Rahner quite infamously defines being as fundamentally self-presence and knowledge as being self-present. These definitions lend his critics fodder for maintaining that Rahner is a subjective Idealist.[8] But the way Rahner lays out his idea of the abstractive return evades this critique. The duality of human knowing and its consequent aesthetic cast are the means for this evasion.

Three sentences about self-presence support this claim. Rahner writes, "Presence to self as being present to oneself and being present to oneself as being placed over against another constitute in this duality the one fundamental constitution of the human intellect." Then he continues, "For if being present to itself were possible to human thought without being placed over against another, then the first-known (proper object) would be the being of the knower himself." And finally, "If, vice versa, the knowledge were presence to self, not as placed over against another, but only as being with the other, then such knowledge would merely be sensibility, which of its es-

---

7. SW 132/109.

8. See SW 68–71/62–64. Long ago Francis Fiorenza exposed this critique of Rahner as a misunderstanding of him, but since the critique perdures in commentators like Burke, McDermott, and a host of Thomists, I still must refute it. See Fiorenza, "Karl Rahner and the Kantian Problematic," xxx–xxxv.

sence excludes being present to oneself."[9] The point is that the duality of the human person must be preserved, lest this person fail to be human.

Most of all, the duality cannot collapse on the side of the intellect. Such a collapse is modern subjectivism's main problem. If the knower's first knowledge is self-knowledge—I think, therefore I am—then that knower is not human. The modern subject, which seals itself off from that which it knows, thus properly knowing itself alone, fails to be human.

Something similar goes for the side of sensibility. The knower who knows another only by being that other is not human, either. But the issue is not so much the excess of sensibility. In fact, sensibility plays an important role in knowing, as the bastion against modern subjectivism's noetic excess. Knowing is "aesthetic" for human persons because it cannot be had without being rooted in sensibility.

One must keep these ideas in mind when one reads that for the Rahnerian Thomas the subject's return to itself is a *complete* return. A complete return to self, *reditio completa in se ipsum,* sounds hauntingly like the key moment of the odyssey of Hegelian spirit, which is widely regarded (correctly or not) as the pinnacle of modern subjectivism. A complete return to self, it would seem, should entail a thorough sealing of a self against the world that it means comprehensively to consume. Is this what Rahner means, or something else?

The answer is "something else." Rahner uses the idea of the "complete return" as another way to safeguard the humanity of human knowing, to prevent it from degenerating into the modern conception of subjectivity. This is why Rahner entitles a crucial section "The *Reditio Completa* Peculiar to Man (*Reditio in Conversione ad Phantasmata*)."[10] The "return" establishes intellection as, so to speak, a middle term in human knowing, bound on either side by human

9. SW 134/110.
10. SW 230–36/176–80, my translation.

aesthetic receptivity. The "return" is knowledge's "taking along" (*Mitnahme*) of what human sensibility gathers from the world. Likewise, the "return" as a "taking along" ensures that what the intellect knows comes not by its own power, but by the power of another. The other encountered in sensibility is the thing that the human subject knows, not some subjective impression. In other words, the human subject is ontologically open to the world and the things in it, not noetically barred from the world and the things in it. The human subject actually relates to the world, not regulatively, à la Kant, but substantively. The human subject does not seal itself off from the world, but really and truly partakes of it, even to the point of becoming determined by what it receives.

Even in the chapter on the agent intellect, then, Rahner remains true to the aesthetic perspective that we examined in chapter 1. The intellect may locate the universal in each particular sensible thing, but the intellect does not outstrip these sensible things. To do so would be to ignore or to destroy them. The Rahnerian Thomas's intellect does not do this. Having said this, though, I have not yet shown how Rahner's idea of the *Vorgriff* complicates matters. To that we now turn.

VORGRIFF

Chapter 1 began examining how Rahner sides at times in his reading of Thomas with the German Idealists. This happens when he insists upon the inherent human drive toward the infinite. As is common knowledge in Rahner studies, he derives this idea from the transcendental emendations of Thomas in Pierre Rousselot and Joseph Maréchal.[11] The main and most controversial way Rahner

---

11. Lest I stray from my argument about Rahner, I shall avoid here any detailed consideration of Rousselot and Maréchal. I direct the reader to search the works of Otto Muck, Joseph Donceel, and Andrew Tallon on the relationship between Rahner and these so-called transcendental Thomists. See Otto Muck, *The Transcendental Method*, trans. William Seidensticker (New York: Herder & Herder, 1968); Joseph Donceel, trans. and ed., *A Maréchal Reader* (New York: Herder & Herder, 1970); Andrew Tallon, "Spirit,

makes his own emendation of Thomas is by treating the agent intellect as a *Vorgriff* of being.

Rahner sets this *Vorgriff* as a condition for the return to the self.[12] Abstraction, that is, the return, is a recognition and release of a universal form from a material object. The subject returns to herself, for instance, by recognizing the oak in her backyard as a limited, material instantiation of the form "tree." Intellectual activity, then, consists in seeing a field of possibilities. *Vorgriff* names the apprehension that prepares for this intellectual activity.

In chapter 1, I pointed out how the *Vorgriff* always remains tied to the human imagination, thus sensibility, and this ensures that the *Vorgriff,* thus human subjectivity, never claims to do the impossible: exit the world. I must now nuance that thought.

We already know that for Rahner, the *Vorgriff* attains somehow to the infinite. In the chapter on abstraction, Rahner identifies a Thomistic distinction between two types of unlimitedness (*Ungegrentztheit*), so as to explain what sort of infinite scope the *Vorgriff* has. First, there is "privative unlimitedness," which belongs to matter, and refers to the "nothing" of space and time.[13] Second, there is "negative unlimitedness," which belongs to form, and refers to "being absolutely."[14] Though the *Vorgriff* encompasses privative unlimitedness, it attains to negative unlimitedness as its proper scope.

This proves significant for at least two reasons. First, at this point Rahner seems to claim that by way of the *Vorgriff* human intellection surpasses the purview of the imagination, thus violating the bounds of metaphysics on the imagination's basis. Second, Rahner

---

Matter, Becoming: Karl Rahner's *Spirit in the World* (*Geist in Welt*)," *The Modern Schoolman* 48 (1971): 151–65. Tallon's translations of Rousselot's works (Marquette University Press) are also significant in this respect.

12. SW 143/116. For this and the rest of the references to *Geist in Welt* in this part, I have modified the ET.

13. This reading combines thoughts on SW 153/122 and 143/116. The ET renders "Ungegrentzheit" as "infinity."

14. SW 153/123, 143/116.

risks this transgression so as to stake a philosophical position resistant to Heidegger.

As is well known, Rahner borrows the term *Vorgriff* from Heidegger.[15] In *Being and Time, Vorgriff,* along with the two companion terms, *Vorhabe* and *Vorsicht,* refers to a set of preexisting structures that orients *Dasein* toward the world. *Dasein* has an anticipatory grasp on, possession of, and vision of the world as constitutive features of its makeup. Thus Dasein feels ready to interpret the world as it comes. Sheehan points out that Rahner's appropriation of Heidegger's *Vorgriff* without its companion terms is a rather "loose" one.[16] The three are, in *Being and Time,* inextricably interlaced. For Sheehan, Rahner should not uncouple them.

Sheehan's critique merits a response, since it has contributed to an overall impression that Rahner reads and appropriates Heidegger selectively and not tremendously well. If one restricts oneself to *Being and Time,* one might hold this opinion. But elsewhere even Heidegger is not as faithful to himself as Sheehan would like. In *Kant and the Problem of Metaphysics,* for example, Heidegger treats the *Vorgriff* alone. Thus Rahner's isolation of the one term from the others is not entirely unfounded. And since the Kant book was so important for him, it stands to reason that he would follow Heidegger's formulation of the *Vorgriff* in this text. There is, though, even more to the story.

Indeed, Heidegger would be dissatisfied with Rahner's utilization of this term, but not because Rahner failed to understand what Heidegger meant by it. Instead, Rahner recalibrates the *Vorgriff* to do something Heidegger would not have it do. Rather than using *Vorgriff* to describe a pregiven structure that orients human interpretation of the world, *Vorgriff* disrupts human orientation toward the world, if "world" means the arena of human finitude.

15. See Heidegger, BT 191.
16. Sheehan, *Karl Rahner,* 204.

To resume our reading of *Geist in Welt,* Rahner states his position, implicating the distinction between privative and negative unlimitedness:

This is always true: man knows the finitude and limitedness of a concrete determination of the being (of an existent) insofar as it is held in the broader "nothing" of its potentiality; but this broader nothing itself is known only when it itself is held against the unlimitedness of its formal actuality as such (of being).[17]

The *Vorgriff* exceeds what seem to be the distinct bounds of the imagination: the "nothing" of potentiality that we call space and time, or privative unlimitedness. Rahner does not mean, though, to set the *Vorgriff* so loose from the range of the imagination that it loses the world. Instead, Rahner wishes to make the point that being grounds nothingness, not the other way around. An orientation toward being — absolute being — ensures the concreteness of things in the world in their finitude. Negative unlimitedness reveals things' limits. Without an awareness of being, the nothingness of space and time would be unrecognizable. Being, in its unrestricted scope, is the ground for any recognition of individual things within the restricted field of the world.

Heidegger claims the opposite in the 1935 course Rahner takes with him, *Introduction to Metaphysics.* He prosecutes a similar thesis in "What Is Metaphysics?" (1929), a text with which Rahner was also familiar. For Heidegger, only by "holding beings out into the nothing" can one properly apprehend them.[18] Rahner's view of the *Vorgriff* specifically and self-consciously opposes this Heideggerian thesis, on the grounds that the thesis derives from an illicit philosophical decision: an apriorism of finitude.

Rahner puts it another way in the lectures that would become

---

17. SW 154/124.

18. Martin Heidegger, *Introduction to Metaphysics,* trans. Gregory Fried and Richard Polt (New Haven: Yale University Press, 2000), 30. Hereafter EM.

Hearer of the Word (given 1937, published 1941). The *Vorgriff* is "not simply a transcendence toward a finite circle of possible objects, nor originally a transcendence toward nothingness."[19] The first half of the sentence evokes the noetic constraints of Kantian critique, and the second half the Heideggerian apriorism of finitude. Both thinkers offer only a "relative" openness that extends "merely to a certain sector of the real or of the possible."[20] Since Heidegger's initial formulation of the *Vorgriff* in *Being and Time* attempts to open the possibilities of *Dasein,* it is rather ironic that this very formulation, and subsequent ones, limits *Dasein's* possibilities. This irony is not lost on Rahner.

For Heidegger, *Dasein's* being bound to the world predicates itself upon *Dasein's* inability to confront its own limits: "So profoundly does finitude entrench itself in existence that our most proper and deepest limitation refuses to yield to our freedom."[21] This may sound like a humble and realistic statement regarding human capabilities. He aims to show how *Dasein* better accounts for human abilities than the modern subject does. While this may be so, Rahner constructs a different alternative to modern subjectivity, one that he believes outstrips *Dasein.*

For Rahner, human existence's being bound to the world does not entail anxious resolve in the face of damnable limitation. It involves a fundamental offer of freedom that moves through the *Vorgriff.* In a later section of *Geist in Welt* subtitled "The Ontological Meaning of 'Nothing,'" Rahner records observations about the *Vorgriff's* ability to recognize the limits of particular beings. He calls this act "negation." Then he contends, "The negation is the index of the freedom of spirit in its being bound to sensibility. Non-being is known, not insofar as being is held up against nothing, but insofar

---

19. HW 122/216.

20. HW 140/250.

21. Martin Heidegger, "What Is Metaphysics?" in *Basic Writings,* ed. David Farrell Krell (New York: HarperPerennial, 2008), 89–110, at 106.

as *esse* as such is apprehended simultaneously."[22] The *Vorgriff*'s freedom, its transcendence, lies in the promise of freedom's actualization, not in freedom's actual breakdown.

The *Vorgriff* is an orienting structure. Rahner retains this from Heidegger. It is an anticipatory sense that orients particular things apprehended by the human intellect toward their sustaining ground. But this sustaining ground is not the privative emptiness of space and time. It is God, the unlimitedness or infinity that is beyond world. S. J. McGrath writes, "Rahner corrects Heidegger's agnostic being-in-the-world by disengaging [the] average and everyday experience of God as one of Dasein's existentials."[23] Rather than rooting human *Dasein* in the world alone, yet without leaving the world, the *Vorgriff* directs the human person toward God, the sustaining ground of the world.

THE POSSIBLE INTELLECT

The foregoing paragraphs on the *Vorgriff,* particularly these last comments on God, ought to suggest that Rahner's discussion of the agent intellect as a *Vorgriff* of being augments the aesthetic perspective we encountered in chapter 1. I shall round out this augmentation by exploring more contours of Rahner's view of the human intellect.

So far we have familiarized ourselves with the agent intellect. I have tried to indicate how different this intellect's activity is from that of the modern subject and of Heideggerian *Dasein,* which explicitly counters modern subjectivity. The difference lies in Rahner's painstaking dual insistence upon (1) the intellect's aesthetic grounding in, yet (2) distinctness from the world. This difference cannot be fully clear, though, unless one understands the importance of the "possible" intellect.

These words are the sine qua non of Rahner's metaphysics of

---

22. SW 298/224, ET modified.
23. McGrath, *The Early Heidegger and Medieval Philosophy: Phenomenology for the Godforsaken,* 236.

human knowing: "possible intellect is the most adequate and simple conception for human knowledge and for human being altogether."[24] Rahner thus reiterates his point that human knowing and being is not primarily characterized by its activity. This flies in the face of the modern subjectivist account of human knowing, which holds it to be primarily and even supremely active. But there is more. Rahner's foregrounding of the possible intellect teaches us something more fundamental about human knowing and being, and in turn about the manifestation of absolute being. This fundamental insight relates to the subject's return to itself.

The potentiality of the possible intellect consists in this: its "coming-to-itself" (*Zu-sich-selber-kommen*) occurs only in the "receptive letting itself be encountered" (*hinnehmenden Sichbegegnenlassen*).[25] The possible intellect's potentiality does not refer mainly to its as yet undeployed power of knowing, but to its ontological conditioning by another. This is an ontological—or ontophanic—not just a noetic claim. The knowing and being of the human person comes about by way of a letting, an allowing of oneself to be met by the other. The "subject's return to itself," then, is hardly a sealing of oneself against infiltration by another. Instead, it is a paradoxical reception-action that invites the other into a cooperative relationship.

Rahner's lengthy and detailed development in part two, chapter three of a theory of emanation corroborates this reading. The spirit's emanation as sensibility is the reception-action of creating a space for another as the ground for establishing the self. Rahner will even state that spirit and sensibility are the receptive origins of each other.[26] In other words, the "subject" for Rahner *is* openness to and for the other. Likewise, the "object" realizes itself in its relationship to the "subject."[27] The cornerstone of the subject-object relationship, then, is mutual enhancement.

24. SW 245/186.   25. SW 247/187.
26. SW 284–86/213–15, 260–61/197–98.
27. See SW 358–66/265–71.

Over the past two sections I have been contesting the claim that Rahner's account of subjectivity accords with modern subjectivism's. The theme of the possible intellect proves critical for ascertaining how Rahner's subject contrasts with the modern subject. The possible intellect introduces us to an idea of receptive-activity, where the classical duo of *passio* and *actio* are disallowed from being held as strict opposites.[28] Rahner's idea of receptive-activity lends an openness to the "return of the subject to itself" that modern subjectivity forecloses. Let me illustrate the difference.

The modern subject, for example Kant's, is a law unto itself, auto-nomous. When the modern subject goes out into the world, it is to the subject's own benefit, and its alone. The modern subject's return to itself lies in closure from the world. The Rahnerian subject's "law" is not properly its own. It is God's law. And when the Rahnerian subject goes out into and returns from the world, the world comes with it. The Rahnerian subject's existence lies in exposure "to all the destinies [*allen Schicksalen*] of this earth."[29] To summarize, while the modern subject's intellectual activity begins with and ends in solitude, the Rahnerian subject's activity consists in relationality. And this relationality's only boundary is the absolute being of God. It is unlimited.

The subject who receives while in action and self-exposes to the destinies of the world: this sort of subjectivity leads us to consider a similar sort in Heidegger. He develops it as he reads the poet Hölderlin.

HEIDEGGER'S FIRST HÖLDERLIN COURSE

Perhaps no other name is more closely associated with Martin Heidegger than Friedrich Hölderlin (1770–1843). This poet captivates Heidegger for the better part of five decades. Out of his read-

---

28. Cf. SW 332–33/247–48.
29. SW 406/299.

ings of Hölderlin's poetry, Heidegger develops some of his best-known "late" ideas, like the fourfold and *Gelassenheit,* the "flight of the gods," and the relationship between the poet (*Dichter*) and the thinker (*Denker*). Whereas in Friedrich Nietzsche Heidegger saw the prophet of metaphysics' collapse, in Friedrich Hölderlin Heidegger glimpsed a new way forward after this collapse. It is noteworthy, then, that during Rahner's first semester at Freiburg, he attended Heidegger's first course on Hölderlin.

Rahner did not leave any notes from this course, or at least none that are yet available. Thus anything I write regarding how Rahner might have reacted to what Heidegger said in this course is a matter of conjecture. However, I shall attempt in this section to pull out of Heidegger's analyses of Hölderlin's poems points that resonate in interesting ways with (1) Rahner's explicit statements about Heidegger, which we have duly examined; and (2) Rahner's other writings, which we shall interpret in later sections.

I shall analyze Heidegger's stipulation in these lectures that poets, and Hölderlin specifically, reveal being through their poetry. This privileging of a certain type of discourse as optimally ontophanic seems to make a positive impression on Rahner. Despite this convergence between Rahner and Heidegger, there are grounds for divergence as well. Heidegger's exaltation of a mythic Germany over against Christianity, for instance, would have presented Rahner with plenty to which he might react. The exposition of the Hölderlin lectures will set some terms for later discussion between Rahner and Heidegger.

THE ESSENCE OF POETRY

Heidegger's first course on Hölderlin interprets two poems, "Germanien," a hymn to the German homeland, and "Der Rhein," one of Hölderlin's many river hymns. From the outset, Heidegger conveys in no uncertain terms that he intends for his reading of Hölderlin's poetry to effect a momentous change in philosophy.

He declares, "We wish to bring ourselves and those to come under the measure of the poet."[30] A "thinking confrontation" (*denkerische Auseinandersetzung*) with Hölderlin promises to transform Western thought, because in his poetry he achieves a "revelation of being" (*Offenbarung des Seyns*).[31] This revelation of being comes through a disclosure of what Heidegger calls the "essence of poetry."

Heidegger chooses "Germanien" to begin because he judges this poem to be among Hölderlin's most difficult.[32] The poem's difficulty derives from its reflection on the "origin" or the "essence" of poetry. Very soon after delivering this lecture course, Heidegger gives a lecture in Rome called "Hölderlin and the Essence of Poetry" (1936), which will become a keystone to the later book, *Elucidations of Hölderlin's Poetry* (first edition 1944). In that lecture, Heidegger declares that Hölderlin is the "poet's poet" who "makes poems about the role of the poet."[33] In so doing, the poet assumes his role as the "founder of being" (*Begründer des Seyns*).[34] The poet is the one who founds being, Heidegger asserts, because "the poetic is the foundational structure [*Grundgefüge*] of historical existence."[35]

During Heidegger's time, the dominant paradigm for interpreting poetry, including Hölderlin's, consisted in conjecturing how the poem expressed the "experiences" (*Erlebnissen*) of the poet. This is a subjective reading of a poet. Heidegger rejects this thinking of "experiences" as a modern, "liberal" misunderstanding of poetry, but even further of human existence in general. Instead, poetry is not individual, subjective expression, but the way that a wider history reveals itself through the poet.[36] This revealed history is being's history.

Were one to formulate it using the term "subjectivity," which

---

30. HGR 4. All translations from this text are mine unless otherwise indicated.
31. HGR 6.   32. HGR 4.
33. Heidegger, "Hölderlin and the Essence of Poetry," in *Elucidations of Hölderlin's Poetry*, trans. Keith Hoeller (Amherst, N.Y.: Humanity Books, 2000), 51–65.
34. HGR 33.   35. HGR 67.
36. HGR 25–29.

Heidegger avoids, one could say that poetic subjectivity is never "subjective" in the way that modern subjectivism is. The poet does not re-present the world (or feelings, or anything else) as the product of his own consciousness. Instead, the poet gives word to a communal spirit that is not his own.[37] That is, the poet receives the poetic word.

For the Heideggerian Hölderlin, poetry comes first and foremost from the gods. The poet receives the "hints of the gods" (*der Winke der Götter*), and passes on these hints to an historical people (*das Volk*): "Thunderstorms and lightning are the speech of the gods, and the poet is the one who unavoidably has to take in, to intercept, and to set up this speech in the existence of the people."[38] The poetic "founding" of history predicates itself upon two things: (1) the poet's sensitivity to godly speech and (2) the act of communicating this godly speech to the poet's people.

At this point in the lecture, Heidegger anticipates his later essay on Hölderlin's saying "Full of merit, yet poetically, man / dwells upon this earth."[39] The poet must be sensitive to the gods' hints. Another way of putting this, Heidegger suggests, is that poetic *Dasein,* or dwelling, lies in an "exposure to being."[40] The poet's *"Ausgesetztheit des Seyns"* is, for Heidegger, the true manner of human existence. One does not have to be a poet, but in order to exist truly, one must dwell poetically. Any other mode of existence is a fall from or a perversion of this original form. It bears asking what exactly this exposure to being implies.

James Risser observes, "Heidegger will turn to the work of Hölderlin ... as a way of encountering the very ground of the historical world of a people. In this poetry, Heidegger can sense the urgency of the question, that he himself feels, of a future yet to come — the

37. In "Hölderlin and the Essence of Poetry," Heidegger addresses the phrase "voice of the people" in Hölderlin's poetry (63).

38. HGR 31.

39. See Heidegger, "Poetically Man Dwells," in *Poetry, Language, Thought,* 209–27.

40. HGR 36.

question of home and homeland."[41] The lectures as a whole detail how Hölderlin's poetry confronts the German people with a call to receive and to struggle for their own proper history. He describes the contemporary age as a "time of turning" (*Wendezeit*), during which a people faced with the abyss (*Abgrund*) awaits a coming future—presumably a better one.[42]

Less than a year later, in his lecture "The Origin of the Work of Art," Heidegger makes several remarks that shed light on these ideas. Heidegger avers, "the nature of art is poetry."[43] And art, thus poetry, has a constitutive relationship to history: "Whenever art happens ... a thrust enters history, history either begins or starts over again. History means here not a sequence in time of events of whatever sort, however important. History is the elevation [*Entrück-ung*] of a people into its given task [*Aufgegebenes*] as entrance [*Ein-rückung*] into that people's endowment [*Mitgegebenes*]."[44] We shall return to these ideas in due course. For now it suffices to say that the "people" whose "history," "task," and "endowment" the poet Hölderlin reveals is the German people.[45] Exposure to being, then, is exposure to the "destiny" (*Schicksal*) of Germany, the *Vaterland*.[46]

Being and its history are tied to the poet's mediation between heaven and earth. The poet's mediation is tied to the German *Volk*. The essence of poetry, then, is tied to the German homeland.

THE POET AND THE DEMIGOD

If Heidegger reads "Germanien" as a poem about the essence of poetry as an exposure to being qua the historical task of the German

---

41. James Risser, "Introduction," in *Heidegger toward the Turn: Essays on the Work of the 1930s*, ed. James Risser (Albany, N.Y.: SUNY, 1999), 1–16, here 5.

42. See HGR 105–7.

43. Heidegger, OWA 72.

44. OWA 74, ET modified. Cf. Martin Heidegger, "*Der Ursprung des Kunstwerkes*," in *Holzwege, Gesamtausgabe Band 5* (Frankfurt: Vittorio Klostermann, 1977), 1–74, here 65.

45. On the "*Sendung*," see the section beginning on HGR 104.

46. HGR 120–22. On "*Schicksal*," see the entire part on "Der Rhein," 163–294.

Volk, he interprets "Der Rhein" as a poem about the poet's relationship to the "demigod" (*Halbgötter*). He singles out the first line of the tenth stanza as central: "Of demigods now I think."[47] He deems this line so important because he interprets the poem as a presentation of the proper realm of being. Hölderlin presents this realm by elucidating the distinction between humans and gods. The demi-god, neither fully god nor merely human, is the vehicle for this elucidation.

Since Heidegger spent the first half of the lecture course defining the poet as the mediator between gods and humans, he quickly draws a parallel between the poet and the demigod. Each is a "between-being" (*Zwischenwesen*).[48] The poet, like the demigod, mediates between gods and humans. The poet is the "middle" (*Mitte*) of being itself.[49]

When the poet thinks of the demigod, Heidegger notices, he considers the "wine god," Dionysos.[50] This "god" is truly a demigod, the son of Semele, a mortal woman, and Zeus, a god. Dionysos is, then, an example of a between-being, in between the being of humans and the being of gods. In fact, Heidegger argues, "Dionysos is not just one demi-god among others, but the most excellent one." Heidegger continues, specifying what makes Dionysos the exemplary demigod: "He is the 'yes' of the wildest aspects of the generative urge of inexhaustible life, and he is the 'no' of the most terrible death of annihilation."[51] Dionysos embodies extremes: the liveliest exuberance of the gods and the lowest depths of finitude.

Heidegger claims that Dionysos's unique way of being a demigod is foundational for Hölderlin's poem, "Der Rhein." The poet al-

47. HGR 163. Friedrich Hölderlin, "Der Rhein," in *Selected Poems and Fragments,* trans. Michael Hamburger (New York: Penguin Books, 1998), 196–209, here 202 (German), 203 (English).

48. HGR 164.

49. HGR 260.

50. See HGR 187–91. Cf. Hölderlin, "Der Rhein," 204 (German), 205 (English).

51. HGR 189: "Dionysos ist nicht nur ein Halbgott unter anderen, sondern der Ausgezeichnete. Er ist das Ja des wildesten, im zeugerischen Drang unerschöpfbaren Lebens, und er ist das Nein des furchtbarsten Todes der Zernichtung."

ludes to this demigod with a mention of "ivy" in its first line, and then in a climactic line from the tenth stanza. Even further, Dionysos proves fundamental for Hölderlin's conception of the "essence and the call of the poet."[52] Borrowing a line from another of Hölderlin's poems, Heidegger contends that the poet is the "priest of Dionysos," the one who gives word to Dionysos's being.[53]

This may not sound like that remarkable of a claim. Dionysos is the god of inebriation and mystery that has long been associated with the poetic spirit. Heidegger's insistence upon the Dionysian character of Hölderlin's poetry has philosophical implications, though. These relate to Friedrich Nietzsche, whom Heidegger references at this point. The reader should recall that three years after this Hölderlin course, Heidegger will commence his lecture series on Nietzsche with a consideration of his philosophy of art.

Above I quoted lines from "The Origin of the Work of Art," in which Heidegger states that art effects a new beginning in history, and history "is the elevation [*Entrückung*] of a people into its given task [*Aufgegebenes*] as entrance [*Einrückung*] into that people's endowment [*Mitgegebenes*]." The final pages of the first Hölderlin course discuss the pair "*Aufgegebene*" and "*Mitgegebene*" with respect to the ancient Greek and German experiences of being.[54] Heidegger grounds this discussion in a letter Hölderlin wrote to his friend Casimir Böhlendorff. The "task" is an experience of being toward which a historical people must work. The "endowment" is the experience of being that comes naturally to them.

The Greek "endowment," according to the Heideggerian Hölderlin, is "the fire from heaven" (*das Feuer vom Himmel*), or a "being-affected by being as a whole" (*Betroffenwerden durch das Seyn im Ganzen*). The German endowment is "clarity of presentation"

---

52. HGR 188.
53. HGR 191.
54. Cf. Julian Young, *Heidegger's Philosophy of Art* (New York: Cambridge University Press, 2001), 40–41.

(*die Klarheit der Darstellung*), or the "ability to grasp being in the acquisitive presentation of beings" (*das Fassenkönnen des Seyns in der erwirkenden Darstellung des Seyenden*). Heidegger concerns himself more here with the Germans than with the Greeks. The Germans must assume the endowment of the Greeks as their task. They must struggle (*kämpfen*) to be affected as the Greeks were by the "force of being" (*die Gewalt des Seyns*).[55] This task is the destiny of the German people. The poet can lead them in this task.

The task relates to Dionysos, and to Nietzsche. Heidegger refers in his closing remarks to Nietzsche's famous distinction in *The Birth of Tragedy* between the Dionysian and the Apollonian.[56] Heidegger claims that Hölderlin draws the same distinction prior to Nietzsche and with greater purity and simplicity.[57] But even though Heidegger seems to give Hölderlin the upper hand, it seems that Heidegger has Nietzscheanized the poet. For Nietzsche, a constitutive element of the Dionysian is its complete and utter finitude. Heidegger adopts this perspective from Nietzsche and applies it to Hölderlin. If the poet "thinks of the demi-god," he thinks of Dionysos as the symbol for human existence's exposure to its own finitude. The "fire from heaven" which the poet mediates for the German people is not precisely from "heaven," but rather is being's power that holds sway over finite beings. In the Hölderlin course, then, Rahner would have heard Heidegger radicalizing his apriorism of finitude. Being is limited to the German people, and their experience of being is the task of being exposed—via the poet—to their own finitude.

RAHNER ENCOUNTERING THE HEIDEGGERIAN SUBLIME

It has become common in the contemporary conversation to refer to the Heideggerian sublime. Jean-François Lyotard, Jacques

---

55. HGR 290–92.
56. Friedrich Nietzsche, *The Birth of Tragedy and Other Writings,* ed. Raymond Geuss and Ronald Speirs (New York: Cambridge University Press, 1999), passim.
57. HGR 294.

Derrida, Jean-Luc Nancy, and Jean-Luc Marion each link Heidegger to discussions of the sublime—particularly the Kantian sublime from the Third Critique.[58] For Kant, the sublime reveals the inadequacy of the subject's faculties of presentation. Since Heidegger critiques the modern subject from the standpoint of *Dasein's* radical finitude, these French theorists see a convergence of the Kantian sublime and Heideggerian thinking. Jan Rosiek's *Maintaining the Sublime* exhaustively justifies the ascription of "the sublime" to Heidegger.[59] Rosiek proposes that Heidegger maintains a view of the sublime as the "religio-literary translation of the metaphysical." Jennifer Gosetti-Ferencei's account of the Heideggerian sublime is also noteworthy.[60] The Heideggerian sublime manifests itself whenever he insists upon the "violence" of the poetic founding of truth. What follows supplements these definitions of the Heideggerian sublime.

The touchstone for my supplement is the German word for the sublime, *das Erhabene*. This word carries connotations of elevation. Despite their other vast differences, most theories of the sublime center on the elevating quality of sublime experience. The Heideggerian sublime is a discourse of the elevation of human existence above the restrictions of metaphysics.

This elevation is as indebted to Nietzsche as it is to Hölderlin. There are positive and negative aspects to this. I have begun to suggest the negatives from a Rahnerian point of view—Heidegger's radicalization of his apriorism of finitude—and I shall address more

58. For texts linking Heidegger to the sublime in general and Kant's sublime in particular, see Jean-François Lyotard, *Lessons on the Analytic of the Sublime*; Jacques Derrida, *The Truth in Painting*, trans. Geoffrey Bennington and Ian McLeod (Chicago: University of Chicago Press, 1987), and Derrida, *Of Spirit: Heidegger and the Question*, trans. Geoffrey Bennington and Rachel Bowlby (Chicago: University of Chicago Press, 1991); Jean-Luc Nancy, *The Ground of the Image*, trans. Jeff Fort (New York: Fordham University Press, 2005); Jean-Luc Marion, *Being Given: A Phenomenology of Givenness*, trans. Jeffrey L. Kosky (Stanford, Calif.: Stanford University Press, 2002).

59. Jan Rosiek, *Maintaining the Sublime: Heidegger and Adorno* (New York: Peter Lang, 2000).

60. Jennifer Gosetti-Ferencei, *Heidegger, Hölderlin, and the Subject of Poetic Language* (New York: Fordham University Press, 2004).

soon. But first it bears noting how Heidegger's application of Nietzsche's Dionysos to Hölderlin's poetry constitutes an advance past modern subjectivity.

We have seen that Heidegger sets up a "Dionysian" task for the German people in the conclusion to the lecture course. He believes that the hour has come for the German nation to cultivate an exposure to being. He envisions this exposure to being as an experience of being that the Germans have forgotten as they have employed their capacity for "clear presentation." The "clarity of presentation" or "ability to grasp" that Heidegger calls the natural endowment of the Germans is the central feature of modern subjectivism: an intellectual taking hold of reality. Though Heidegger concedes that this natural endowment has helped the Germans in their planning of reality and their scientific accomplishments, it has covered over a more originary experience of being that the Germans vitally need. Thus in recovering the endowment of the Greeks, "being-affected by being," the Germans can become more truly and vitally German.[61] They can become more vitally German by overcoming modern subjectivism.

This is an interesting, if somewhat vague, proposal. It dovetails interestingly with Rahner's insistence in *Geist in Welt* that human subjectivity ought to be characterized by exposure to being, rather than self-enclosure. Rahner may, then, have positively appropriated some central themes from the first Hölderlin course.

Nevertheless, the lectures offer plenty to make Rahner uncomfortable. We shall encounter these reasons over the next few pages. Before this, I shall enumerate some propositions that sum up the analysis to follow. They indicate some main lines of what I am call-

---

61. See HGR 293. It is notable that this is the task that Heidegger believes has the potential to unify and fortify the German nation. Though this does not excuse his enthusiasm for Nazism, as some Heidegger supporters would have it, it does show that Heidegger had something entirely different in mind than the Nazis did when he spoke of a national task.

ing the Heideggerian sublime. (1) The Heideggerian sublime exalts finitude and has nothing to say about infinitude. (2) The Heideggerian sublime elevates poetic existence over Christian existence. (3) And worst, the Heideggerian sublime is a deformation of Christianity à la Nietzsche.

Heidegger defines the "basic attunement" (*Grundstimmung*) of Hölderlin's poem "Der Rhein" as "co-suffering" (*Mit-leiden*) with the demigod Dionysos—thus he parodies the Christian's participation in Christ's Paschal Mystery.[62] Heidegger's view of history in his explication of "*Germanien*" derives from yet distorts the Christian view. Instead of the period of waiting between Christ's Ascension and his Second Coming at the end of time, Heidegger regards history as the time of mourning the flight of the old gods and anticipating the advent of the new gods.[63] Dionysos is the demigod who accompanies the *Volk* through this time of mourning. And most notably, in a move that recalls Nietzsche's famous quote, "Have I been understood? Dionysus versus the crucified,"[64] Hölderlin's poetry occasions Heidegger's pitting of the "Führer"—as a Dionysian figure—against Christ.

I shall quote the passage in question at length. But first it bears noting that the critical comments to follow, though they may accord somewhat with the damning charges in Emmanuel Faye's overblown exposé, *Heidegger: The Introduction of Nazism into Philosophy* (2005),[65] do not endorse Faye's method or his conclusions. One need not, as so many French thinkers have done (Faye being the apex),

62. See especially HGR 181–86.

63. See HGR 78–104.

64. Friedrich Nietzsche, *Ecce Homo*, in *The Anti-Christ, Ecce Homo, Twilight of the Idols, and Other Writings*, trans. Aaron Ridley and Judith Norman (New York: Cambridge University Press, 2005), 151.

65. Emmanuel Faye, Heidegger: *The Introduction of Nazism into Philosophy*, trans. Michael Smith (New Haven, Conn.: Yale University Press, 2009), esp. 103–12. For a trenchant but apt rejoinder to Faye's book, see Laurence Paul Hemming, "Introduction," in *The Movement of Nihilism: Heidegger's Thinking after Nietzsche*, ed. Laurence Paul Hemming, Bogdan Costea, and Kostas Amiridis (New York: Continuum, 2011), 1–7.

prejudge Heidegger's thinking as a whole as Nazi theory. Though Heidegger's participation in the Nazi party during the 1930s and his refusal publically to acknowledge Nazism's nefariousness later in his life are horrible things, there are many more ways of critiquing his thought. Rahner would not have known as he listened to Heidegger's Hölderlin lectures the unspeakable things that the Nazis were planning and would do over the next decade. Instead, he would have heard how viciously Heidegger distorted Christianity as he baldly dismissed it in favor of a mythic Germany.

Heidegger declares, "Even today from the pulpits they speak of Christ as the leader, which is not only an untruth, but what is worse, a blasphemy against Christ. Indeed, the true and only leader ever points in his being into the realm of the demi-gods. Being-leader is a destiny and therefore finite being."[66] Heidegger thus rebukes Christian preachers, including Catholic priests (perhaps like Rahner's fellow Jesuit, Alfred Delp, who would die at the hands of the Nazis in 1945). These preachers would bypass the political leader of Germany in search of a more sovereign leader, Christ. By contrast, Heidegger draws a relationship between the "true and only *Führer*" and the demigods, and he insists upon this Führer's finitude. Heidegger makes his position clear, then, but that is not enough for him.

He proceeds to explain Christian dogmatics: "Christ, however, is for church dogmatics, according to the decision of the Council of Nicaea, *deus verus ex deo vero—consubstantialis patri—homo/ousios to patri,* of equal in essence with the father, not *homoiousios,* not only of similar essence." Heidegger claims that this remark is made "in

66. HGR 210: "So spricht man auch heute auf den Kanzeln von Christus als dem Führer, was nicht nur eine Unwahrheit, sondern was noch schlimmer ist, Christus gegenüber eine Blasphemie. Der wahre und je einzige Führer weist in seinem Sein allerdings in den Bereich der Halbgötter. Führersein ist ein Schicksal und daher endliches Sein. Christus aber ist der kirchlichen Dogmatik, gemäß der Entscheidung des Konzils von Nicaea, *deus verus ex deo vero—consubstantialis patri—homo/ousios to patri,* wesensgleich mit dem Vater, nicht *homoiousios,* nicht nur wesensähnlich." I have transliterated the Greek.

passing," in order to correct the confused thinking of his time. He assumes, though, that his "clarity" is legitimate.

Heidegger's rendering of "church dogmatics" is on the one hand correct, but on the other misleading. He quotes Nicaea, as opposed to Chalcedon, which must always be paired with it, so as to emphasize Christ's divinity, and thus to dismiss him from the world. Christ cannot "lead" in this world, because this world is utterly finite, and he is infinite. No Christ, no full divinity can appear in history. So goes Heidegger's Dionysian worldview, which in this case serves to exalt Adolf Hitler as the head of history.

We shall see in the next two parts how Rahner sets up a version of the sublime that differs sharply from Heidegger's. Heidegger believes that an exposure to the destiny of Germany, evidently via the Führer, can overcome modern subjectivity's grip on the world. Even in 1935, let alone 1945, Rahner would have found this approach insufficient. The nub of his disagreement with Heidegger is Heidegger's Dionysian worldview, which replaces the self-sealing of modern subjectivity with a self-sealing of the nation of Germany. Rahner pursues a more holistic sublimity—an exposure to being in the fullness of its scope.

RAHNER'S SUBLIME CONTRIBUTION

The current part begins in earnest my argument that Rahner presents aesthetic insights that might be consolidated into his own version of the sublime. The Rahnerian sublime emerges first in *Geist in Welt,* which contests modern subjectivity by setting up an alternative to it. That alternative predicates itself upon aesthetics in a twofold sense: (1) the encounter with a sensible other and (2) God's movement through the imagination in every event of sense reception and intellectual action. More important for Rahner's view of subjectivity are its noncognitive aspects, those properties of the subject that do not involve intellectual mastery. Instead of the modern subject's goal of noetic control of objects, the Rahnerian subject's goal lies in a mutually enhancing encounter with the reality of things, modeled on God's loving things into being. This is what lies behind Rahner's extensive discussion of "inner-worldly, efficient causality," which he reduces to a formal causality of emanating and received influences.[67] The Rahnerian subject cooperates with beings as they manifest themselves, and this subject cooperates with God as God manifests God's self through the world.

Existing discussions of Rahner's aesthetics in the literature have focused largely on his few writings on art and poetry.[68] This is not a bad start, though it must be supplemented with a more wide-ranging perspective such as I am offering in this book. But like these other texts on Rahner's aesthetics, I shall commence my presentation of the Rahnerian sublime with his main text on poetry, "Priest and Poet," particularly since we have just left a part on Heidegger and poetry, and will continue to discuss his readings of poetry.

There is another reason, which corresponds to my discussion of the "*reditio completa in se ipsum.*" Rahner writes in "Priest and Poet" that the true poet "attains that coming-to-himself and being-with-himself which St. Thomas calls the *reditio completa in se ipsum.*"[69] We shall explore what Rahner means by this, and what implications this has for his view of the sublime, his resistance of modern subjectivity, and his convergent-divergence with Heidegger. The crux of the matter will be Rahner's contrast of the poet with the priest, who represents a Catholic way of life. The priest's ethos in this text will give us a glimpse of the Catholic ethos that Rahner presents in his wider corpus: the Catholic sublime.

One more note before we proceed: thus far our focus has been on the Rahner of the mid-1930s. The text we shall examine here was written in 1958. I aim in discussing this text here to show the conti-

---

67. See SW 309–83/231–83.
68. See this book's introduction, under "II.1: An Aesthetic Rahner," for the relevant citations.
69. PP 309.

nuity between the "early" and the "later" Rahner. The similarities
are overwhelming and illuminating.

PRIEST AND POET

"Priest and Poet" was originally published as the foreword to a
book of poems by a fellow Jesuit, Jorge Blajot. The essay presents a
general reflection on the meaning of the coincidence and mutual re-
inforcement of the poetic and priestly tasks. Rahner notes that his
general remarks might be seen as "very obscure."[70] Indeed, the essay
delves into dense obscurities. These might be clarified if one reads
them as deeply engaged with Heidegger.

While it is unlikely that Rahner would have set out to reflect
specifically on Heidegger's poetic thinking, by the essay's fourth
page Heidegger enters. After acknowledging that he has raised some
conceptual obscurities, Rahner asks, "Is 'being' clear? But of course,
says the shallow mind, that is being which is not nothing. But what
is 'is' and what is 'nothing'? Whole books have been written, and
from this ocean of words there has been obtained only a little jug
of stagnant water."[71] These words are Rahner's, but they could be
Heidegger's from *Introduction to Metaphysics,* during which Rahner
heard Heidegger castigate the metaphysical tradition for ignoring
such questions.[72]

It is not surprising, then, how resonant this essay is with Heidegger's interpretations of Hölderlin in the course Rahner attended, and other poets like Rainer Maria Rilke, whom Rahner cites at
two key points in the essay.[73] Like Heidegger, Rahner finds in the
poet a person who is open to reality in a way that others—particularly modern scientists—are not. Unlike Heidegger, Rahner proposes that the poet's openness to reality's manifestation reaches its full

70. PP 297.
71. PP 297.
72. See Heidegger's critique of ontology, EM 42–44.
73. He quotes the *Duino Elegies* on 298–99, then a different saying of Rilke on 300.

scope only when the poet's mission coincides with that of the Catholic priest.

There are three key pieces to Rahner's case: first, his bivalent view of language; second, his description of the poet; and third, his characterization of the priest. We shall examine the first two in this section, and the third in the following one. The first two pieces establish points of contact with Heidegger. The third comprises the breaking point from Heidegger.

First, Rahner distinguishes between two types of words: "primordial words" (*Urworte*) and "utility words" (*Nutzworte*). The former words are "obscure because they evoke the blinding mystery of things." The latter words "are clear because they are shallow and without mystery; they suffice for the mind; by means of them one acquires mastery over things."[74] Rahner adds to these descriptions that the primordial word presents the thing itself. The primordial word assists the thing it evokes to fulfill its reality in the hearer of the word. This cooperation of the thing with its human counterpart contrasts with the relationship of mastery that the technical word founds. Thus we have Rahner's bivalent view of language. The difference between the two types of language hinges on whether words foster aesthetic cooperation with reality or noetic manipulation of reality.

Stephen Fields compares Rahner's distinction between primordial and technical words to Heidegger's distinction between earth and world in "The Origin of the Work of Art."[75] To his helpful reflection I add that Heidegger makes an even more proximate distinction in the first Hölderlin course. He distinguishes between the "*Erstlinge*" and the "*Gemeiner*," the "firstborn" and the "common," or "essential" versus "inessential" language.[76] The former language is poetry and the latter prose and useful everyday talk.[77] Later in the

74. PP 296.   75. Fields, *Being as Symbol*, 92–96.
76. HGR 62–65.
77. Cf. Rahner's mention of the Heideggerian phrase from *Being and Time*, "chatter of daily life," on PP 308.

lectures, Heidegger makes a parallel distinction between "the poetic understanding of nature" and "the natural-scientific representation of nature."[78] Such a distinction appears in Rahner: "When the poet or the poor man of Assisi exclaims 'water,' what is meant is greater, wider and deeper than when the chemist, debasing the word, says 'water' for his H_2O."[79] He agrees with Heidegger that scientific language is a decline (*Verfall*) from poetic, primordial language, because of natural science's pretension to control its object.

The convergence with Heidegger continues when Rahner applies Rilke's phrase "the intimacy of being" to the process by which a thing is known through primordial words.[80] Heidegger speaks near to the end of the lectures on "Der Rhein" of the "intimacy" (*Innigkeit*) that the poem conjures with the mystery of being (*Geheimnis des Seyns*).[81] Rahner echoes Heidegger's words: "All realities sigh for their own unveiling. They want themselves to enter, if not as knowers at least as objects of knowledge, into the light of knowledge and of love. They all have a dynamic drive to fulfill themselves by being known. They, too, want to 'put in their word.'"[82] These remarks are not precisely consonant with the Heideggerian Hölderlin, since they stem more nearly from a Thomistic metaphysics of knowledge. Nevertheless, they resonate with the Heideggerian poet.

Second, then, Rahner enhances this resonance by maintaining that the poet is the one to whom the primordial word is entrusted.[83] The poet speaks primordial words in a compressed form that amplifies their power to bring things to light, and makes clear that primordial words are "doors to infinity, doors to the incomprehensible."[84] Rahner says that the poet is the "minister" of the "sacrament of all realities," the one who indicates the reference of all finite, limited realities to the infinitude of God.[85] The poet has a high calling, then—one reminiscent of Heidegger's poet.

78. HGR 195.
80. PP 300.
82. PP 300.
84. PP 301, 316, ET modified.

79. PP 296.
81. HGR 248–59.
83. PP 301.
85. PP 302.

Rahner's remarks later in the essay, though, suggest that the poet's deployment of primordial words, though exalted, is not the highest testimony to God's infinite movement through finite creation. Rahner describes the poet's exaltation:

The poet experiences the blissful, but also perilous, extremely perilous, pleasure of an aesthetic kind of identity between his being and his consciousness. He attains that coming-to-himself and being-with-himself which St. Thomas calls the *reditio completa in seipsum.* ... Oh what a sublime blessedness it is to be so reconciled with oneself, so near to oneself, so close to one's immeasurable remoteness, to be able to understand oneself, by uttering oneself, even while one appears to speak of something quite different![86]

The vocabulary here calls to mind Rahner's metaphysics of knowing from *Geist in Welt,* and the aesthetic implications I drew from it above. Rahner refers to the *reditio completa.* When the poet poetizes about "another," the poet realizes the poet's self. And since the poet speaks primordial words, the poet helps the "other" to its own realization. Thus it seems that the poet is an ideal example of the sublime-aesthetic subjectivity that Rahner details in *Geist in Welt.* But there is more to the story, just as there is in *Geist in Welt.* The "more" concerns the movement of God's grace in the priest.

PRIEST OF CHRIST VERSUS PRIEST OF DIONYSOS

The third part of Rahner's argument in "Priest and Poet" consists in a description of the priest's word, which contrasts with the poet's. The priest is the one to whom not just the word, but "God's efficacious word" is entrusted.[87] The priest's word differs from the poet's because it is not his own word, constructed through a *reditio completa in se ipsum.* It is God's word. When the priest speaks, he is a channel for the "infinite *katabasis* of [God's] self-revelation."[88] The

---

86. PP 309.   87. PP 303, 307.
88. PP 303.

priest's word is "efficacious" because it proclaims the love of God, and without this proclamation there could be no salvation, since salvation entails a response to God's call. The most efficacious of the priest's words occurs at the moment of Eucharistic consecration, when the priest assumes the person of Christ to evoke the body broken and blood shed for the world's salvation.[89] Everything that the priest says as his priestly word, then, does not express anything about him, and does not exalt him. Instead, the priest is humbled in two ways: (1) by being "wholly absorbed into Christ" and (2) by being "unmasked" as a sinner and one not fully able to pronounce God's word.[90]

Priest and poet differ in that the former never speaks his own word, and the poet always speaks his own word. The priest gives word directly to God's infinity by uttering the words of Christ. The poet only indirectly articulates God's infinity by using primordial words. Though the priest never relinquishes his own finitude, he is overtaken in large part by the infinitude of God—Rahner alludes to the classical Christian doctrine of theosis.[91] The poet as poet, on the other hand, remains finite. The poet exclaims, "Look, there go I!"[92] while the priest is more inclined toward Paul's, "Not I, but Christ who lives in me" (Gal 2:20).

This typology brings us back to the question of how this essay, which alludes early on to Heidegger, relates to his thinking about poetry. In the first Hölderlin course, Rahner would have heard Heidegger calling the poet the "priest of Dionysos."[93] Rahner refers in passing to such a "priesthood" of the poet, when he writes of the "unmasking" of the Catholic priest. He clarifies that the priest's unmasking occurs "not with that perhaps sublime, perhaps sometimes also masochistic self-unmasking of the poets."[94] The Dionysian spirit, post-Nietzsche, often involves this paradoxical self-abusing/

89. PP 306.
91. PP 311.
93. HGR 190–91.

90. PP 307, 309–10.
92. PP 309.
94. PP 309.

self-exalting behavior—this over and above the fact that Dionysos is a god often associated with masks. We may have here, then, a "masked" reference to Heidegger.

We know from our analysis above that Heidegger champions the poet because he reveals the constitutive finitude of human existence. Though Heidegger gives the poet the high designation of "priest of Dionysos," he intends for this name to suggest the humility of the one who recognizes human existence's proper limits. The poet is humble enough to receive and to accept the place that being assigns him. This "humility" necessitates a bracketing of Christ, who for Heidegger symbolizes the Christian version of metaphysics' forgetting of being. Christ is a figure for the infinite. The priest of Christ, were Heidegger to classify him, would be the one who obscures being, rather than revealing it.

Rahner sees things differently. Although Rahner holds the poet in high regard, he notices that the poetic task often issues in self-exaltation. Instead of glorifying the one who gives the poet words to speak, the poet self-glorifies. Instead of humbly acknowledging his own limits, the poet narcissistically adulates over his own accomplishments. The "priest of Dionysos" is a false priest.

The true priest exercises true humility. Rather than insisting that he himself appears when he speaks, the priest lets the grace of God appear. In this way, the priest does not express the human cleverness of the poet. The priest confounds poetry with the foolishness of the Cross of Christ.[95] Language reaches its highest heights only through the humility that sets aside its own finitude so that the infinitude of God may shine.

As Brent Little has noted, "Rahner's ideal is that the charismata of the priest and poet merge."[96] Indeed, for Rahner the priest has much to gain from the poet. The poet presents a model of how one's total existence might accord with the word one speaks. This rein-

---

95. See Rahner's rephrasing of 1 Cor 1:26–29 on PP 314.
96. Brent Little, "Anthropology and Art in the Theology of Karl Rahner," 945.

forces Rahner's appeal throughout the essay that priests live out the holiness to which God calls them. But more to our concerns here, the priest offers the poet an opening toward the God who inspires the poet: "The priesthood releases poetic existence and sets it free to attain its ultimate purpose."[97] Even further, "The priest calls upon the poet, and the poet's primordial words may become consecrated vessels of the divine word, in which the *priest* proclaims the word of God."[98] Against Heidegger, who would restrict the scope of the poetic word to finitude alone, Rahner insists that the poet needs the priest, so that the poet may disclose the full range of language.

THE QUESTION OF ETHOS

Though theological discussions of aesthetics and the sublime often reduce the field to the arts, and though we have just considered Rahner's essay on poetry, the reader should have a sense that my raising of the idea of Rahner's sublime does not concern art alone—or even primarily. The idea of a Rahnerian sublime concerns the manifestation of being. Since, for Rahner's philosophical work *Geist in Welt*, God is absolute being, the Rahnerian sublime concerns the manifestation of God. Since the God of Rahner's philosophical work opens toward the God of Jesus Christ, the Rahnerian sublime concerns the revelation of the Trinitarian God. And the constitutive feature of the Rahnerian sublime is its expansiveness, which reflects God's infinity.

I have already begun to argue that this Rahnerian sublime opposes modern subjectivism in ways both convergent and divergent with Heidegger's own version of the sublime. In the introduction to this book I suggested that in resisting subjectivism and Heidegger, Rahner presents the ethos of Catholicism. I indicated that the Catholic sublime, which is Rahner's sublime, is another name for this ethos of Catholicism. At the end of this section on Rahner's sublime contribution, I wish briefly to introduce the question of ethos.

97. PP 310.
98. PP 316, emphasis in original.

Ethos is a form of life. Modern subjectivism implies a form of life. Its chief attributes are the primacy of the intellect and autonomy, the intellect legislating rules for itself. These attributes lead to an ethos of self-sufficiency and privatism. To use the language of *reditio completa in se ipsum,* the modern subjectivist ethos comprises a grand return or reduction of all things to the self. All objects must, at least in principle, be mine for the taking. All thoughts must accord with my logic. All times must center on my time—the present.

Heidegger proposes in his thinking to diagnose and to struggle against the ethos of modern subjectivism. Though he believes that to some extent nothing can actively be done to combat modern subjectivism, because it is a dispensation of being and only being can cancel this dispensation, he does aim to effect a change in attitude that might welcome a new dispensation.[99] As a counterpoint to the self-sufficient autonomy of the modern subjective intellect, Heidegger develops his idea of poetic subjectivity, where receptivity as opposed to activity holds sway. The poet receives words from the gods and communicates them outward to his people, rather than claiming them as property. The poet breaks the logic of modern subjectivism by refusing to acknowledge its rules. The poet rejects the temporality of modern subjectivity by centering on the future of the gods' advent, rather than my present.

The strength of Heidegger's approach lies in his refusal to endorse the strictures of modern subjectivism. The modern subject, for Heidegger, represents modernity's unwillingness to acknowledge the proper scope of human life. If all things can be reduced to the "I," the whole world becomes lost in the process. Heidegger's questioning after being, then, aims to root out this problem by opening thinking—and life—once again.

Rahner seems to have recognized in Heidegger's thinking a set

---

99. For a brief statement on being and "dispensation" (*Schickung*), see Martin Heidegger, "The Turning," in *The Question Concerning Technology,* trans. William Lovitt (New York: Harper & Row, 1977), 36–49.

of strategies he might adapt to his own, Catholic alternative to modern subjectivism. Rahner's rethinking of subjectivity centers, as we have already seen, on the scope of thinking and life.

Heidegger and Rahner converge, then, but they diverge on the question of how wide one may draw the scope of thinking and life. Their disagreement over the "priest of Dionysos" and the priest of Christ epitomizes this divergence. And to be clear, this divergence consists in a disagreement over ethos—what one's form of life should be. Heidegger's Dionysian perspective leads to a form of life where one revels in the hope of a better destiny for the German people. Though he aims to combat the modern subjectivist ethos of privatism by broadening its scope, Heidegger's scope, and thus his ethos, narrows when it comes to the question of destiny. Heidegger's ethos is wrapped up in his homeland.

Rahner's sublime contribution is, at least in part, to redirect the Heideggerian impulse against the modern subjectivist ethos toward a more universal scope. This is why it proves very significant that Rahner maintains that true subjectivity involves exposure to "all the destinies of the earth."[100] The ethos of the priest gives a glimpse of this universal scope, also. Whereas the Dionysian priest exalts one historical people, the Christian priest exalts all historical people, by drawing them into the universal offer of salvation in Christ. The ethos of the priest is one sketch among many of Rahner's Catholic sublime.

THE DISAGREEMENT OVER THE "HOME"

The Rahner-Heidegger split over the question of ethos centers largely on the question of how this world serves as home for human existence. Rahner's version of the sublime centers, as Heidegger would have it, on being in the world. Such sublimity works against modern subjectivity, whose ethos works to isolate it from the

100. SW 406/299.

world. But Rahner's sublime elaborates this being in the world as nevertheless being called beyond the world, since God's Spirit infuses human being. Heidegger would reject this, because he deems it a flight from the world and its history, tantamount to a subjective self-sealing from it.

Thus Rahner and Heidegger's ways of defeating the modern subject split over the issue of the "home." For both Rahner and Heidegger the question of the home lays bare a paradox. Human existence is most at home in the world when it faces that which exceeds the everyday world. The different ways that Rahner and Heidegger articulate this "beyond" of the world further entrench their disagreement over ethos.

THE PARADOX OF THE HOME

William McNeill claims that "the question of the home is second to none in Heidegger's work, not even to the question of being."[101] McNeill elaborates this thesis through a painstaking tracing of the German word root "-heim," in various important terms in Heidegger's corpus, from *Being and Time* through his readings of Hölderlin to the later works on language. As Heidegger's career progresses, words like "*Heimat*," "*heimlich*," "*unheimlich*," and "*Geheimnis*" (home, homely, uncanny, mystery) become ever more important. We have seen above how the German homeland, the poet's return to the homely, and the poet's exposure to the mystery of being figure as themes in the first Hölderlin course. The adjective "*unheimlich*" and its substantive "*das Unheimliche*" do not appear in

---

101. William McNeill, "*Heimat*: Heidegger on the Threshold," in *Heidegger toward the Turn*, 319–49, at 320. On this theme of the "home" in Heidegger, see also Richard Capobianco, "Heidegger's Turn toward Home: On Dasein's Primordial Relation to Being," *Epoché* 10, no. 1 (2005): 155–73; Robert Mugerauer, *Heidegger and Homecoming: The Leitmotif in the Later Writings* (Toronto: University of Toronto Press, 2008); and Lina Börsig-Hover, ed., *Unterwegs zur Heimat: Martin Heidegger zum 100. Geburtstag* (Fridingen: Börsig-Verlag, 1989). And for a damning critique of Heidegger, qua Nazi homecomer, see Charles Bambach, *Heidegger's Roots: Nietzsche, National Socialism, and the Greeks* (Ithaca, N.Y.: Cornell University Press, 2003).

the first Hölderlin course, but will feature prominently in Heidegger's later discussions of Hölderlin. And these words are centrally important in *Being and Time*.

In *Being and Time,* Heidegger develops at length what it means for *Dasein* to be at home in the world. Being at home, as Heidegger sees it, entails being confronted with something unlike the home. From this insight we shall find a point of comparison and contrast with Rahner.

The question of *Dasein*'s home pervades *Being and Time*. This question revolves around what Heidegger calls two primordial phenomena: the "they-self" (*das Man-selbst*) and the "authentic self" (*eigentlichen Selbst*).[102] Each is an originary and constitutive of *Dasein*. The "they-self" is *Dasein*'s everyday being in the world, where *Dasein* always already finds itself thrown. The "idle talk" and "common understanding" of the "they-self" orient *Dasein* in the world, providing *Dasein* with the sense of a "protecting shelter."[103] The "authentic self" appears when *Dasein* finds itself in this sheltered world and takes hold of it in its own way. The manner in which Heidegger describes *Dasein*'s traversing of these two selves raises two questions: how the world is home to *Dasein* and what being home entails.

The shelter offered existentially to *Dasein* in the "they-self" masks "an ever-increasing groundlessness."[104] *Dasein* loses itself, abandons itself, is absorbed into the "they," and in this way, one can speak of *Dasein* as "falling."[105] *Dasein* as inauthentic, that is, tempted, tranquillized, alienated, and entangled by the world, does not recognize itself as dispersed in the otherness of the neutral "they," and does not realize that everyday life is actually a flight from something. Heidegger observes, "When in falling we flee *into* the 'at home' of publicness, we flee *in the face of* the 'not-at-home'; that is, we flee in the face of the uncanniness which lies in *Dasein*."[106] This

---

102. BT 167.
104. BT 214.
106. BT 234, emphasis in original.

103. BT 211–14.
105. BT 228.

Unheimlichkeit—unhomeliness—is the key to *Dasein's* reaching authenticity.

According to Heidegger, certain moods (*Stimmungen*) lay bare this uncanniness, the most notable being anxiety (*Angst*). Anxiety brings *Dasein* "back from its absorption in the 'world.'" *Dasein* must encounter the world in such a way that it "can show itself in an empty mercilessness."[107] Anxiety facilitates this encounter. Such facing up to the world as insignificant, simply there as the milieu into which it has been thrown, unveils *Dasein's* "naked uncanniness," with which it becomes fascinated.[108]

Dasein likewise experiences the uncanny through the call of conscience. *Dasein*, as conscience, summons itself "back to the stillness of itself, and is called back as something which is to become still."[109] Through *Dasein's* "desire to have conscience," uncanniness chases *Dasein*: "uncanniness pursues *Dasein* and is a threat to the lostness in which it has forgotten itself."[110] The uncanny silence of conscience attacks the home that *Dasein* believes it has built among the "they."

The uncanny call of conscience for Heidegger summons *Dasein* to its "ownmost distinctive possibility." *Dasein* opens itself in anticipation (*Vorlauf*) of death to its unavoidable finitude. Grasping this finitude of existence "snatches one back" from a field of multiple possibilities to the only one.[111] The act of grasping finitude, prompted by the call of conscience, issues in a return to a different home than the home of the "they-self." The home of the authentic self is, then, a home "beyond" the world.

The reader may have noticed structural similarities here with Rahner's account of human knowing in *Geist in Welt*. The "they-self" plays a similar role for Heidegger as does sensibility for Rahner. Rahner's knower is absorbed in the sensible world, confused with it, until the knower returns to itself in abstraction. The process of taking hold of the "authentic self" in Heidegger bears some resemblance to the knower in the process of abstraction in Rahner. And the "having-come-into-one's-own" of the "authentic self" looks very much like the conversion to the phantasm in Rahner, where the subject who has returned to herself goes back out into a world that she has in-spired.

The analogy breaks down, though, in that Heidegger's beyond the world of the they-self is still a finite world. The central feature of Rahner's abstraction is a *Vorgriff,* an anticipatory sense of the God who is actually beyond the world—infinite. The outer limit of Heidegger's world is still the world. The "unhomely" is still part of the home. This, for Rahner, makes for a narrowed ethos. A Catholic home has a wider plan.

FLIGHT FROM OR JOY IN THE WORLD

In a vitally important section of *Geist in Welt* from which I have already quoted, Rahner writes, "And even if man wanted to flee this world as the place of all his questioning—by mysticism or suicide or any other way—and could thus reach some other place for an understanding of being, he would still have to begin on this earth."[112] Given the contrast I just drew between the Rahner of *Geist in Welt* and the Heidegger of *Being and Time,* we should ask what we ought to make of Rahner's rejection of a "flight from the world" in this quotation.

The same year that he completed *Geist in Welt,* Rahner wrote a brief essay on Ignatian spirituality that examines the theme of flight from the world, "Die ignatianishe Mystik der Weltfreudigkeit" (1936).[113] Rahner did not choose the title of the essay. He indicates in

---

112. SW 62–63/58.

113. The essay was originally published in the *Zeitschrift für Aszese und Mystik* 12 (1936): 121–37, and was published twenty years later in the third volume of *Schriften zur Theologie,* 329–48. At least two translations exist in English: Rahner, "The Ignatian Mysticism of Joy in the World," in TI 3, 277–93, and Rahner, "The Mysticism of Loving All Things in the World according to Ignatius," in *The Mystical Way in Everyday Life,* trans.

a footnote to the *Schriften zur Theologie* version that a request for the paper specified the title. Nevertheless, Rahner uses the title to great effect, setting up a twofold description of Ignatian spirituality: its tendency toward flight from the world, and its requirement of active life in the world. Rahner treats the former aspect of Ignatian spirituality as the one that overarches the whole. Ignatian life in the world always stands under the sign of life beyond the world. Rahner states, "The basis of flight from the world constitutes the intrinsic possibility of Ignatian acceptance of the world."[114] For this reason, the essay appears to contravene the perspective of *Geist in Welt,* if for that text flight from the world is impossible.

Indeed, Rahner presents Ignatius's piety as fundamentally monastic, it is a piety of the "*monachos,* of one alone in God far from the world."[115] Ignatius and the Jesuits who follow his spiritual path dedicate themselves to the Cross of Christ, taking vows of poverty, chastity, and obedience, thereby dying to the world. This dying to the world is complemented by a singular devotion to the "God who is beyond the whole world and who freely reveals himself."[116] In contrast to spiritual movements — Rahner mentions Western metaphysics and various types of non-Christian mysticism — that attempt to bring God down to the level of the world, Ignatian spirituality insists upon God's utter sovereignty over the world.[117] Without this insistence, the Christian way of the Cross would be merely another system of ethics or ascetical program that aims at self-mastery. Christians aim for something more than this.

The "more" is, as it sounds, not a negative gesture. Ignatius does not believe in God out of spite for the world. To the contrary, since Ignatius focuses on God's being beyond the world, he underscores how God chooses to relate God's self to the world, freely and out of

---

and ed. Annemarie Kidder (Maryknoll, N.Y.: Orbis, 2010), 139–56. I shall rely mainly on the TI translation, with some minor modifications. Hereafter IM.

114. IM 283.   115. IM 281.
116. IM 283.   117. IM 283–85, 287–89.

love.[118] This God differs sharply from the metaphysical God who either stands aloof and silent from the world, or who collapses into the world, becoming an Apollo or a Dionysos.[119] The God who is more than the God of metaphysics, "more-than-the-world," is the God of Jesus Christ, the God who willingly revealed God's self as a self-gift on the Cross. The God beyond the world is a God of openness as opposed to the metaphysical God of closure. Rahner adds, "The Christian knows that his flight from the world is only an answering gesture, though a necessary one, when faced with the God who freely reveals and opens himself, who gives himself to us out of a voluntary love."[120] Just as God's being beyond the world issues in love for the world, so does the love of the Christian for the God beyond the world foster love for the world.

This paradox comes most clearly to light, Rahner explains, in the Ignatian maxims of "indifference," "finding God in all things," and "contemplatives in action." Indifference means "an ultimate attitude toward all thoughts, practices, and ways: an ultimate reserve and coolness toward them." This attitude consists in "the courage to regard no way to [God] as being *the* way, but to seek him in all ways." Indifference stems from a willingness to fly from the world, because it provisionalizes all created things. It is most pertinent here, though, because indifference does not privilege a flight from the world. In fact, it encourages the practitioner of Ignatius's spirituality to find God in all things *in the world*. "Finding God in all things" means seeking God "in the world if he wants to show himself in it."[121] The world is not the dialectical opposite of God, as some mystical spiritualities and metaphysical systems risk believing. Instead, the world is a horizon for God's revelation. The Ignatian motto *in actione contemplativus*—contemplative in action—sums up this space beyond the dialectic. The Christian seeks God wherever God might be found.

118. IM 287.
119. IM 285.
120. IM 289.
121. IM 291, emphasis in original.

Though this essay would seem to contradict *Geist in Welt,* then, by putting forward a strong case for flight from the world, Rahner makes no such case. Nor, though, does he discount the possibility that some people might be called to attempt a flight from the world. The upshot of this essay is that human spirituality, though it always bears some reference to the world—even to the world as its home—must regard God as the "beyond" who opens the possibility of truly affirming the world as home. This essay does not contravene the perspective of *Geist in Welt.* It elucidates the book's perspective: one does not truly understand the world until one glimpses what exceeds it.

REFRAMING RAHNER'S EARLY THOUGHT ON WORLD

Three passages, two from Rahner and one from Heidegger, bear consideration before I end this chapter on Rahner's sublime. Each involves the theme of this world as "home" for human existence. Each suggests also that this world, as home, is not immediately homely. A comparison of all three passages will sum up how Rahner's version of the sublime derives from his early thinking on the world, particularly in *Geist in Welt,* and how this sublime resembles yet differs from Heidegger's.

The first passage comes from the article we have just examined. It describes Ignatius's point of view, but also indicates how Rahner, the faithful interpreter of Ignatius, deals with the question of the world and its "beyond":

Ignatius approaches the world from God, not the other way around. Because he has delivered himself in the lowliness of an adoring self-surrender to the God beyond the whole world and to his will, for this reason and for this reason alone he is prepared to obey his word even when, out of the silent desert of this daring flight into God, he is, as it were, sent back into the world, which he had found the courage to abandon in the foolishness of the Cross.

One should note three elements. First, when Ignatius views the world, he does it through the prism of God. Second, God is a priority for Ignatius because he has cultivated a disposition of adoring self-surrender to God beyond the world. This disposition relates in-eluctably to the self-sacrifice of Christ on the Cross. Third, though Ignatius gives up the world in order to approach God, he is always sent back into the world to obey God's will within it.

The second passage appears on the final page of *Geist in Welt*. I have already made reference to this page, but it merits further reflection because it is the most hermeneutically significant of the entire book. In this passage Rahner surveys the philosophical and theological dimensions of the book's interpretation of Thomas. Philosophically speaking, "Abstraction is the opening of being in general that places man before God; conversion [to the phantasm] is the entrance into the here and now of this finite world, which makes God the distant unknown." Theologically speaking, "If Christianity is not the idea of an eternal, omni-present spirit, but Jesus of Nazareth, then Thomas's metaphysics of knowledge is Christian when it calls man back into the here and now of his finite world, because Eternal has also entered into it, so that man may find him."[122]

One should note here the similarities to the passage about Ignatius. Abstraction, which we examined in the first part of this chapter, relates to Ignatius's flight beyond the world toward God, so that the world might become knowable. Conversion to the phantasm relates to Ignatius's being sent back into the world. And theologically speaking, this world is the arena for God's self-revelation in Jesus of Nazareth. Being called back into the world, then, is being called to encounter God through Jesus Christ. Abstraction and conversion to the phantasm are not simply epistemological faculties. Instead, they tell the story of how being is revealed—and for Rahner being is revealed first and foremost through Jesus Christ.

---

122. SW 408/300, ET modified. Metz adds to the final line "and in Him might find himself anew." I have omitted this for two reasons. First, these words are not from the 1939 edition. Second, at this point Rahner is not writing so much of, so to speak, the return of the subject to himself, but of the subject's encounter with God. It is ironic that Metz, who criticizes Rahner for the danger of egocentrism in his theological approach, introduces this potentially egocentric wrinkle.

The third passage, from Heidegger, resonates with the two passages from Rahner because it concerns a poet's return to the "homely earth." According to Heidegger, the poet comes into his position as *Mitte des Seyns* by way of an "assault" (*Überfall*). Heidegger continues, "This assault brings him back to the homely earth, that is, engages him in historical existence and its earthly, landscapely rootedness."[123] Though Heidegger will a year later draw a distinction between earth and world, here he uses "earth" synonymously with Rahner's word, "world."[124] We have, then, another odd parallel to Rahner's conversion to the phantasm. Being attacks the poet, forcing him back into the world. There he may participate in the mission of the people, who are rooted in the land. This attack comes after the poet's "rapture" (*Entrückung*) into the being of the demigod. This rapture is somewhat akin to Rahner's abstraction, which places the human person before God. Again somewhat of a convergence between Rahner and Heidegger shows itself, but the divergences are wider and more interesting.

For Rahner, the world's being home to human existence means that the human person finds her proper place here and now, but insofar as she encounters this here and now as the place and time through which God moves to effect salvation. The world and its "beyond"—the infinite God—are intimately intertwined. This God has entered this world through Jesus Christ. Rahner notes that this last point cannot be reached philosophically, but one can prepare philosophically to receive it. At the very least, one can leave its possibility open. The Rahnerian sublime strives for this openness of philosophy—and of the world—to its beyond.

Heidegger's thinking of the world, though it constructs some

123. HGR 181. Since Heidegger's idiosyncratic German leads to an odd English rendering, I give the German: "Dieser Überfall bringt ihn an die heimatlichen Erde zurück, d.h. rückt ihn ein in das geschichtliche Dasein und seine erdhafte, landschaftliche Verwurzelung."

124. Cf. OWA 43 and 47. Even further, Heidegger posits a "strife" between world and earth. Those ideas are not in play in HGR.

sort of "beyond," maintains his apriorism of finitude. The world's being home to human existence means that the human person finds his proper place here and now only insofar as he enters into a historical destiny. The world's "beyond," then, is never really beyond the world. The gods are tied to the world, but only inasmuch as their flight or awaited return reinforce a historical destiny. And the demigod maintains this destiny. All players reinforce the radical finitude of the world, and the being that sustains it. For Heidegger, poetry and thought consist in barring the possibility that the "home" of the world might have some true beyond.

I began this chapter by discussing Rahner's idea of the return of the subject to itself, which I noted would seem to be proof positive that he espouses modern subjectivism in *Geist in Welt,* thus determining his theology in advance as "turning to the subject." To put it in this section's terms, the fear is that the subject would be a home unto itself. Over the past several pages I have argued that Rahner's *reditio* involves no such turn to the subject. Instead, the subject, in "returning to itself," places itself before God. Then it turns back toward the world as its home, a home in which God has entered and made God's mark.

Rahner's early thinking of "the world" in *Geist in Welt* should be reframed in at least three ways: (1) as resistant to modern subjectivity's representation of the world as the raw material for its own self-realization; (2) as resistant to Heidegger's view of the world as the radically finite stage for historical projects that is closed to any true "beyond"; and (3) not merely as an epistemological venture, where world would be the arena for human cognition. Instead, Rahner's thinking of world should be seen as a theory of the sublime. It tells of God's saving exaltation of all things in the world, and it intimates a form of life that affirms, appreciates, and acts upon this exaltation.

3 RAHNER AND THE SPIRIT OF THE AGE

Our age is aware of the reality of the deliberate destructiveness in the human spirit and our age is troubled to its very depths. Therein lies its greatest opportunity: to grasp the truth by breaking away from the optimisms of the modern mind.

Romano Guardini, *The End of the Modern World,* 78–79

WHEN RAHNER'S supporters and critics alike characterize him as a theologian of a "turn to the subject," they assume a few things: (1) "subject" equals "spirit"; (2) "subject" equals the post-Cartesian subject; (3) "spirit" thus equals the subjectivity of the post-Cartesian subject. Depending on the commentator, Rahner has been praised for adopting or blamed for capitulating to the modern spirit. My focus in this chapter lies in constructing a counterpoint to these readings of Rahner.

The two foregoing chapters have worked to disarticulate Rahner's understanding of subjectivity in *Geist in Welt* and other texts from modern subjectivity. This chapter continues and develops that line of argumentation. It explores how Rahner's theology, which is overwhelmingly consonant with *Geist in Welt,* opposes the "spirit" of the modern subject. Again, Heidegger serves to evoke and to amplify Rahner's countersubjective resonances.

First, an examination of angels in several Rahnerian texts shows how Rahner sets up a field of resistance against the modern subject's self-sufficient intellection. This part reinforces the idea of Rahnerian spirit at which we first arrived in chapter 2—spirit is not a self-sealing intellect, but a sublime-aesthetic receiver. Second, I enhance this view of Rahnerian spirit by investigating a Heideggerian text on the angel in Rainer Maria Rilke's poetry. Rilke's angel, according to Heidegger, looks ahead to a kind of spirit not beholden to modern subjectivity. This spirit harmonizes with Rahner's. Third, I consider Rahner's texts on Ignatius as an exemplary site in the Rahnerian corpus where he reshapes and looks beyond the spirit of the modern age. Fourth, I juxtapose Rahner's essay "Christian Humanism" (1966) and Heidegger's famous "Letter on Humanism" (1946) to reflect further on Rahner's parting from modern subjectivism.[1]

Rahner's theology, even when it looks "anthropological," seeks a person not modeled on the all-capable Renaissance man, Descartes's *cogito,* the Leibnizian monad, the Kantian *Aufklärer.* That is, Rahner does not turn to the modern subject.[2] Even further, Rahner's theology can be seen as opposing today's substitutes for the modern subject: the businessperson, the consumer, or what Romano Guardini calls "mass man."[3] Rahner's theology so far outstrips the narrowness of modern subjectivism—and its heirs—that one can hardly compare them.

1. Karl Rahner, "Christian Humanism," in TI 9, 187–204, hereafter CH; Martin Heidegger, "Letter on Humanism," in *Basic Writings*, ed. David Farrell Krell (New York: HarperCollins, 2008), 217–65, hereafter LH.

2. A commendable article by Kevin Hogan is the closest example of an inquiry akin to the one proposed in this chapter. See Hogan, "Entering into Otherness: The Postmodern Critique of the Subject and Karl Rahner's Theological Anthropology," *Horizons* 25, no. 2 (1998): 181–202.

3. Romano Guardini, *The End of the Modern World,* introduction by Frederick Wilhelmsen, foreword by Richard John Neuhaus, trans. Joseph Theman et al. (Wilmington, Del.: ISI Books, 1998), 58–63.

RAHNER, THOMAS, AND THE ANGEL

Why am I writing of the angel? This seemingly odd choice of subject matter has to do with a critique of Rahner from the foreword to the first English volume of *Theological Investigations*. The translator, Cornelius Ernst, states that for Rahner "every entity ... is a more or less deficient angel."[4] Ernst means by this that in Rahner's estimation, the central being is the intellectual being. Any being that does not possess strong subjectivity is deficient. If Rahner holds that every being is a more or less deficient angel, his thinking is indelibly marked by a turn to the modern subject.

This part of the chapter will demonstrate how the angel does play a role in Rahner's thought in *Geist in Welt* and elsewhere, but not the role that Ernst thinks it does. The angel helps to define human spirit, but not by rendering human spirit deficient. Even further, the angel's spirituality helps Rahner to articulate a wider interrelationship of spirit and matter, beyond the human, and thereby spirit's constitutive receptiveness toward the other.

THOMAS'S ANGEL

In treating the angel, Rahner intends to follow Thomas's procedure in ST I.84.7, where he distinguishes between angelic and human intellection based on the incorporeality of the former and the corporeality of the latter. Furthermore, Rahner states that Thomas does not intend anything he says about angels in this article to apply to the essence of angels, since specific knowledge regarding angels is impossible for the philosopher. Instead, Thomas's words on angels "are the way in which Thomas treats the possibility of a knowledge which is based on an intellectual intuition." Angelic intellection as an idea stands in for "precisely what human knowledge is not."[5] We can discover how this is so by examining Thomas's own observa-

---

4. Cornelius Ernst, "Introduction," in TI 1, xiii n9.
5. SW 36–37/39–40.

tions about the angel in the *Summa theologiae*. In the next section we shall see what alterations to Thomas's angel Rahner makes when he himself discusses the angel.

As I pointed out in chapter 1, Thomas's mature treatise on angels in the *Summa theologiae* (ST I.50–64) appears within the larger sweep of his theology of creation (ST I.44–119). In the "Prooemium" to this treatise, Thomas indicates that it is the first of three parts that will expound the distinction between bodily and spiritual creatures.[6] He defines angels as spiritual creatures who are entirely incorporeal.[7] An angel is pure form. By its very essence as a spiritual creature, it is unrelated to matter.[8] Thus an angel is called a "separated substance." The angel's only relationship to a body occurs when the angel assumes a body so as to become visible to a human being, as with Abraham and Sarah's angelic visitors in Genesis, or Raphael's relating to Tobiah and Sarah in Tobit.[9] An angel is an intellect without need for a body.

The angel's spirituality without materiality has implications for how it knows. We know from Rahner's reflections on the human intellect that it consists in both an agent intellect and a possible intellect. For angels the case is different: "In the angel there is no agent and possible intellect."[10] Angels do not arrive at knowledge through a process of sensation, abstraction, and a conversion to the phantasm: "Knowledge … is not generated in an angel, but is there naturally."[11] God imprints knowledge directly on the intellect of the angel. The angel thus has no need for, and does not have, an imagination.[12] Without an imagination and a possible intellect, the angel's intellection and therefore its knowledge look rather different from human intellection and its resultant knowledge.

The main difference lies in the completeness of angelic knowledge. Thomas writes that human knowledge gradually approaches

6. ST I.50.prooemium.

7. ST I.50.1.corpus.

8. ST I.50.2.

9. ST I.51.2.corpus and ad 1.

10. ST I.54.4.sed contra. Translations are mine.

11. ST I.54.4.ad 1.

12. ST I.54.5.ad 3.

completeness by deriving it from the things it encounters in sensibility. For angels it is different: "The power of understanding is naturally complete by way of intelligible species, insofar as they hold connaturally intelligible species for all intelligible things [*omnia intelligenda*] that they can know naturally."[13] This is Thomas's complex way of expressing that anything an angel needs to know in fact it already knows in principle.

Thomas later infers that angelic knowledge is nondiscursive.[14] Thomas elucidates angelic knowledge by describing the sort of knowledge humans, who depend on discourse, lack: "For if they possessed the fullness of intellectual light, like the angels, then in the first aspect of principles they would at once comprehend their whole range, by perceiving whatever could be reasoned out from them."[15] Angelic knowledge, then, comprises knowledge of principles from which the whole range of knowledge derives. The mode of this derivation is not a movement from unknown to known, but from that which is not actively being known at a given moment to being actively known at another moment.

To summarize, Thomas's angel exhibits many characteristics that sharply distinguish it from its fellow creature, the human person. Thomas's view of the angel would have had great currency among Rahner's contemporaries, particularly during his years of formation. And as I have pointed out, Rahner feels compelled at important points of *Geist in Welt* to engage Thomas's view of the angel. Twenty-five years after writing *Geist in Welt*, though, Rahner feels equally compelled to distance himself from Thomas's angel: "The Thomistic speculation regarding the metaphysical essence of angels is an opinion which one is free to hold or not."[16] We must figure out why.

---

13. ST I.55.2.corpus.   14. ST I.58.3.ad 1.
15. ST I.58.3.corpus.
16. Karl Rahner, "Angels," in *Encyclopedia of Theology: A Concise Sacramentum Mundi*, ed. Karl Rahner (New York: Continuum, 1975), 4–13, at 11.

THE ANGEL AND HUMAN DEFICIENCY?

Above I quoted briefly from Cornelius Ernst, who worries that for Rahner "every entity ... is a more or less deficient angel." This comment comes in a footnote in which Ernst objects to the foundation of Rahner's philosophical perspective in *Geist in Welt*, which Ernst takes to be fundamental for the writings in *Theological Investigations*. His concern stems from Rahner's definition of being as self-presence (*Beisichsein*). Ernst continues, "My main objection to this approach is that what is said *cannot* be said if the Thomist thesis which the book is supposed to be maintaining is true, namely that our metaphysical knowledge derives from our experience of the world, or, putting it in Fr. Rahner's (and Heidegger's) terms, that our 'ontological' knowledge derives from our 'ontic' knowledge."[17] There are a number of problems with Ernst's reading of the situation, but I shall name only the most pertinent ones.

Given our close examination of "*Beisichsein*" in the last chapter, it should be clear that though Rahner does define being as *Beisichsein,* he qualifies it in the case of human beings. And more importantly, this qualification on behalf of human beings points to a fundamental alteration of *Beisichsein* in general. *Beisichsein* is a matter not of being by oneself (as *Beisichsein* might be literally translated), but rather of being with the other. Ernst and many others in his wake do not attend adequately to Rahner's nuancing of this initial definition. This would answer Ernst's objection that Rahner does not remain consistent with the overall aim of his project, that is, developing a metaphysics based on the imagination.

It should be noted that Ernst seems to intend his remark as somewhat hyperbolic. However, if one holds Ernst to his choice of words—every being for Rahner is a deficient angel—then one must ask the question of how exactly the angel functions for Rahner. Who is the angel for Rahner?

17. Ernst, "Introduction," xiiin9, emphasis original.

In *Geist in Welt,* the angel becomes a "limit-idea" (*Grenz-idee*) for highlighting the peculiarity of human intellection. The angel is pure intuitive intellection, and human intellection is not intuitive but, as we saw in Thomas, discursive.[18] Rahner's discussion of the angel centers on its nonreceptivity, its inability to relate to the "other" of matter, and the impossibility of the material object to "encounter" it.[19] Also, Rahner points out that since Thomas's angel always already has its knowledge, the angel has no possible intellect (the reader should recall that Rahner's concise definition for human being is the possible intellect). When Rahner calls the angel a limit-idea for human intellection, it may sound as if this denigrates humanity in favor of a superior angelic intelligence. Ernst takes it this way. But if one notices that Rahner's presentation of the angelic intellect emphasizes what the angel does *not* have, then if a deficiency appears, it appears on the angel's side. That is, if there has to be a deficiency.

It is true, and Ernst could have pointed this out, that Rahner cites Thomas's portrayal of the human intellect as the "lowest rank among intellectual substances."[20] This "ranking" holds only if one assumes in principle that a purer intellect is "higher," that the angel is pure intellect, and that the human's intellect is rendered impure by it involvement in matter. Rahner does not adopt these principles.

Rahner addresses this question of rank in his 1961 entry on angels in the theological encyclopedia *Sacramentum mundi.* He contends that "the problem of the nature of the angels as 'higher' than that of man was affirmed [in traditional, Thomistic angelology] in a way that took for granted too readily and indiscriminately neo-Platonic conceptions of scales and degrees." Rahner continues, "The intellectual nature of man cannot so easily be characterized as inferior to that of the angels."[21] If Rahner finds this "ranking" so problematic, it is difficult to see why he would have set up such a ranking in his own work.

---

18. SW 38/40, 243/185.
20. SW 250–51/190.

19. SW 243/185.
21. Rahner, "Angels," 8.

His interest in *Geist in Welt* is not to rank God, angels, and humans, but rather to find how specifically human intellection occurs, and what this tells us about how God reveals God's self through the world. There is not, nor does there have to be, a deficiency on the human side vis-à-vis the angel. Instead, the angel helps to open the question of how human spirituality relates to God's self-manifestation.

RAHNER'S ALTERNATIVE ANGELOLOGY

Rahner returns to the topic of the angel in the late essay, "On Angels" (1978).[22] The text has three parts: (1) on whether we can know about angels; (2) on the "existential-ontological question" of angels, that is, what angels and demons are; and (3) on the question of the theology of the cosmos. I shall focus on the second part, though the entire essay bears a close reading. The second part involves a theological critique of prior angelologies, and Rahner's proposal of an alternative. While it is true that Rahner sets out in part to "demythologize" some "primitive" or "folkloric" ideas about angels, his more proximate targets for theological critique are illegitimate technical, philosophical assumptions about angels. It is not clear, Rahner states, what angels are. One must ask this question.

Most concerning to Rahner is the common assumption regarding angels that Thomists, regular believers, and modern skeptics share: that angels "must be seen as 'pure' spirits without necessarily possessing an essential relationship to matter."[23] Rahner notes that this philosophical belief about angels comes from Neoplatonism as it is filtered through Thomas, and it takes root in "scholastic speculation" post-Thomas.[24] The idea of the angel as a pure spirit without

---

22. Karl Rahner, "On Angels," in TI 19, 235–74. There is also a remarkable two-page treatment of the angel in Rahner, "The Unity of Spirit and Matter in the Christian Understanding of the Faith," in TI 6, 153–77, at 157–59, and some interesting comments in Rahner, *The Theology of Death,* trans. W. J. O'Hara (New York: Herder and Herder, 1961), 23, 52–53, along with scattered references to angels elsewhere.

23. Rahner, "On Angels," 253–54.

24. Rahner, "On Angels," 254; Rahner, "Angels" 12.

any relationship to matter, though it may have roots going back to the Church Fathers, is by and large a modern invention.

The main problem with understanding the angel as entirely unrelated to matter lies in its contravention of the scriptural witness. In scripture, angels are "powers and authorities of this material world." They "have something to do with the winds, fire, and water." They "are localized in this earthly world." And "in the last resort [they] form together with human beings one and the same history of salvation, can be angels of individual nations, and are understood as actively helpful and tempting in this world and its history."[25] The idea of an angel as a "separated form" contradicts this varied biblical testimony, all of which is tied together by the presupposition that angels relate to matter.

Rahner suggests a different approach to angelology. Instead of conceptualizing the angel as a spiritual form separated from matter, Rahner proposes positing a priori an "essential intrinsic relationship" between angels and matter. This relationship would not be the same as the human relationship to matter. It would, in a certain sense, be "higher." Lest this sound like it lends credence once again to Ernst's charge that every being for Rahner is a deficient angel, Rahner intends a different "height." The angel's "superhuman" character would not come from its separation from matter, but instead from its production of a "greater material unity and configuration" than human beings could achieve.[26] Its being would not be an aloof *Beisichsein,* but *Miteinandersein.*

This account of the angel would fit better with the scriptural evidence, or at the very least would not be as far afield from it as the idea of a separated form. Rahner's alternative account of the angel would address another difficulty, too. It would underscore how spirit can be seen as receptive toward another. Rahner's angel would reinforce the sublime-aesthetic perspective of *Geist in Welt* in a way that

25. Rahner, "On Angels," 255, ET modified.
26. Rahner, "On Angels," 255.

Thomas's angel could not. In doing so, it would contest modern subjectivism.

As I observed above, Ernst's charge that for Rahner every being is a deficient angel is so vexing because it insinuates that Rahner turns to the modern subject. It is interesting, then, when during Rahner's critique of Thomistic angelology he mentions an influential figure for the modern subject: the "Leibnizian monad."[27] It also is worth noting that Rahner studied Gottfried Wilhelm Leibniz's text *Monadologie* in a seminar with Heidegger (1936), in which Heidegger teaches that the "monad" is the "logical subject."[28]

Rahner writes, "In traditional angelology the angels are set up as Leibnizian monads which can draw the content of their existence (apart from its relationship to God) purely from their own internal resources, since as *formae separatae* they are always aware of themselves from the outset without the mediation of another being."[29] One can see from the passages I quoted above from Thomas how one might arrive at this "monadic" view of the angel. For Thomas, angels have innate and complete knowledge without any need for mediation from matter, or even from another angel. One could also add that for Thomas, no two angels are of the same species. Each angel is its own kind of being, absolutely. This follows from the angel's lack of a relationship to matter.[30] Just like the monad, an angel is autonomous and wholly self-sufficient. Were this view of the angel applied to the human person, we would have the ideal person of modern subjectivism.

When Rahner chooses the phrase "Leibnizian monad," then, it is not just a convenient metaphor. And when he opposes the angelology that coheres with the Leibnizian monad, he is not just engaging in a provincial exercise of interest to Catholic theologians only.

27. Rahner, "On Angels," 254. Cf. Rahner, "Angels," 8.
28. See Rahner's notes from this seminar in *Geist in Welt,* 421–26.
29. Rahner, "On Angels," 254.
30. ST I.50.4.corpus.

Rahner shows how the angel can be incorporated into a wider philosophical and theological discussion on spirit, and how a more careful definition of what spirit is might work against the spiritual pathology of the modern age: its inability to relate, its false sense of autonomy, its closure.

Likewise, the angelic spirit might be used to oppose modern subjectivism's close correlate, anthropocentrism. Rahner affirms in his encyclopedia entry on angels that angelology "makes man recognize a section of the world of persons of which he is a member for the decision of faith and prevents him from diminishing its dimensions—he realizes that he stands in a more comprehensive community of salvation and perdition than that of mankind alone."[31] This is why the question of the angel's being gives way to a theology of the cosmos.[32] Rahner's opening of human subjectivity widens the scope of human subjectivity beyond modern accounts of it. His alternative angelology promises, if only in sketch form, to open reality even further, via a "higher" spirit. Let us now move on to an analogue to this "higher" spirit in an essay of Heidegger's.

HEIDEGGER, RILKE, AND THE ANGEL

Heidegger's 1946 essay, "Wozu Dichter?" (ET "What Are Poets For?), presents a reading of Rilke's poetry.[33] If Hölderlin is the poet most important to Heidegger's thinking, Rilke is second. Heidegger borrows several terms from Rilke's poetry, including "the Open" [das Offene] and "play-space" [Spielraum]), which help Heidegger to articulate his view of language. Most importantly for us here, though, Heidegger reads Rilke as one who writes of the angel. Rilke's angel becomes for Heidegger a poetic figure for a being who

---

31. Rahner, "Angels," 6.

32. Rahner, "On Angels," 260–74.

33. Heidegger, "What Are Poets For?" in *Poetry, Language, Thought,* 89–139, hereafter WPF. For the German, see Heidegger, "Wozu Dichter," in *Holzwege: Gesamtausgabe* 5 (Frankfurt: Vittorio Klostermann, 1977), 269–320.

stands at the center of being,[34] in a way similar to the demigod of Hölderlin's hymn "Der Rhein."

Rahner most likely would not have read "What Are Poets For?," though we do know he read Rilke, since he cites *The Duino Elegies* (1922) in "Priest and Poet."[35] Heidegger's essay, though, with its thinking on the angel, may be read as a remarkable complement to Rahner's revision of Thomas's angel. The Heideggerian-Rilkean angel works against modern subjectivity. I aim here to evoke some resonances between this angel and the Rahnerian-Thomistic angel. Thus I shall identify another way that Rahner's convergence with Heidegger belies the conventional reading of Rahner's turn to the subject.

RILKE AND MODERN METAPHYSICS

In order to understand the Rilkean angel, it is important to recognize the figure with whom Heidegger contrasts this angel. And in order to recognize this figure, one must be clear on the Heideggerian conception of history that undergirds his portrayal of this figure. In chapter 2 I noted a key component of Heidegger's view of history. The current age is the age of the "flight of the gods." Heidegger derives this idea from Hölderlin's poem "*Germanien*." Heidegger begins "What Are Poets For?" by referring to this idea of the flight of the gods. The title of his essay is an abbreviation of a line from one of Hölderlin's poems, "what are poets for in a destitute time?" Heidegger interprets the destitution of the current age as the absence of a god who gathers people and disposes the world's history. Heidegger adds that this default of a God has become so entrenched that it can no longer be recognized as a default.

Since the gods cannot be encountered, Heidegger contends, human persons—or "mortals"—fail truly to experience the conditions

---

34. WPF 131.
35. Rahner, PP, 298–99.

of their mortality: "pain, death, and love."[36] Mortality remains concealed, where it would be more proper for it to reveal itself. Rilke poetizes from within this situation, which is exacerbated in modernity because of the modern age's metaphysical constitution.

During the modern age, the being of beings appears as human, self-assertive will.[37] The world and everything within it become objects for human calculation and manipulation: "Man places before himself the world as the whole of everything objective, and he places himself before the world. Man sets up the world toward himself, and delivers Nature over to himself."[38] The goal of this objectification lies in a denial of death.[39] The world is set up, so the self-assertive human subject thinks, to evade the danger of death.[40] The key to modern metaphysics, then, is human willing's active forgetting of its mortal condition in its development of technology and its corollary: business.

Heidegger believes that Rilke recognizes something like this in his poetry. This recognition appears in conjunction with the poetic word, "the Open." Heidegger states that Rilke uses "the term 'the Open' to designate the whole draft to which all beings ... are given over."[41] This "Open," particularly in the eighth of the *Duino Elegies,* does not include the human being. In a letter to one of his readers, Rilke insists that plants and animals "are admitted into the Open," while the human being is not. The reason Rilke states is vitally important for understanding his stance toward modern metaphysics. Plants and animals are "*in* the world," in contrast to the human being who "stands over against the world."[42] In other words, plants and animals that do not objectify the world stand more securely within it, while the human being who willfully opposes the world is barred from being secure within it. The human being turns against the Open, thus becoming "unshielded."[43]

36. WPF 95.   37. WPF 107–9.
38. WPF 107.   39. WPF 122.
40. WPF 114.   41. WPF 103.
42. WPF 105–6.   43. WPF 117.

Rilke proposes as an antidote to this metaphysical situation that self-assertive calculation be inverted. If the modern human will aims by objectifying the world to deny death, the one who inverts this will must affirm death. Heidegger cites another saying from Rilke's letters: "the point is to read the word 'death' without negation." Rilke envisions this affirmation as a "turning of unshieldedness into the Open." It reverses the calculative will that turns away from the Open. To turn unshieldedness "into the Open is to renounce giving a negative reading to that which is."[44] Instead of subscribing to a calculative logic wherein everything—death or anything else—is assigned a negative or positive value, Rilke advocates a turn toward a more expansive logic of the heart, which exposes itself to an "overflow beyond number." Heidegger indicates that Rilke has a predecessor in Blaise Pascal, who opposed his "logic of the heart" to Descartes's "logic of calculative reason."[45] Heidegger summarizes Rilke's proposed turning of the objectifying will: "The conversion of consciousness . . . is an inner recalling of the immanence of the objects of representation into presence within the heart's space."[46]

While Heidegger admires Rilke's poetry and his efforts to poetize a counterpoint to modern calculative logic, he notes a glaring insufficiency of this approach. Rilke's "logic of the heart" remains beholden to the representational logic of calculative willing.[47] The logic of the heart is not different enough from its opposite. They are mere reciprocals of one another.

That said, Heidegger deems Rilke's poetry remarkable in that it approaches the end of metaphysics. Though Rilke does not find

44. WPF 122, 124.   45. WPF 125.
46. WPF 127.

47. See WPF 130. In the 1942 course on Parmenides, Heidegger prosecutes an even more trenchant critique of Rilke. He charges Rilke with misunderstanding the historical role of humanity as a recipient of the event of being, and thus a misconstrual of the poet's role in history. The critique of Rilke here is lighter, and shows that Heidegger has aligned Rilke more closely with the model poet, Hölderlin. See Martin Heidegger, *Parmenides*, trans. André Schuwer and Richard Rojcewicz (Bloomington: Indiana University Press, 1992), 151–61.

an exit from modern metaphysics, he diagnoses its blindness to being. And though, like Nietzsche, Rilke remains within metaphysics' sway, he identifies a transitional figure—one who points to while not yet accomplishing a new age in history. For Nietzsche, that figure is Zarathustra, the preacher of the "*Übermensch.*"[48] For Rilke, it is the angel.[49]

The only glimmer of hope in a world destitute of gods lies in Dionysos, the wine god who communicates the traces of the gods to the godless.[50] The poet is, of course, the proxy of Dionysos. And Rilke the poet passes on the hint of the angel as a trace of the gods that might assist the mortal in his night of destitution into a new day.

RILKE'S ANGEL

Heidegger draws his reading of the angel from Rilke's *The Duino Elegies.* Indeed, the angel plays a substantial role in these poems. Rilke commences by crying out to the angelic orders.[51] His descriptions of angels are captivating: "Every angel is terrifying" (*Ein jeder Engel ist schrecklich*).[52] The angel, as compared to the human, "more feelingly feels" (*fühlender fühlt*).[53] The angels are the ones to be praised when this life's grim vision has ended ("*an dem Ausgang der grimmigen Einsicht*").[54] And most importantly, the angel elucidates a contrast of the modern age with prior ages, like the one preserved in the biblical book of Tobit. Rilke refers to Tobiah's amicable encounter with the angel Raphael. The young man does not find the angel's

48. See Martin Heidegger, "Who Is Nietzsche's Zarathustra?" in *Nietzsche: Volume Two,* trans. David Farrell Krell (New York: Harper & Row, 1984), 211–33.

49. WPF 131: "Only a more primal elucidation of the nature of subjectness will serve to show how, within the completion of modern metaphysics, there belongs to the being of beings a relation to such a being, how the creature which is Rilke's Angel, despite all differences in content, is *metaphysically the same* as the figure of Nietzsche's Zarathustra."

50. WPF 91.

51. See Rainer Maria Rilke, *The Duino Elegies and Sonnets to Orpheus* (bilingual edition), trans. A. Poulin Jr. (New York: Houghton Mifflin Books, 2005), 1.1–2. I shall cite the *Duino Elegies* (hereafter DE) by elegy and line number.

52. DE 1.7, 2.1.   53. DE 9.55.

54. DE 10.1.

presence too much to bear. The poet surmises that should Raphael confront us today as he did Tobiah, our hearts would burst in his presence.[55]

Though I have said that the angel's role in these poems is substantial, it is not immediately clear what this role is. Heidegger notices this. He discovers in one of Rilke's letters the poet's own interpretation of the angel: "The angel of the *Elegies* is that creature in whom the transmutation of the visible into the invisible, which we achieve, seems already accomplished. The angel of the *Elegies* is that being who assures the recognition of a higher order of reality in the invisible." Even this statement allows some room for defining the angel's role. Heidegger takes this opportunity. He contends that Rilke's angel is "the being who governs the unheard-of center of the widest orbit and causes it to appear."[56] The angel brings to light the widest scope of being that Rilke can imagine. Though Heidegger finds this scope to be not quite wide enough, he deems instructive Rilke's attempt to open it.

Rilke proposes that the human will to objectify be reversed and converted into an "inner recalling of objects." This, Rilke hopes, will save the human being from her "unshieldedness" by affirming that unshieldedness as a part of life. It behooves the human being to attempt this conversion and finding of a new security because the human rapport with the Open differs from the plant and the animal.

During his exposition of the angel, Heidegger returns to the topic of the plant and the animal in order to illustrate how the angel differs from the human being. He details how each being relates to the "balance" of being. "Plant and animal," Heidegger writes, "are held carefree in the Open." They are "lulled" into the Open, and they belong there completely un-self-consciously. They are secure and still in the balance, as opposed to humans who are "unstilled." The angel is like the plant and animal in its stillness, but also some-

55. See DE 2.3–9.
56. WPF 131.

how different: "The balance in which the angel is ventured also remains outside of the unstilled—not, however, because it does not yet belong to the realm of the unstilled, but because it belongs there no longer."[57] In a manner of speaking, Heidegger categorizes Rilke's plant and animal as "prior" to modern, willing humanity, and Rilke's angel as "after" it.

Heidegger illustrates this "after" with a late, fragmentary poem of Rilke's in which the poet envisions a passing over of the balance from the "merchant's hand" to the angel.[58] The thinker notices that for the poet the "merchant" is a figure for modern humanity, that is, the modern subject. Modern humans attempt to achieve stillness through "businesses" and "exchanges." They risk their "nature in the vibration of money and the currency of values."[59] Everything— every being—is assigned a number. Self-assertive willing "subjects all beings to the trade of a calculation that dominates most tenaciously in those areas where there is no need of numbers."[60] This is the "customary life of contemporary man." The angel points to an alternative existence: "By contrast, the passage of the balance to the angel is uncommon."[61]

Heidegger's invocation of the "uncommon" should recall to us last chapter's discussion of how human existence comes truly to light only through an encounter with a "beyond" of some sort. Rilke's *Duino Elegies* provide a different vocabulary for describing this "beyond." The angel is the word for a "beyond," a rapport with the world that does not evaluate it and assign it a price, an existence above number: "*Überzähliges Dasein*."[62] Rilke facilitates an encounter with the "beyond" of modern subjectivity by poetizing the passing of the balance from the merchant to the angel.

Rilke's angel is for Heidegger the "worldly oneness" that appears amid the "unholiness" of the modern world. The angel is a figure for

57. WPF 132, ET slightly modified.   58. WPF 133.
59. WPF 132–33.   60. WPF 112.
61. WPF 134.   62. DE 9.79.

the "singing" that constitutes an effective "saying" in contrast with the "propositional assertion" of modern, willing human beings. The angel is, then, a sign for the "venturesome" language of poets who turn language back toward being, that is, toward the "soundness of worldly existence."[63] In the angel Heidegger finds a harbinger of an age superior to the age of objectivism and business. Rilke's angel inscribes Heidegger's hope that the current age's default of being will give way to an age of being's nearness.

RAHNER AND THE HEIDEGGERIAN-RILKEAN ANGEL

On the face of it, Rahner's writings on angels and Heidegger's meditation on Rilke's angel evidence few similarities. Everything Rahner says about the angel derives from either Thomistic metaphysics or Catholic dogmatic theology. Everything Heidegger observes about the angel in "What Are Poets For?" comes from the poetic imagination of Rilke.[64] But insofar as both Rahner and Heidegger set the angel against the modern subject, their disparate texts converge.

In *Geist in Welt,* Rahner uses the angel to highlight the constitutive features of human subjectivity by way of contrast. He posits the angel as a placeholder for the idea of a completely intuitive intellect. This limit-idea enhances our view of the "possibility" and "discursiveness" of human intellection. These aspects of the human intellect oppose modern subjectivism's ideal of the self-sufficient intellect. In the other texts we examined, Rahner moves beyond the use of the angel as a mere limit-idea to his own alternative angelology. He supplements the Thomistic view of the angelic intellect as a "separated form." He hypothesizes an angelic intellect that is constitutionally related to matter, though in a different way than the human intellect. Likewise, he looks to the angel as a way to break the illu-

---

63. See WPF 134–39.

64. Heidegger does reflect on angels elsewhere, since Hölderlin mentions them in his poetry. See, for example, Martin Heidegger, *Hölderlin's Hymn "The Ister,"* trans. William McNeill and Julia Davis (Bloomington: Indiana University Press, 1996), 134.

sion that human subjectivity is the only kind of rational subjectivity. This contextualizes human thought and life within a more cosmic scope, thus tempering modern subjectivism's narcissism.

Heidegger's thinking dovetails with Rahner's at this point. Anything Heidegger writes about the angel does not say so much about the angel as about the human. Heidegger enlists Rilke's angel to make his point that the modern subject's way of relating to the world is not humanity's only option. The angel, singing the poet's song, can entice humanity beyond the fallenness and forgetfulness of calculative reason to a new way of being. The angel, though a being entirely different from the human, can show humanity an existence more proper to it. As with Rahner's angel, this existence is more proper to humanity because it sets the human within the wider context of the world: plants, animals, angels, gods. And it is notable that Heidegger, at Rilke's prompting, specifies his objection to modern subjectivism by taking aim at business. In Heidegger's day and more so in our own, the businessperson has become the dominant heir to modern subjectivism and its baneful effects on the life of the world. In fact, the businessperson is the one who has overthrown the modern subject's intellection and replaced it with a completely thoughtless willing—the will to acquire and to concentrate wealth.

Although Rahner and Heidegger converge in their deployment of angels to turn the tide against modern subjectivism, they diverge, also. Heidegger's reading of Rilke's angel has a distinctively Dionysian cast. It is important to remember that the angel fits with Rilke's desire to affirm death. The proper human existence that the angel means to show is a radically finite existence, bounded ineluctably by pain and death. The angel as a "beyond," just like the "*Unheimlichkeit*" of *Being and Time,* is a finite beyond. In short, Heidegger conscripts Rilke, as he did Hölderlin, to reinforce, to elaborate, and to intensify his apriorism of finitude.

If Heidegger chooses Dionysos, Rahner opts for Christ. In at least two texts, Rahner makes a plea that consideration of the angel be transposed from the area of metaphysical speculation to the theology of Jesus Christ. He writes, "Angelology draws its ultimate measure and basis from Christology."[65] And elsewhere, "A really Christian angelology must, from the start, fit in with the fact of the God-man."[66]

Thus far what I have written about angels concerns Rahner's comparison and contrast of angels to human subjectivity so as to clarify what sort of subjectivity it really is. The point at issue in these quotes adds a crucial layer to Rahner's thinking on the angel. Angelology must cohere with Christology, lest one lose sight of the fact that angels, though they may seem self-sufficient, receive everything by the grace of Christ. Grace is the layer that must subtend all consideration of subjectivity, whether human or angelic. Rahner diverges from Heidegger on this count because instead of an apriorism of finitude, Rahner sets forth an apriorism of the infinite grace of Christ.

Heidegger and Rahner both oppose a modern subjectivity that *takes* when it would be better to receive. Heidegger's essay on Rilke articulates a vision of poetic receptivity within the world. The poet receives the world instead of turning against it. Heidegger criticizes Rilke for his conception of the Open, suggesting that Rilke's Open is not wide enough. It remains determined by modern subjectivism.

Rahner could direct a similar objection toward Heidegger. His Dionysian perspective, though he claims that it opens beyond modern subjectivism, fails fully to open. It remains closed to anything beyond the world of danger, pain, and death. Rahner's cosmic-Christological perspective sets human subjectivity on a wider plain, an infinite horizon. Receptivity to the world is important, but one

---

65. Rahner, "Angels," 6.

66. Karl Rahner, *The Trinity,* trans. Joseph Donceel, introduction, index and glossary by Catherine Mowry LaCugna (New York: Crossroad, 2004), 36.

cannot rule out in principle receptivity to the sustaining ground of the world—the God of Jesus Christ, who saves the world through outpoured grace.

RAHNER'S IGNATIUS AGAINST MODERNITY'S SPIRIT

Though I have dispatched the objection that the spirit behind Rahner's subjectivity is a modern spirit, and elaborated my reply to the objection by testing the resonances between Rahner and Heidegger, a potential problem still remains. When Rahner writes in his theology, particularly his spiritual writings, that God can be experienced immediately,[67] it seems that the problem of the angel rearises. In his metaphysics of knowledge, Rahner rejects the idea of intellectual intuition, or a direct infusion of knowledge from God. This idea cannot apply to human knowledge. Yet in his theology it appears that Rahner allows an analogue to intellectual intuition—a direct spiritual intuition of God. Rahner evidently retreats from his work to differentiate the human person from the angel. Does he, then, recant his distancing of the human person from the modern subject? Does the modern spirit return in the spiritual experience of God?

Rahner claims to get his idea of the immediate experience of God from Ignatius Loyola (1491–1556), the founder of the Society of Jesus to which Rahner belonged. Ignatius lived at the beginning of the modern era. He has been alternately credited and disparaged for being a founding father of modern spirituality—individualistic,

67. The locus classicus for this is Karl Rahner, "Ignatius Speaks to a Jesuit Today," in *Ignatius of Loyola*, introduction by Paul Imhof, trans. Rosaleen Ockenden (London: Collins, 1979), 11–38. Since this text is notoriously difficult to locate, it bears consulting Karl Rahner, *Spiritual Writings*, ed. Philip Endean (Maryknoll, N.Y.: Orbis, 2004), in which Endean has translated several selections from the text; see especially 36–43. See also the most widely available German: Karl Rahner, "Rede des Ignatius von Loyola an einen Jesuiten von heute," *Wissenschaft und christlicher Glaube: Schriften zur Theologie XV*, ed. Paul Imhof (Zürich: Benziger, 1983), 373–408. For exposition of this text, see Endean, KRIS 12–31, and Declan Marmion, *A Spirituality of Everyday Faith: A Theological Investigation of the Notion of Spirituality in Karl Rahner* (Grand Rapids, Mich.: Eerdmans, 1998), 252–61.

willful, anthropocentric.[68] If Rahner espouses a spirituality under-girded by modern subjectivity, it would make sense to many that Ignatius prompts Rahner to do so.

In the last chapter we investigated an earlier Rahnerian text on Ignatius. This part will consider more of Rahner's writings on Ignatius. These writings are extensive.[69] Here I shall analyze just a few of them: "Ignatian Spirituality and Devotion to the Sacred Heart of Jesus" (1955), "The Logic of Existential Decision in Ignatius Loyola" (1956), "Being Open to God as Ever-Greater: On the Significance of the Aphorism 'Ad Majorem Dei Gloriam'" (1959), and "Modern Piety and the Experience of Retreats" (1974).[70] The focus will be twofold: (1) how Rahner presents Ignatius as simultaneously taking up and disrupting the spirit of the modern age and (2) the implications of this reading of Ignatius for Rahner's theology.

68. A famous disparagement of Ignatius with which Rahner would have been familiar occurs in Jacques Maritain's *Integral Humanism* (1936). Maritain accuses Ignatius of an "exaltation of the heroic will" that reflects the "heroic humanism" of the Renaissance and presages the twentieth-century "heroic humanism" of Lenin. For Maritain, Ignatius's "human, too human" heroism is epitomized in the motto, "ad majorem dei gloriam," which encourages those who espouse it "to augment the glory of God." Rahner would have recognized the violent misinterpretation in this reading of Ignatius, and it would have given him incentive to reread Ignatius as a countermodern. See Jacques Maritain, *Integral Humanism*, trans. Joseph Evans (New York: Charles Scribner's Sons, 1968), 155–56.

69. For the definitive bibliography of Rahner's Ignatian writings, see Endean, KRIS, 268–74, and for a brief schematization of these texts, see ibid., 8. The best resource in German for Rahner's Ignatian writings is the *Sämtliche Werke* volume devoted to them: Karl Rahner, *Ignatianischer Geist: Schriften zu den Exerzitien und zur Spiritualität des Ordensgründers, Sämtliche Werke 13*, ed. Andreas Batlogg, Johannes Herzgsell, and Stefan Kiechle (Freiburg: Herder, 2006). See also Andreas Batlogg, *Die Mysterien des Lebens Jesu bei Karl Rahner: Zugang zum Christusglauben* (Innsbruck: Tyrolia, 2001).

70. Karl Rahner, "Ignatian Spirituality and Devotion to the Sacred Heart of Jesus," in *Christian in the Market Place,* trans. Cecily Hastings (New York: Sheed & Ward, 1966), 119–46, hereafter ISD; Rahner, "The Logic of Concrete Individual Knowledge in Ignatius Loyola," in *The Dynamic Element in the Church,* trans. W. J. O'Hara (New York: Herder, 1964), 84–170, hereafter LED (N.B. the ET's title is misleading, hence my emendation of it in the text). Cf. the German: Rahner, "Die Logik der existentiellen Erkenntnis bei Ignatius v. Loyola," in *Das Dynamische in der Kirche* [Freiburg: Herder, 1958], 74–148]; Rahner, "Being Open to God as Ever Greater: On the Significance of the Aphorism 'Ad Majorem Dei Gloriam'" in TI 7, 25–46, hereafter AMDG; Rahner, "Modern Piety and the Experience of Retreats," in TI 16, 135–55, hereafter MPER.

Ignatius's language of individuality, will, decision, and freedom may seem to accord with the early modern spirit, which will become modern subjectivity. But to Rahner's mind, Ignatius inflects his language—thus his spirituality—in such a way that he sets up an alternative to modernity. Though he lives at the beginning of the modern age, Ignatius sees beyond it. Rahner stands convinced that Ignatius's age is yet to come. If this is true of Ignatius, then Rahner's appeal to the Ignatian experience of God means something different from the experience of the modern subject.

THE QUESTION OF IGNATIUS AND MODERNITY

Prior to reading Rahner's Ignatian texts, it would help briefly to set up a hermeneutical structure for understanding Rahner's Ignatius. I shall lay out two components. The first comes from a text Rahner did not know, since it was written long after his death. Nevertheless, its diagnosis of what characterizes modernity echoes Rahner's description of modernity in his Ignatian writings. The text is Louis Dupré's *Passage to Modernity* (1993), which includes a short section on Ignatius that treats him as subverting modernity's spirit.[71] The second comes from a book Rahner did know: *The End of the Modern World* (1950) by Romano Guardini, Rahner's predecessor at the University of Munich. Rahner read this book, which originated in a set of lectures on Pascal, and cites it frequently during the 1950s and 1960s, most notably in two essays I discuss below.[72] From Dupré we shall get a sense of how Ignatius works at the dawn of the modern worldview to transform it. From Guardini we shall learn how a transformation of the modern worldview heralds that worldview's terminus.

Dupré argues that modernity began with a "combustive mixture" of two factors: late medieval nominalist theology's removal of

71. Louis Dupré, *Passage to Modernity: An Essay in the Hermeneutics of Nature and Culture* (New Haven, Conn.: Yale University Press, 1993), 224–27.
72. MPER 135n2; AMDG 32.

God from creation and Renaissance humanism's assignation to the human person of God's former role of meaning giver.[73] This "mixture" transformed the cosmos supported by the Creator God into an object, and the human person as a microcosm of God's cosmos into the subject that constituted every object. Thus came the dominance of modern subjectivism and modern science, but Dupré argues strongly that modernity had already been afoot before the rise of the subject in Descartes or Francis Bacon. This is an interesting claim in itself, but it becomes even more so when Dupré contends that alternatives to modern subjectivism arose before it took hold. One of these proleptic alternatives took shape in what Dupré calls the "devout humanism" of Ignatius.[74]

To some extent Ignatius is a product of his time. He reflects its prevailing attitude: "In truly modern fashion ... Ignatius places the person at the center of his universe." He specifies this anthropocentrism by developing a spiritual book, the *Spiritual Exercises,* which assumes that human persons can shape their own wills through systematic training. Dupré likens this training to the method of reasoning that Descartes will develop in the next century. Dupré notes that the insistence in the *Exercises* "on making the most effective use of one's spiritual potential resembles so closely contemporary secular attitudes as to cast suspicion on its religious nature." And he asks, "Does Ignatius's trust in nature not hide a secret naturalism which merely aggravates a condition that had reduced grace to a supplement of an autonomous natural order?" Does not Ignatius's confidence in the natural power of the human will—which could be construed as operating without the help of God's grace—derive from and further entrench the nominalist dismissal of God from creation, and the humanist elevation of the human person to meaning giver?[75]

After having set up the case for the ascription of "modern" to Ignatius, Dupré contends to the contrary that Ignatius's spiritual-

---

73. Dupré, *Passage to Modernity,* 3.   74. Dupré, *Passage to Modernity,* 224.
75. Dupré, *Passage to Modernity,* 224.

ity countervails the spirit of modern humanism. Modern humanism promotes an ideal of human self-realization. Human creativity
is self-sustaining and self-completing. Ignatius inverts this ideal. For
him, "Grace must first liberate nature from a state of unfreedom in
order to enable it to reach its natural potential." Ignatius entirely redefines the emerging modern idea of freedom. In contrast to his humanistic contemporaries, and more like the Protestants, he defines
freedom as "a divinely inspired surrender within which action itself
becomes grounded in passivity."[76] Freedom is primarily God's, and
God shares this with human creatures.

This conception of freedom likewise "subverts ... the anthropocentric attitude." Instead of human persons working out their au-
tochthonous capabilities and ascending toward God, Ignatius judges
human action to be rooted in a divine descent to creation that enables a return to God. Dupré states, "Ignatius transforms the anthropocentric ideal of creative self-development by placing it within
a radically theocentric perspective." Dupré characterizes this transformation of anthropocentrism as a sacralization of "Renaissance
naturalism from within."[77] This is important to understand.

We have noted already that Ignatius is not simply a modern. He
is also not a late medieval intruder in a burgeoning modern world.
He is a modern of a different sort, a modern who dislocates modernity as it takes shape.[78] He does so by adopting the language of modern culture while infusing it with the perennial spirit of Christianity.
Dupré notes how even an eminent scholar meets Ignatius's contribution with incomprehension: "The Basque mystic did the exact opposite of what [Hans] Blumenberg considered characteristic of modern
culture, namely to fill traditional religious forms with a modern content. He conveyed to the modern worldview a traditional spiritual

---

76. Dupré, *Passage to Modernity,* 225. This, incidentally, is exactly the conviction behind Rahner's theology of the supernatural existential.

77. Dupré, *Passage to Modernity,* 225.

78. Dupré, *Passage to Modernity,* 225–26.

content."[79] Thus Dupré identifies for us how Ignatius presents a paradox. Rahner explores this paradox in his Ignatian writings.

In addition to Dupré's reading of Ignatius as the alter-modern within modernity, we should briefly consider two points from Guardini's book about the end of modernity. The first concerns Guardini's depiction of modern subjectivity, and the second a choice that Guardini identifies as pressing upon people at the end of the modern world.

First, Guardini presents the "experience of subjectivity" as one of the crucial experiences of modern life. He finds in the idea of "personality" the most distinctive revelation of subjectivity: "Conceived as that which most expressed the human, as flowering from roots intrinsic to itself, as shaped in its destiny through its own initiative, personality became ... something primary and absolute which could not be questioned or doubted." This "personality" bred in human persons a new ethos: "An ethos based on objective goodness and truth was discarded for an ethos based in the subjective where nobility and truthfulness to one's own self prevailed."[80] Guardini's picture of personality is especially significant for us because we shall see Rahner alluding to it in connection with Ignatius.

Second, Guardini finds that at the end of the modern world, the ideal of personality no longer applies to human persons. If modernity exchanged the medieval ethos of a cosmos under God for an ethos of the subject, the end of modernity witnesses another shift in ethos. The autonomy of "personality" is ousted by its opposite, "the mass man."[81] This person's life is organized technologically, standardized. Conformity is valued over creativity. Furthermore, "it is taken increasingly for granted that man ought to be treated as an object."[82] Individuality in the modern sense is being lost, both for better and for worse.

79. Dupré, *Passage to Modernity,* 226.
80. Guardini, *End of the Modern World,* 39.
81. Guardini, *End of the Modern World,* 58.
82. Guardini, *End of the Modern World,* 61.

While recognizing the danger in this situation—mass objectification of people—Guardini discovers an opportunity in the rise of the "mass man." The loss of the modern sense of autonomy can allow for a greater "comradeship" between people, and a recovery of communal values like "benevolence, understanding, and justice." And, for the Christian in particular, this new "mass" experience can lead to a new conception of the human person and a new appropriation of the Christian ethos.

The Christian at the end of the modern world is faced with a choice: to conform to the "mass man," or to assert her obedience to God, thereby differentiating herself from the mass in a postsubjective way.[83] Guardini expresses a hope that people will take the second option: "We feel justified in assuming at this time that the genuine 'person' is destined to stand forth with a spiritual resoluteness never demanded of man before."[84] The new person, after modernity, is an individual individuated not by her own inherent capacities, but by the creative freedom of God, and by an obedient standing before God within the Church. This postmodern person sounds like Dupré's Ignatius and, we shall learn, like Rahner's Ignatius.

RAHNER ON IGNATIUS AND MODERNITY

Harvey Egan writes, "Because of Ignatius's emphasis on the subject, interiority, the subjective striving for self-reflection, self-responsibility, and salvation, Rahner views him as *the* modern par excellence."[85] Since I have introduced the idea of Ignatius as one who disrupts modernity, and since by the end of this part I shall show how Rahner develops this idea, it would seem that I disagree with Egan's estimation of the Rahnerian Ignatius. Is Ignatius *the* modern par excellence for Rahner? He is; I do not disagree with Egan. The

---

83. Cf. Guardini, *End of the Modern World,* 106–9.

84. Guardini, *End of the Modern World,* 65.

85. Harvey Egan, *Karl Rahner: Mystic of Everyday Life* (New York: Crossroad, 1998), 30, emphasis original. See the entire chapter from which this quote comes, "Karl Rahner—Ignatian Theologian," 28–54.

question is what Rahner means by "modern" when he ascribes it to Ignatius.

We have seen already how in many of his works Rahner redefines "subjectivity" so as to counter the modern version of subjectivity. For similar reasons in his Ignatian writings he redefines "modern." Modern subjectivism has the market cornered on neither "subjectivity" nor "modern." Ignatius's modernity is an alternative to the modernity that has hitherto prevailed. We shall now see how Rahner makes this case in four of his essays on Ignatius.

The best place to start is the 1955 essay on Ignatian spirituality and the sacred heart. After reflecting on the pillar of Ignatian spirituality, indifference, Rahner describes how Ignatian spirituality might be called "existential" as opposed to "individualist":

The indifferent man is not so much an individualist as is the Renaissance man, who sets a value on the lofty, unique, individual richness of his own personality and defends it as of high if not supreme worth. Ignatius has not, at bottom, much connection with the Renaissance.... An understanding of the world which is reached as the fruit of a mystical death, and in which everything can be held valuable because there is not very much value in anything, makes him precisely the opposite of the men who arrived at a new love of the world in the Renaissance.[86]

Rahner's invocation of the "mystical death" here recalls the 1936 essay on Ignatius that we examined in the last chapter. There I likened Rahner's metaphysics of the *Vorgriff* to the Ignatian experience of the Cross—dying to the world in coming before God. Rahner has the same thing in mind here. Being brought before God and in a sense "away" from the world, which is made "of secondary rank to God," allows Ignatius to love the world in a way much stronger than the Renaissance love of the world. Ignatius's love of the world is not directed *toward* himself. It is directed *by* the God who loves the world into being.

86. ISD 125.

Rahner is willing to call Ignatius an individualist, but one "not of personality but of the person."[87] Here he evokes Guardini's *End of the Modern World,* which calls the individualism of modernity "personality." The individualist of "personality" "was a man who had to be taken inevitably upon his own terms."[88] The individualist of "the person," Ignatius, is one who lives on God's terms: ready to serve anywhere and in any situation for which God calls.[89] Guardini says that "person" denotes "the incommunicable being possessed by man, an inviolability which deepens neither on special talents nor on social station. It simply emerges from the fact that a man has been called forth by God."[90] Rahner intends a similar meaning. Instead of bending the world to his will, Ignatius's will is formed by God's call.

Rahner continues these thoughts in a footnote in the lengthy essay "The Logic of Existential Decision in Ignatius Loyola." Rahner castigates those who facilely categorize Ignatius as a modern, Renaissance, or Baroque individualist:

He has nothing that really belongs to the Baroque or the Renaissance about him. The features that are held to justify an interpretation in those terms, his individualism, deliberate reflection, his almost technically regulated self-mastery, his silence and discretion, his subordination of the highly self-aware person to the objective task, the slight skepticism which pervades everything though without lyrical self-expression or self-conscious melancholy, these and similar traits are not really "Baroque" and "modern," even if in other connections the distinguishing mark of the "Baroque" and of "modern times" is the individual's awareness of himself as individual, exulting in himself or intoxicated with his own problems and complexity, a self-mirroring individuality. None of that is to be observed in Ignatius.[91]

87. ISD 125.
88. Guardini, *End of the Modern World,* 39.
89. ISD 126.
90. Guardini, *End of the Modern World,* 62.
91. LED 86–87n1.

We have, then, another categorical dismissal of Ignatius's "modernity" if this means his "self-mirroring individuality." Still, though, it is undeniable that Ignatius is a "modern." His "modernity" is a different one from the one that prevailed, whether one calls it modern subjectivism, personality, or anything else.

"Being Open to God as Ever Greater" deepens Rahner's reflection on Ignatius and modernity. He explicates the motto of the Jesuits, "ad majorem dei gloriam (to the greater glory of God)" as it relates to the modern age. During Ignatius's time there is a "turning to the subject, to subjective striving for salvation, to the subjective viewed as a task for the Church, to the attitude of reflection upon one's self" and other subject-related activities. Rahner summarizes: "This is, in short, a turning to self-responsibility." The motto "ad majorem dei gloriam," if it is conditioned by this early modern turn to the subject, is a statement about subjectivity. The human subject gives greater glory to God.[92]

But as in Rahner's other Ignatian writings, Ignatius differs from the spirit of his age: "Although Ignatius stands in the midst of this revolutionary change he in turn is, nevertheless, the one who has already, to a certain extent, transformed something which was subject to the conditions of this particular modern world into something lasting." For Rahner, Ignatius makes this "lasting" achievement by being a "man of the Church," and he does this "'in spite of' his subjective approach." Rahner disputes the normal "history of ideas" approach to Ignatius, which holds that his "initial inspiration . . . is not the Church but modern man considered as a personal subject." Ignatius does, indeed, live out of the experience of early modern subjectivism, but in an alternative—an ecclesial—way. It bears noting, too, that Ignatius's ecclesial subjectivity has an aesthetic cast: he is "the man to whom the phrase '*sentire cum ecclesia*' may supremely be applied."[93] Ignatius's subjectivity feels, or senses, with the Church. Ig-

92. AMDG 32–33.
93. AMDG 33.

natius opposes this "feeling-with" to the autonomous, auto-affective modern subject.

Rahner's later essay on the *Spiritual Exercises,* "Modern Piety and the Experience of Retreats" suggests the difficulty of maintaining the above position on Ignatius's spirituality. Rahner discusses at length the "modern" tendency of the *Exercises* to privilege the individual retreatant over the Church.[94] This would appear to vindicate the standard reading of Ignatius as a quintessential modern.

Again, though, Rahner depicts a different Ignatius. To discover this Ignatius, one must dig deeper than the textual surface of the *Exercises.* Rahner points to the fact that Ignatius did not consider himself the founder of the Jesuits. Instead, he shared this founding with his companions. Rahner observes that Ignatius "knew and practiced the '*deliberatio communitaria*' with his companions (deliberation not only *in* the group but *of* the group), where the logic of existential choice was to apply and operate for the group as a whole." This affected Ignatius's view of the Church—it was a community of "shared testing and decision making which was to take place dynamically in such a group."[95] Ignatian spirituality is, contrary to superficial interpretations, an ecclesial way of being—cooperating, feeling-with.

This view of Ignatius should command our attention because Rahner sets it within a section entitled "Ignatius and the End of the Modern Era." This section stands at the center of the essay, and over the remaining pages, Rahner attempts to devise a variation of the *Exercises* for what he calls a postmodern era, which will answer to this coming era's "cultural and ecclesial demands."[96] He does not jettison the traditional, individual *Exercises.* Like Guardini, he does not want to discard the fruitful elements of modernity. But Rahner believes that in the future the *Exercises* should be used to help the Church attain a "higher degree of socialization," beyond the "purely secular" socialization of the modern period.[97]

94. MPER 142–45.
96. MPER 148.

95. MPER 145–46, emphasis original.
97. MPER 153.

Rahner leaves this idea of "socialization" unelaborated, but the drift of his argument, irrespective of its possible content, coheres with our foregoing discussion of the angel. An honest look at the modern subject reveals that, like the angel, it does not relate well to others. Leibniz's idea of the monad is paradigmatic in this respect: the modern subject is a world unto itself. The importance of Rahner's reimagining of the Ignatian spiritual heritage in this essay lies in his emphasis on communal, cooperative subjectivity, as opposed to individual, autonomous subjectivity. At the beginning of the modern age, Ignatius's spiritual attitude and practice was communal and cooperative. Whether he knew it or not, his spiritual heritage at the end of the modern age may prove to be shepherding the Church beyond modern subjectivism.

Rahner's writings on Ignatius in the 1950s and 1960s concern how he relates to the modern age and its representative, the modern subject. Rahner opposes Ignatian spirituality to the modern spirit on three remarkable counts: (1) love of God versus self-love, (2) God's will versus self-will, and (3) ecclesial versus individual subjectivity. Ignatius arrives at his spiritual perspective at the time of the modern subject's arrival, and as a result his spirituality sounds at times like the spirit of modern subjectivity. But Ignatius's spirit resists the spirit of his age. Ignatius is the modern par excellence because he guides modernity to transcend itself.

IGNATIUS AND THE CATHOLIC SUBLIME

Throughout this book I have engaged not only in exegesis of Rahner's (and Heidegger's) writings, but also in a constructive reframing of them. The chief locus of this reframing is the idea of the Catholic sublime. I give this name to the ethos of Catholicism as it comes to light in Rahner's works.

Rahner's texts on Ignatius, particularly as we have read them through the prism of Dupré and Guardini, raise anew the question of ethos. Ignatius presents us with a modern appropriation of the Catholic ethos. Ignatius reshapes Catholicism in modern terms, but in a way that resists the ethos of modernity, be it expressed through Renaissance humanism or later subjectivisms. Thus Rahner's Ignatius introduces us to the idea of an alternative modernity, and insofar as Ignatius leads modernity beyond itself, an alterative aftermodernity.

In the introduction to this book I indicated preliminarily my disagreement with several recent theorists like Milbank, Blond, Bauerschmidt, Betz, and Hart, who view the "sublime" as hopelessly wedded to the pathologies of modernity and postmodernity. I do agree with them that the sublime can be taken as a figure for modernity. I disagree that it *has* to be equated with the pathologies of modernity. Instead, the sublime can be rendered Catholically. As Dupré says Ignatius did, we can take up the fruitful forms of modernity and convey to them a traditional spiritual content. If, according to the sublime's detractors, the modern/postmodern sublime is a hopeless imitation of Christian transcendence, the Catholic sublime is a hopeful reaffirmation of Christian transcendence, with an eye to modern deformations of it.

Heidegger remains relevant here. In the "Letter on Humanism" (1946), which we shall analyze more below, Heidegger discusses Hölderlin in a way parallel to Rahner's portrayal of Ignatius. Hölderlin functions strategically for Heidegger like Ignatius does for Rahner. It is at least plausible that Rahner learned his strategy for depicting Ignatius from Heidegger, whether from his reading Kant's First Critique against the traditional grain or from his lectures on Hölderlin's hymns as setting a new agenda for philosophy.

For Heidegger, Hölderlin is a modern, yet an alter-modern. He lives among the German humanists of the late eighteenth and early nineteenth century, but he "does not belong to 'humanism,' precisely because he thought the destiny of man's essence in a more original way than 'humanism' could."[98] Hölderlin's poetizing of the essence

---

98. LH 225.

of humanity abides beyond modern humanism, even if it seems to come out of modern humanism's idiom. The key here is that Heidegger notes that the modern standard for humanism cannot dictate the measure for all thinking of humanity in modernity. Similarly, Rahner discovers that the modern subjectivist spirit cannot be regarded as the spiritual standard for the whole modern age.

By extension, I argue that the modern sublime, especially the post-Kantian trajectory, cannot speak for all of modernity. The modern sublime is a set of discourses supporting an ethos of autonomy in the sense of immanentist self-sufficiency. This ethos was not the only way of being in modernity. Ignatius provides an alternative ethos, and Rahner narrates this alternative in his Ignatian and his other writings. To modern immanentism, individualism, autonomy, it opposes God-directed ascent back to God, exposure to the will of God and feeling with the Church, and thus community. Modern sublimity is a misdirection of the sublime; the Catholic sublime, a proper redirection.

We can agree with Milbank that the problem with modern theories of the sublime is that they sunder the sublime from the beautiful.[99] There may be a consequent worry that Rahner, if he develops a version of the sublime, sunders it from the beautiful. Such a worry seems to be behind Balthasar's critiques of Rahner, where he accuses Rahner of sundering the transcendental from the categorial. This does not happen in Rahner, though. One significant example from his Ignatian writings can serve to illustrate this.

With respect to Rahner's view of Ignatius, the concern would seem to be that Rahner overemphasizes indifference, which above we saw him calling "the mystical death." If taken by itself, one might object, Ignatian indifference could look like the modern or postmodern sublime: a negative experience of indeterminacy or disorder, a heightened awareness that the world is not God and that

99. Milbank, "Sublimity: The Modern Transcendent," 209 and passim.

God is not in the world. Were Rahner unaware of this danger, his frequent invocation of indifference, of an immediate experience of God, or of "consolation without prior cause" could result in an other-worldly spirituality that would fail to be Christian.

But Rahner recognizes this danger. In "Ignatian Spirituality and Devotion to the Heart of Jesus," he specifically names this danger. Indifference is always in danger of becoming a false rendition of itself: "stoic apathy," "meanness of heart," "blindness to the magnificence of reality and the splendor of the world," or "lonely individuality"—something like the spirituality of the angel.[100] The mystical element of Ignatius's spirituality must never be separated, Rahner contends, from its source: the love of Jesus Christ. He remarks, "The sublime gift of indifference is saved from being a deadly poison only when it is received by someone with an adoring devotion to love; someone who dares to have a heart being an adorer of *the* Heart."[101] Sublime indifference and beautiful love of Jesus' Heart mutually enhance one another. They can never be sundered. Thus Rahner entitles one section of this essay "Devotion to the Sacred Heart as the Interior Counterbalance to Ignatian Spirituality," and the next "Ignatian Spirituality as a True Flowering of Devotion to the Sacred Heart."[102] Given our prior analyses in this book, it is interesting also that Rahner traces his maintenance of the sublime and the beautiful back to Thomas Aquinas's metaphysics of knowledge. He points to the twofoldness of Thomas's view of knowledge: a "returning upon oneself" which is completed only by a "making over of what is one's own to what is other than oneself . . . the beloved person."[103]

If Rahner emphasizes the sublime, he never does it in the same way that modern and postmodern purveyors of the sublime do. He learns from Ignatius's *Exercises,* which are a call both to indifference

100. ISD 131, 133.
101. ISD 132, emphasis original.
102. ISD 128, 137.
103. ISD 138–39.

and to discover love in Jesus Christ, that the sublime and the beautiful must remain together.[104]

RAHNER, HEIDEGGER, AND NEGATIVE HUMANISM

The last part discussed humanism as an early modern predecessor to subjectivism. This part continues the chapter's rejection of readings of Rahner as a theologian of the "turn to the subject" by treating his thinking on humanism in the mid-1960s. Rahner's dialogues with Marxists especially attuned him to the question of the relationship between Christianity and late modern humanism.[105]

Like Ignatius, Rahner relates to humanism positively and negatively. Rahner's positive disposition toward humanism stems from his conviction that God's salvific work in Christ has ineluctably tied the human destiny to God's own destiny.[106] As long as "humanism" truly concerns itself with humanity, its projects have theological reference and possibly redemptive value. On the negative side,

---

104. ISD 143. This example of the importance of the Sacred Heart for Rahner is not an isolated one. Rahner wrote extensively on this devotion: Rahner, "'Behold This Heart!': Preliminaries to a Theology of Devotion to the Sacred Heart," in TI 3, 321–30; Rahner, "Some Theses for a Theology of Devotion to the Sacred Heart," in TI 3, 331–54; Rahner, "The Theology of the Symbol"; Rahner, "The Theological Meaning of the Veneration of the Sacred Heart," in TI 8, 217–28; Rahner, "Unity–Love–Mystery," in TI 8, 229–47; and see the related short meditation, Rahner, "Christmas in the Light of the Ignatian Exercises," in TI 17, 3–7.

105. Several of Rahner's writings provide a written record of his interactions with Marxists. For instance, see the preface to the fifth volume of TI (1962), where Rahner dedicates the book to the Paulus Gesellschaft, a society that facilitated dialogue between Catholics and Marxists: TI 5, ix. The lectures, "Marxist Utopia and the Christian Future of Man," in TI 6, 59–68 (delivered in 1965 to the Paulus Gesellschaft), and "The Theological Problems Entailed in the Idea of the 'New Earth,'" in TI 10, 260–72 (given in 1967 to a humanist conference in Salzburg) are exemplary. Important also are Rahner, "Christianity and the 'New Man,'" TI 5 135–53; Rahner, "The Experiment with Man: Theological Observations on Man's Self-Manipulation," TI 9, 205–24; Rahner, "On the Theology of Hope," TI 10, 242–59; and Rahner, "Utopia and Reality: The Shape of Christian Existence Caught between the Ideal and the Real," TI 22, 26–36; which span the time period from the early 1960s to the early 1980s.

106. CH 189. Cf. Karl Rahner, "Christlicher Humanismus," in *Schriften zur Theologie VIII* (Einsiedeln: Benziger, 1967), 239–59, at 241. The use of "destiny" (*Schicksal*) is Rahner's own.

Rahner finds that modern humanisms often fall short of this high potential. A remark from one of Rahner's latest essays (1982) illustrates this point well: "Although we may still hear the last echoes of a triumphant humanism that claims to have reached the limits of its self-made fulfillment, today we are assailed by a feeling that we have lost our way, a feeling that our beautiful ideals are quickly becoming threadbare."[107] Insofar as a "triumphant humanism" based on the modern subjectivist ideal of "self-made fulfillment" speaks for humanism, Rahner feels compelled to reject it.

This part argues that though Rahner is often portrayed as a theologian beholden to something like modern humanism, this portrayal does not suit him. This is precisely because he opposes modern subjectivity and envisages a human way of being after the subject. We shall see that Rahner's negative disposition toward humanism accords largely with Heidegger's rejection of humanism in his "Letter on Humanism." Rahner's rejection of humanism is unlike Heidegger's, though, because it refers the human person to God's infinite incomprehensibility instead of being's finite evasiveness.

HEIDEGGER'S LETTER ON HUMANISM

A comment from Rahner's "Logic of Existential Decision in Ignatius Loyola" can set the tone for our reading of Heidegger's "Letter on Humanism." Rahner writes in a footnote, "Ignatius cannot be subjected to the alternative either of being a pure existentialist or of knowing and living ... what can be comprised within the contents of an ethics of universal essences."[108] Ignatius evades the binary opposition of existentialism or essentialism, which is another way of saying the classical modern distinction between subjectivism and objectivism. Ignatius is not an existentialist, and he is not a humanist.

I have already protested against the conventional view of both Rahner and Heidegger under the rubric of "existentialism." It is true

107. Rahner, "Utopia and Reality," 35.
108. LED 92n5.

that Rahner leaves himself open to this label, due to his rather liberal use of its derivatives in many of his writings, including the essay on Ignatius and "existential decision." And since Heidegger was regarded very soon after *Being and Time*'s publication as a father of existentialism, the label seems to fit.

But famously Heidegger rejects the name "existentialist" in the "Letter on Humanism," which is an extended critique of Jean-Paul Sartre's lecture "Existentialism Is a Humanism" (1945). Heidegger dissociates himself from Sartre because the French philosopher's existentialist humanism predicates itself upon a turn to the Cartesian subject.[109] Although Rahner likely did not read the "Letter," his own critical disposition toward modern humanism (and existentialism) reflects Heidegger's.

Heidegger writes the "Letter on Humanism" in response to several questions addressed to him in a letter by his colleague, Jean Beaufret. The first among them is how to restore meaning to the word "humanism."[110] Heidegger notes two things latent in this question: (1) "a desire to retain the word 'humanism,'" and (2) "an admission that the word has lost its meaning."[111] He objects to Beaufret's desire precisely because of what Beaufret admits. On Heidegger's view, humanism has rightly lost its meaning because it has reached a dead end. Humanism attempts to think and to advocate on behalf of the human, but it has revealed itself as utterly incapable of completing its task. Humanism falls short because it "remains metaphysical. In defining the humanity of man humanism not only does not ask about the relation of being to the essence of man; because of its metaphysical origin humanism even impedes the question by neither recognizing it nor understanding it."[112] Humanism has lost its meaning because it never knew how to seek it.

---

109. See LH 232–34. Cf. Jean-Paul Sartre, *Existentialism Is a Humanism,* trans. Carol Macomber, introduction by Annie Cohen-Solal, notes and preface by Arlette Elkaïm-Sartre, ed. John Kulka (New Haven, Conn.: Yale University Press, 2007), 69.

110. LH 219, 247.   111. LH 247.

112. LH 226.

Heidegger is responding to late modern humanisms like Sartre's existentialism. He provides a genealogy of humanism to show how it was bound to run aground from the beginning. From ancient Rome to the Renaissance, Christianity, Marxism, and existentialism, all humanisms "agree in this, that the *humanitas* of *homo humanus* is determined with regard to an already established interpretation of nature, history, world, and the ground of the world, that is, of beings as a whole."[113] Being (*humanitas*) is confused with beings, closing humanists off from the apprehension of being's advent, so that they miss and misconstrue "the essential unfolding of ek-sistence in the history of being."[114] Humanisms fail because they share in the metaphysical tendency to provide answers before the proper question has even been identified.

Heidegger finds *modern* humanisms particularly impotent. Even their "highest determinations of the essence of man ... still do not realize the proper dignity of man." Heidegger treats it as patent that modern humanisms' determinations of the human essence miscarry: "Of course the essential worth of man does not consist in his being the substance of beings, as the 'subject' among them, so that as the tyrant of being he may deign to release the beingness of beings into an all too loudly bruited 'objectivity.'"[115] Though there may be various modern humanisms, they all in some way presuppose the metaphysics of subjectivity, which prides itself upon its control of objects.

In place of modern subjectivism's assertion of humanity's essence, Heidegger urges an opening toward a primordial questioning of the essence of humanity. This would involve a thinking of the "dimension" in which the human feels "at home," or as Heraclitus calls it, "ethos."[116] Such thinking would transpire as an "open resistance to 'humanism,'" which would "risk a shock that could for the first time cause perplexity concerning the *humanitas* of *homo huma-*

---

113. LH 225.
115. LH 234.

114. LH 264, 231.
116. LH 248, 256–59.

nus and its basis."[117] Heidegger asks the question so that "wider vistas" might be opened.[118]

Heidegger does not specify what will come to light in these "wider vistas," and this is largely the point. Against humanism's all-too-quick specification of the essence of the human person, Heidegger seeks a kind of thinking and a kind of language that will let the human be human, and thus will let being be being. He states the goal of his questioning resistance of humanism: "The one thing thinking would like to attain and for the first time tries to articulate in *Being and Time* is something simple. As such, being remains mysterious, the simple nearness of an unobtrusive governance."[119] With this appeal to mystery, we are now ready to consider Rahner's own critical probing of humanism.

RAHNER ON CHRISTIAN HUMANISM

In 1966, Rahner was invited to deliver a paper at a conference on "Christian Humanity and Marxist Humanism." The requested paper was given the title "Christian Humanism." Rahner expresses discomfort with this title. He points out, "Nowadays everyone wants to be a humanist. And at the same time there is less agreement than ever as to what a *human* really is."[120] The title assumes the clarity of two very hard-to-define terms, and of the relationship between them. He questions four tacit assumptions in the lecture's title: (1) that Christianity and humanism form a unity, (2) that Christianity is easily definable, (3) that humanism is easily definable, and (4) that Christians confess "an absolute humanism."[121] Rahner assesses each of these assumptions as follows: (1) possibly true, (2) mostly false, (3) mostly false, (4) and only true if carefully described.

"Christian Humanism" is less a title than a question: "Christianity accepts the experience of its own humanism as one which re-

---

117. LH 248.   118. LH 250.
119. LH 236.   120. CH 187.
121. CH 187–88.

mains constantly questionable."[122] Christianity stands in a time when "'europeanism' (and its colonialist export)" has been unmasked as hegemonic.[123] Europe's main export during the modern age was humanism, which initially spread via Christianity, though a Christianity that in many cases was a violent *Ersatz* of Christianity. At the end of modernity, humanism has been unmasked as inhumane, and its close relative, modern science, has shown its inability to account for human persons.[124] These "humanisms" are as questionable as ever. Christianity is, too, whenever it imitates modern humanism and fails to give a sense of the whole.

Rahner raises all these caveats in order to set Christian humanism and "enlightened" or Marxist humanisms on equal footing. Given the situation Rahner has described, each humanism is questionable, and thus must ask what its particular understanding of the human person is, and from where it derives. As a Christian theologian, Rahner inquires as to what Christian anthropology has to say about the human person. He gives a curt yet pregnant answer: "he is the being who loses himself in God. Otherwise nothing."[125] Rahner pairs this statement with a description of God as the "ineffable, intractable Mystery."[126] Christian theology offers, then, a negative picture of the human person, an "*anthropologia negativa*," where the human person is defined by "loss" into a "mystery." Rahner acknowledges that compared with humanisms that claim concrete, specific knowledge of human persons, this theological approach would likely seem quite unsatisfactory. This unsatisfactoriness would appear to be compounded when Rahner states that Christianity "does not erect a particular *concrete* humanism" and that it "relativizes every

---

122. CH 194.   123. CH 196.

124. CH 192: Though scientific anthropology provides a great deal of knowledge about human beings, "all the same the theologian will still maintain that all the empirical, scientific anthropologies, which can only exist now in a permanent state of pluralism, can only bring a person to himself *whole* and *single* provided that he hears the message of Christianity" (emphasis original).

125. CH 192.   126. CH 193.

concrete humanism."[127] Rahner offers, one might surmise, a rather thin Christian definition of the human and of humanism.

At a pivotal moment of the "Letter on Humanism," Heidegger anticipates (or perhaps recounts) objections to his own resistance of humanism. The objections center on the "logic" of his opposition. Logically, if he opposes humanism, he must be championing the inhuman: "With the assistance of logic and *ratio* ... people come to believe that whatever is not positive is negative and thus that it seeks to degrade reason."[128] Similar objections might be leveled against Rahner—if you define the human person negatively, how will you have anything to offer? Heidegger rejects the "logic" of his critics as fallacious. He chastises them for their overzealousness to provide answers when they should be identifying questions. A similar chastisement could apply to Rahner's potential critics.

Rahner's "negative anthropology" and his relativizing of concrete humanisms might seem to turn Christianity into an engine of indeterminacy and an advocate of relativism. He does not intend this. Like Heidegger, Rahner deems himself privy to a humanism more concrete and more effective than the modern ones surrounding him. Heidegger finds his "humanism" in *Dasein*'s thrownness into the truth of being. Rahner locates it in the person of Jesus Christ and the people of Christ's Church. Heidegger invokes the "mystery of being" so as to clear a space for human existence's entrance into the home being prepared for it. Rahner invokes the "intractable mystery of God" to imply that *we* do not create our humanism. Christianity does not construct a particular humanism. God does.

Rahner summarizes his position: "Christianity's *concretissimum*, for which alone it stands, is Jesus Christ, who, in accepting death and suffering *for us* (and in no other way) has created our relationship of immediacy before God, and the Church, which looks for the Kingdom which has yet to be fulfilled and which is *not* identical with the humanism we ourselves have produced or shall produce in the

127. CH 194, emphasis original.   128. LH 249–50.

near future."[129] Because of its rootedness in Christ and the Church, not because of some purely otherworldly ethereality, Christianity's ethos demands that it reject purely worldly humanisms.

Christian humanism is, then, a question. Let us move on to the final section of this chapter, which will specify the question of Christian humanism, its opposition to modern subjectivism, and its divergence from Heidegger.

HUMANIZATION AND GOD

To Rahner's mind, modern humanism, as it arises from or colludes with modern subjectivism, demands resistance for two main reasons. We shall call them contemporaneity and inhumanity.

The 1965 lecture "The Man of Today and Religion" begins by expressing the concern that contemporary people want only to be people "of today." Rahner observes that today's person "is always in danger of oversimplifying, in danger of wanting to design everything in his life from one *single* angle and of wanting to determine everything as a function of one single, definite entity which is familiar to him and controllable by him." In sum, "contemporary man is in danger of wanting to be nothing but a man of today."[130]

The paradigm for this contemporary danger is the "manager type." This type narrows his entire life to derivatives of entrepreneurial enterprise. He lives only for today—only for how much money he can make today. Marriage, art, religion, friendship, and anything else can, in the hands of this type, "come to bear no more pregnant and justifying meaning in themselves than the limits of what they signify for business and its undertakings." Rahner laments that this reduction of everything to business results in a "disappearance of the meaning of human life, which becomes fatal for man."[131]

---

129. CH 195, emphasis original.
130. Karl Rahner, "The Man of Today and Religion," in TI 6, 3–20, at 3, emphasis original.
131. Rahner, "Man of Today," 4.

Business was supposed in Rahner's day and is still supposed in our day to be a very human enterprise. It is supposed to make life more livable, existence more fulfilling and fulfilled. Business is, then, supposed to be a humanism. But Rahner suggests that the dominance of the manager type proves fatal for humanity. The manager type does not humanize the world. Business is a false humanism.

Business stands in the line of many false humanisms, from the Renaissance through the present. Later in the same lecture, Rahner makes a distinction that points to the difference between a false humanism and a true humanism:

> The world remains "demythologized," secularized and hominized even though this by no means signifies that it has been humanized since, even out of this hominized world, there can rise once more the specter of the inhumanity of man himself in the face of the devastation of nature by ABC-weapons and similar horrors.[132]

Modern humanisms "hominize" the world. They stamp it with the spirit of the modern *homo*. The inhumanity that arises out of the modern spirit reveals that this spirit is not fully human. Though the modern person may laud himself for his technological, scientific, and financial accomplishments, he must face the fact that these achievements have often come at the cost of his humanity. Atomic, biological, and chemical weapons are surely astounding from the standpoint of technology, science, and finance—what control of energy! what productive inquiry! how lucrative!—but their capacity to kill the body comes with the death of the souls of those who fund and deploy them. Their impact "today" resounds eternally.

Rahner argues that this loss of humanity comes in the first place from a loss of God. The modern person chased God out of the world so that he—not God—might rule over it.[133] The hominized world without God is a sinful distortion of what Rahner calls a legit-

132. Rahner, "Man of Today," 11.
133. Rahner, "Man of Today," 12.

imate, humanized conception of the God-world, God-human, and human-world relationships.[134] Properly speaking, God is beyond world and God is absolutely other than humanity. God does proceed at some "distance" from the world. In a manner of speaking, the world is "demythologized," in that it is not "holy" in the sense of being the home of a purely immanent god. This means that the human person can operate on the world with some modicum of independence from God, so that this person might become a "free, responsible subject before God." Even so, the view of human freedom behind modern humanisms does not get the picture right. Pride over what he controls blinds the modern humanist to what remains uncontrollable. And God, the one dismissed by modern humanism, is the uncontrollable par excellence.

True Christian humanism, like the "devout humanism" of Ignatius Loyola, demands that human freedom be set in the proper context. This contextualization sheds light on the inhumanity of other humanisms:

In its conviction of human freedom, rooted in and orientated towards God, Christianity opens up the permanent possibility of an inhuman "humanism." But in consequence the only humanism which is inhuman is one which denies human dependence on and relation to the intractable and incomprehensible One, thus positing itself as absolute and refusing to allow its own nature to be called in question by possibly taking a new decision to embrace *another* future, materially determined by history, which realizes in concrete form the will to accept God's absolute future.[135]

The proper context for any humanism is God. Human freedom must direct itself toward God. A human freedom that does not do this, and turns inward to absolutize itself, is inhuman—no matter how much it may "hominize" the world. *God* is the absolute, not the human subject. God is absolute because God is utterly "intractable" and "ungraspable." God evades all human attempts at control.

---

134. Rahner, "Man of Today," 17.   135. CH 195–96, emphasis original.

The most interesting aspect of this passage on "inhuman 'humanism'" lies in its invocation of the future. As with the passages we examined from "The Man of Today and Religion," Rahner aligns modern humanism's inhumanity with its exclusive focus on the present. In "Christian Humanism" Rahner prescribes that a replacement of the concern for the present with a focus on the future lends Christian humanism a consummate humanity.

The humanity of a humanism lies in its refusal to limit itself. Humanism becomes more human when it opens itself to a fuller breadth of being human. The future figures in here because a humanism becomes more human when it opens itself to future humanisms. Christianity's devotion to God's futurity sustains its rejection of too narrow, too contemporary, and thus inhuman, humanisms: "Christianity pronounces judgment on any humanism which sets itself up as absolute and thus explicitly or implicitly tries to inhibit man's openness to further concrete history and hence to God's absolute future."[136] The hominization of modern humanisms, reliant on the self-sufficiency of the subject, does not compare in breadth with the humanization offered by Christian humanism, which relies on the God who opens the subject beyond himself.

In the previous section we read how Heidegger's efforts toward a more humanistic humanism in his "Letter" compare favorably with Rahner's "Christian Humanism." As always, signs of divergence also show. The divergence relates to God's absolute futurity, which is another way of saying God's infinity.

A telling passage of the "Letter on Humanism" includes an apologia by Heidegger against those who think that he rejects "transcendence" and that he denies the existence of God. He claims that he makes no such denials. Instead, he does not concern himself with these questions. He pleads that "the boundaries" set for thinking by the "truth of being" keep these questions outside his purview.[137] His response to the objections, far from being satisfactory, actually

136. CH 197.   137. LH 252–54.

proves that they hit the mark with respect to his apriorism of finitude. It decides *tout court* against the appearance of Christ and thus,
if not against God's existence, against God's action in the world.
The "boundaries" he sees as imposed by being's truth are, rather,
self-imposed. His attack on modern humanism from the standpoint
of *Dasein*'s home in the truth of being, then, is questionable.

The contrast between Heidegger and Rahner and each thinker's capacity to resist modern subjectivism can be illustrated in conjunction with a Heideggerian rejoinder to Sartre. Heidegger quotes
Sartre's statement of the foundation of his existentialist humanism:
"Précisément nous sommes sur un plan où il y a seulement des hommes."
He proposes instead, *"Précisément nous sommes sur un plan où il y a
principalment l'Être."*[138] For Sartre's subjectivist humanism, there are
only humans. For Heidegger's nonmetaphysical humanism, there is
principally being. His perspective removes Sartre's anthropological
restriction, but we must keep in mind Heidegger's self-imposed restriction of thinking to finitude.

For Rahner, things are not so simple. Would he state a position
on humanism, he would say *"il n'y a pas de seulement"*—there is no
"only." God's infinity sets the context for humanism, for thinking,
for living, but since this context is infinite it is unrestrictedly open:
not closed by the subject, whose quasi-angelic self-sealing limits
everything; not closed by Heidegger's apriorism of finitude. Rahner's humanism consists in a sublime dis-closure: there are angels,
humans, animals, plants, and all creation. In principle, everything,
unless it is bound by sin, participates in the life of God through
God's gift of life in the Son and the Spirit. Everything is of interest
to this humanism, because God may be found in all things.[139] In this
Ignatian way, Rahner transcends the spirit of the modern age.

138. LH 237: "Precisely we are in a situation where there are only humans." "Precisely we are in a situation where there is principally being."

139. For background on Rahner's retrieval of this pillar of Ignatian spirituality, see
Endean, KRIS, 69–80.

4 RAHNER REFOUNDING THEOLOGICAL LANGUAGE

THE CONVERGENT-DIVERGENCE between Rahner and Heidegger covers the general area of an opposition to modern subjectivism. That point is now well established. The following two chapters will specify this insight by elaborating the themes of language and history, respectively.

These topics first arose in chapter two, when I exposed Heidegger's first Hölderlin course and observed what Rahner stood to gain from it. The Heideggerian sublime, as it takes shape in the first Hölderlin course, grounds itself in the poet's unique relationship to language and history. The poet founds history by communicating the mysterious language—"hints"—of the gods. As we saw, these ideas at once resonate and conflict with Rahner's view of the relationship between human persons, the world, and God.

This chapter returns to the question of language. Like chapter three it juxtaposes later Rahnerian texts with later Heideggerian texts, in order to trace how these two thinkers develop convergent yet divergent ideas even after Rahner stopped reading Heidegger. This tracing will reveal the importance of language for Rahner, in particular a use of language that does two things: (1) allows God's mystery to remain mysterious, (2) without despairing of language's capacity to speak truly of God.

Part one describes Rahner's view of language in such essays as "The Concept of Mystery in Catholic Theology" (1959) and "Reflections on Methodology in Theology" (1969).[1] This account of language centers on God's incomprehensibility. Part two shows how this account resembles in interesting ways Heidegger's in texts like *Gelassenheit* and *On the Way to Language* (both 1959).[2] These texts describe a way of thinking about language that overturns the metaphysical tradition's privileging of assertion, thus laying bare the mystery that comprises language's essence. Part three compares Rahner's Mariology with Heidegger's thinking of "the thing," to show how both thinkers develop and perform a nonobjective use of language. The chapter's final part indicates how the convergence between Rahner and Heidegger again issues in a divergence, this time over the "openness" that each thinker's view of language supports.

The upshot of all this work is an enriched description of Rahner's version of the sublime. The Catholic sublime is a form of life that faces up to the formlessness of God's incomprehensibility, without trying to domesticate or to give shape to it. Unlike the sublime associated with modern subjectivism, the Catholic sublime is not the sublimity of human noesis, nor is it a sublime sundered from the aesthetic or the beautiful. Unlike the Heideggerian sublime, which we shall see bears pernicious overtones, the Catholic sublime is not

1. Karl Rahner, "The Concept of Mystery in Catholic Theology," in TI 4.36–73, hereafter CM; cf. Rahner, "Über den Begriff des Geheimnisses in der katholischen Theologie," in *Schriften zur Theologie 4*, 51–99; Rahner, "Reflections on Methodology in Theology," in TI 11.68–114, hereafter RM; cf. Rahner, "Überlegungen zur Methode der Theologie," in *Schriften zur Theologie 9*, 79–126.

2. Martin Heidegger, *Discourse on Thinking*, trans. John M. Anderson and E. Hans Freund (New York: Harper and Row, 1966), hereafter G. I shall refer throughout to this text's original name because "Discourse on Thinking" is rather nondescript. See Heidegger, *Gelassenheit* (Pfullingen: Neske, 1959). See Heidegger, *On the Way to Language,* trans. Peter D. Hertz and Joan Stambaugh (New York: Harper and Row, 1971), hereafter OWL; cf. the German, Heidegger, *Unterwegs zur Sprache: Gesamtausgabe 12* (Frankfurt: Vittorio Klostermann, 1985).

the sublimity of finitude. The Catholic sublime is properly God's, and becomes proper to finite human persons only by a divine gift — in the *Word* made flesh.

RAHNER SAYING MYSTERY

Rahner's *Worte ins Schweigen* (1937) and *Geist in Welt* explore many of the same themes, if in very different ways. Perhaps first among the common themes is theological language. The title *Worte ins Schweigen,* or *Words into Silence,* poses an interesting philosophical-theological statement. Throughout the text, Rahner prayerfully reflects on the interplay of speech and silence, the things we can affirm of God and those things we cannot apprehend well enough to affirm. All words have some bearing on God. At the same time, any words one sends into the silence of God do not grasp God. Instead, by these words God grasps the one who says them: "You have seized me; I have not 'grasped' You."[3]

Given its resistance to "grasping," the thinking on language that Rahner begins to develop during this period of time resonates rather well with Heidegger's thinking on language from *Being and Time* forward. I shall turn first to *Geist in Welt* for some background, and then commence detailing Rahner's theory of theological language—how he thinks we can say mystery.[4] Then in the next part we will compare this thinking on language with Heidegger's.

LANGUAGE IN *GEIST IN WELT*

The third objection in Thomas's *Summa theologiae* I.84.7 suggests that some human knowledge can be had without a conversion to the phantasm. The objection rests on the conviction that a human

---

3. Rahner, *Encounters with Silence,* 31.

4. This idea of a Rahnerian theory of language derives primarily, for me, from Stephen Fields, "Rahner and the Symbolism of Language," *Philosophy and Theology* 15, no. 1 (2003): 165–89. Fields's article proves helpful, also, because of its defense of Rahner's reading of Heidegger against Heideggerian critics.

knower can know the truth, God, and angels without direct sensation of them.[5] Thomas answers that, indeed, we do not know incorporeal realities directly. He proposes first that one can know such
things by way of comparison with the sensible world. Then, citing
Dionysius the Areopagite, Thomas indicates that in the case of God
there are three ways of knowing: "as cause" (*ut causam*), "through
excess" (*per excessum*), and "through remotion" (*per remotionem*).[6]
Thomas's reference to Dionysius implicates the question of theological language.

The citation comes from *The Divine Names,* the central treatise
in the Areopagite's reflections upon theological language. Dionysius
is more famous for his radically apophatic text *The Mystical Theology.* But *The Divine Names* proves more important because of its sustained attention to Scripture's affirmations about God, set within a
wider awareness that God "is gathered by no discourse, by no intuition, by no name."[7] Though God is infinite and incomprehensible,
because of God's self-disclosure in Christ, in Scripture, and in raising the faithful into the divine life, God may be named.

Rahner deems the three linguistic acts that Thomas borrows
from Dionysius to be vital for his study of Thomas's metaphysics of
knowledge. He relates *comparatio, excessus,* and *remotio* to his schematization of Thomistic metaphysics. *Comparatio* and *remotio* cohere with the conversion to the phantasm (i.e., sensibility) and *excessus* with abstraction and the *reditio subjecti in se ipsum.*[8] Since
comparison and remotion refer to the sensible world, Rahner asks
how these acts can produce knowledge of nonsensible realities, like
truth, God, or angels. Comparison, for instance, would involve some
purchase on the two realities to be compared. Remotion, too, would
imply some sense of what can properly be denied of the nonsensible

5. ST I.84.7.arg 3.

6. ST I.84.7.ad 3.

7. Pseudo-Dionysius, *The Complete Works,* trans. Colm Luibheid and Paul Rorem
(Mahwah, N.J.: Paulist Press, 1987), 50 (DN 1, 588B).

8. SW 52/49–50.

reality. For this reason, Rahner believes that comparison and remotion are grounded in a third act: excess. This insight coheres with Rahner's thesis that *excessus* is the "fundamental human act."[9]

Late in *Geist in Welt* Rahner passes on the opportunity to discuss in detail how *excessus,* negation, and comparison relate to "the familiar three ways of knowing God," "causality, eminence, and negation," which are staples of Thomistic theology.[10] Had he done so he may have expounded helpfully and concretely upon how theological language works. He does not do this, but he does allow himself several pages that bear tangentially on the question of language. Rahner's comments concern a complex interplay of affirmation and negation.

Comparison and negation, as they relate to God, are both founded on a prior affirmation. *Excessus* as an anticipatory sense (*Vorgriff*) of absolute *esse* founds all knowledge of the world. It does so by affirming "absolute being as possible and real beyond the world."[11] This means that all sensible being is referred to sensibility's "beyond," and thus that sensible beings can rightly be compared with and contrasted to nonsensible ones. Categorial affirmations and negations are possible only on the condition of a transcendental affirmation of God as the sustaining ground of all that is.[12]

Rahner makes clear that this affirmation is *not* a decision on what God is if this "what" would involve an objective determination of God's essence. Instead, absolute *esse* is the negation of the limitation of *esse* to worldly being. The *Vorgriff* as the fundamental human act amounts to a negation of the representational consciousness whereby a subject reduces each worldly thing to an object. God resists objectification, and the *Vorgriff* does not attempt to deliver God as an object.

This talk of affirmation (under which Rahner files comparison) and negation, although he may not self-consciously associate

9. SW 393/290.
10. SW 394/290–91.
11. SW 398/293.
12. Cf. SW 405/298.

it with language, cannot be dissociated from language. For Thomas, comparison and negation are strategies for accessing knowledge of metaphysical realities. Such knowledge cannot be had, and thus these linguistic strategies cannot be employed, without the linguistic probing of *excessus*—Thomas's "way of eminence," which uses the name of God to signify that which exists above all things.[13] Rahner writes, "Thus negation and comparison appear as inner moments within the *excessus* itself, through which the *excessus* is first completely itself."[14] If negation and comparison are inner moments of *excessus*, this means that language derives first from the nonobjective experience of God in the *Vorgriff*.

This, of course, plays into a fear that Rahner's critics have about him—that he sunders a transcendental, nonobjectively encountered God from the God who takes concrete form in Jesus Christ. There are two problems with this critique. First, it ignores the second half of the quote from the last paragraph, which states that *excessus* "is first completely itself" only through negation and comparison. One has to remember that earlier in *Geist in Welt* Rahner aligned negation and comparison to the conversion to the phantasm, thus to this world, and given his comments on the final page of the book, to Jesus of Nazareth. The transcendental, nonobjective affirmation of God in the *Vorgriff*, then, is never released from its tie to categorial affirmation or negation.

Rahner's brief mention of the "analogy of being" late in *Geist in Welt* reinforces this point. He believes that his account of the *Vorgriff* ensures an analogous view of being, where God completely transcends worldly being. Rahner likens the conversion to the phantasm, as a turn from abstraction back to the world, to a turn from analogous to univocal being.[15]

13. See ST I.13.8.ad 2.
14. SW 399/294.
15. SW 402/296. Cf. Rahner, "Mystery" in *The Concise Sacramentum Mundi*, 1000–1004, at 1002: "Analogical knowledge [*analogia entis*] is not the limiting case of a knowledge which in itself is univocal and which brings the particular object of knowledge into

Second, Rahner follows the example of Dionysius the Areopagite in his discussion of affirmation and negation. Dionysius is not an unhinged mystic. Instead, his praise for God as hidden and beyond all names comes from a conviction that God communicates God's self concretely in Christ and through the Church and its liturgies. Rahner has such confidence in the *Vorgriff*'s nonobjective experience of God because he shares Dionysius's faith in God's self-disclosure in sensible things.

But also like the Areopagite, Rahner wants assiduously to avoid the impression that theology represents God with full adequacy. Anything we say about God, God tailors to our capacities. These capacities are not God's, but ours. We can have confidence in our words about God insofar as God gives them. We must be modest, though, inasmuch as these words disclose God in a human way. *This is Geist in Welt*'s teaching on language. This teaching reverberates throughout Rahner's later reflections on theological language.

THE CONCEPT OF MYSTERY

Rahner's set of lectures "The Concept of Mystery in Catholic Theology" (1959) was a watershed moment in twentieth-century theology. The lectures call for and preliminarily step toward a comprehensive overhaul of Catholic fundamental theology. Within them, Rahner formulates a theory of theological language. In accordance with this theory, he recalibrates the relationship between faith and reason by questioning what model of reason Catholicism ought to assume as its own. Rahner intimates throughout, particularly in the first lecture, that Catholic theology has sacrificed something essential by adopting—unwittingly—a modern, subjectivist, positivist version of reason. To reiterate, in these lectures, Rahner contests the predominant paradigm in the Catholic theology of his day *not* because it

---

a firm and humanly intelligible system of coordinates (of the *prima principia*). It is the fundamental open and upward movement of the spirit towards the uncircumscribed mystery."

is not modern enough, but because it is too modern. Neo-Scholasticism is Thomas filtered through modern scientific reason.

The lectures center on two difficult questions regarding the framework for understanding Christian dogmatics:

Is Christian doctrine, where it covers real mysteries, really a highly complicated system of orderly statements? Or is it rather a mysteriously simple thing of infinite fullness, which can be propounded in an immense variety of statements while its mysterious and simple unity remains unchanged?[16]

Rahner's posing of these questions indicates that he will explicate two things: (1) two different theological concepts of mystery, and (2) how each concept inscribes a certain view of language.

The first theological concept is operative for the Catholic neo-Scholasticism of "the current manuals of dogmatic and fundamental theology." For this school theology, "mysteries are affirmations whose truth can be guaranteed only by a divine communication and which do not become perspicuous even when communicated by divine revelation but remain essentially the object of faith."[17] Rahner underscores that on this view, a mystery is a statement, an affirmation, an assertion, a bit of language that in principle should be clear but does not achieve its proper clarity.

A mystery, then, is provisional. It is a deficient truth. At this time it does not meet the demands of human reason — perspicuousness, evidence, strict proof — but one can hope that in the future it will meet these demands. Rahner points out that this view of language (clear assertion) and reason (ordered toward proof), which the neo-Scholastics tacitly hold as universal, derives from the ideal of modern science.[18] In a later essay (1974), Rahner will accuse this "classical" theology of cleaving to "a defective form of the true knowledge in which the mystery itself unfolds."[19] The defect of

16. CM 37.
17. CM 38.
18. CM 40. Cf. Rahner, *The Trinity*, 50.
19. Rahner, "The Hiddenness of God," in TI 16.227–43, at 236.

neo-Scholastic theology is its modern objectivism, which is a corollary of modern subjectivism.[20]

Rahner seeks a more "authentic and primordial" concept of mystery, one that regards a theological mystery not as "the limitation of a knowledge which should by right be perspicuous," but the precognitive condition that makes perspicuous knowledge possible.[21] This thesis demands explanation. We shall arrive at it by considering a passage from later in the lectures:

> As long as we measure the loftiness of knowledge by its perspicuity, and think that we know what clarity and insight are, though we do not really know them as they truly are; as long as we imagine that analytical, coordinating, deductive and masterful reason is more and not less than experience of the divine incomprehensibility; as long as we think that comprehension is greater than being overwhelmed by light inaccessible, which shows itself as inaccessible in the very moment of giving itself: we have understood nothing of the mystery and of the true nature of grace and glory.[22]

This quote suggests that the second concept of mystery, which Rahner espouses as his own, will be defined by positive and negative attributes. It will regard divine incomprehensibility as a positive reality. It will take as its norm being overwhelmed by divine light. It will *not* lament the divine incomprehensibility as a trap or a block to human flourishing. It will *not* despair when it realizes that the beatific vision will not be a momentous solution to a seemingly impossible problem. Instead, it will rejoice at the thought that even in the be-

---

20. This accusation against Neo-Scholastic Catholic theology is the necessary context for understanding the types of passages that perplex commentators like Francis Caponi, who accuses Rahner of treating "objectifications" of the faith as "necessary but unfortunate." Rahner does not affirm a "speechless grace," as Caponi's title would have it. Instead, Rahner concerns himself with what sort of speech theologians apply to the truths of faith. If the speech is infected by modern subjectivism/objectivism, Rahner will surely reject it—not because of his merely "notional acknowledgement of the importance of the categorical and linguistic," but because of his refounding of the categorical and linguistic, outside of objectivity. See Francis Caponi, "A Speechless Grace: Karl Rahner on Religious Language," *International Journal of Systematic Theology* 9, no. 2 (2007): 200–221, at 211–12.

21. CM 42.

22. CM 56.

atific vision God will remain incomprehensible, in a mode of near-ness and perfect love.[23]

This concept of mystery, like the first one, reflects a view of language. Rahner explicates this view of language in terms reminiscent of *Geist in Welt*. Language originates in the "'whither' of transcendent experience," that is, God as anticipatorily sensed. Rahner observes, "The whither of transcendental experience is always there as the nameless, the indefinable, the unattainable. For a name distinguishes and demarcates, pins down something by giving it a name chosen among other names. But the infinite horizon, the whither of transcendence cannot be so defined." Theological language comes not from human capacities for masterful labeling. Theological language comes from that which exceeds language: "the name from the experience of the nameless."[24] Fundamentally, language is received. As Terrance Klein captivatingly puts it, "God appears not as that which is forged by language, but rather as the forge upon which language itself is produced."[25]

This view of language coheres with an account of reason. Rahner calls reason, properly understood, the "faculty of mystery."[26] He contrasts this type of reason with the modern one: the faculty of mastery. Rahner's rationality revolves around a question. He articulates it in several different, rather poetic ways.

I shall recount two. He asks the knower, "whether he loves the island of his so-called knowledge better than the ocean of infinite mystery," or "whether he thinks that this little light with which he illuminates this little island—we call it science—should be the eternal light that shines on him forever (which would be hell)." The reasoning person must choose either an "uncharted, unending adventure where he commits himself to the infinite, or—despairing and

23. See CM 41.54–55.

24. CM 50.

25. Terrance Klein, "The Forge of Language," *Philosophy and Theology* 15, no. 1 (2003): 143–63, at 147.

26. CM 43.

embittered—of taking shelter in the suffocating den of his own finite perspicacity."[27] These questions and images about reason indicate Rahner's dissatisfaction with modernity's narrowed conception
of reason, and consequently of language. He directs this dissatisfaction primarily at his fellow Catholic theologians, who have capitu-
lated to modern reason and its misconstrual of language.

We could add to Rahner's questions two more, which will elucidate the problematic to which Rahner was alerting his fellow theologians: What do we want reason to give us, God or ourselves? What
do we want language to give us, God or ourselves? His descriptions
of the choice facing people suggest that isolation comes with the
modern concept of mystery. As with modern subjectivism, whose
logical conclusion is an individual human person who is a world
unto himself, the modern view of mystery threatens to make each
person his own island. And this would be hell.

REDUCTIO IN MYSTERIUM

The theological concept of mystery that Rahner advocates is
not a new one, except that—and this is a noteworthy exception—it
responds to a new situation, the status of late modern Catholic theology. The "primordial" concept of mystery is primordial in a twofold sense: (1) it arises from the ground of human thinking and language, and (2) it retrieves premodern experiences of and thinking
about God. This section treats primarily the retrieval component of
Rahner's concept of mystery.

In the "Concept of Mystery" essay, Rahner cites Dionysius the
Areopagite, Maximus the Confessor, and Gregory of Nyssa as his
forbears in emphasizing the suprarationality of God's incomprehensibility.[28] He also quotes Thomas at length to show the Angelic Doctor's agreement with his concept of mystery. Rahner will pursue this
thought further in the late essay "An Investigation into the Incom-

27. CM 57–58.
28. CM 58.

prehensibility of God in St. Thomas Aquinas" (1974).[29] Perhaps just as important as these explicitly invoked predecessors, though, is one who remains unnamed, yet with whose thought Rahner spent considerable time, specifically during the 1930s: Bonaventure.

In 1933, Rahner published an essay in French on the spiritual senses in Bonaventure.[30] He expanded the article in 1934 and then rereleased it in 1975 in the twelfth volume of the *Schriften*.[31] In the list of sources at the end of this volume, he explains that he includes the article, which was written decades prior to many of the other texts in the volume, because of its close relation to his philosophy of religion and his later theological works. Indeed, many of the themes Rahner identifies in his historical work on Bonaventure have direct bearing on later inquiries, mystery being chief among them. And the concerted attention Rahner pays to the affective nature of the experience of God in Bonaventure coincides nicely with my perspective on Rahner in this book. In Bonaventure, Rahner locates a thoroughgoing aesthetic that structures philosophy and theology.[32] *Affectus* precedes and grounds *noesis*. Bonaventure's is an aesthetic subjectivity that is qualitatively different from a subjectivity governed primarily or exclusively by pure intellection. Though Rahner does not follow this path, in Bonaventure he may have located resources for an aesthetic defeat of the modern subject.

Bonaventure is important in yet another way for Rahner, though a more implicit and understated way. The Seraphic Doctor's importance comes to light in a phrase Rahner employs to describe the concept of reason that accords with his concept of mystery. He writes, "All

29. Karl Rahner, "An Investigation into the Incomprehensibility of God in St. Thomas Aquinas," in TI 16.244–54.

30. Karl Rahner, "La doctrine des 'sens spirituels' au Moyen-Age en particulier chez Saint Bonaventure," *Revue d'Ascétique et de Mystique* 14 (1933): 263–99.

31. Karl Rahner, "Der Begriff der ecstasis bei Bonaventura," *Zeitschrift für Azsese und Mystik* 9 (1934): 1–19; Rahner, "The Doctrine of the 'Spiritual Senses' in the Middle Ages: The Contribution of Bonaventure" in TI 16.104–34, hereafter "Bonaventure."

32. See especially Rahner, "Bonaventure," 123–28. Cf. Stephen Fields, "Balthasar and Rahner on the Spiritual Senses," *Theological Studies* 57 (1996): 224–41.

understanding of any reality whatsoever is in the last resort always a *'reductio in mysterium,'* and any comprehension which is or seems to be devoid of the character of mystery, is only arrived at through the unspoken convention that this *'reductio in mysterium Dei'* should be excluded from the start."[33] The phrase "reduction into mystery" means a leading of all things back to the incomprehensibility of God. This phrase relates to Bonaventure because he uses the word *"reductio"* in a technical sense in several of his works, most notably and obviously in *De reductione artium ad theologiam,* but also in the *Breviloquium* and his *Commentary on the Sentences.*[34]

French philosopher Emmanuel Falque has recently shown how a "reduction into mystery" impels Bonaventure's thought. The act of this "reduction" Bonaventure calls *"persucratio."* Falque defines *persucratio* as a "boundless, bottomless penetration into mystery" or a "dive into mystery without either destroying the mystery or priding itself on the discovery of it."[35] When Rahner says *"reductio in mysterium,"* he means something similar.

Rahner illuminates this phrase most completely in his three-lecture series "Reflections on Methodology in Theology," where he uses the phrase to summarize the contents of the third lecture.[36] The third lecture begins with a problem that we have encountered already: theology's difficult relationship with the demands of scientific reason. As Rahner depicts the situation in this lecture, modern science has backed theology into a corner. Theology either must jus-

---

33. CM 62.

34. Bonaventure, *De reductione artium ad theologiam,* in Emma Thérèse Healy, *Saint Bonaventure's* De Reductione Artium ad Theologiam: *A Commentary with an Introduction and Translation* (St. Bonaventure, N.Y.: Franciscan Institute, St. Bonaventure University, 1955). On the other works, see Emmanuel Falque, *Saint Bonaventure et l'entrée de Dieu en théologie: La Somme théologique du Breviloquium* (Paris: Vrin, 2001); and Falque, "The Phenomenological Act of *Persucratio* in the *Proemium* of St. Bonaventure's Commentary on the Sentences," trans. Elisa Mangina, *Medieval Philosophy and Theology* 10 (2001): 1–22.

35. Falque, "Phenomenological Act of *Persucratio*," 9–10.

36. Rahner, "Reflections on Methodology in Theology," in TI 11.68–114, at 101–14, hereafter RM.

tify itself scientifically or pride itself on being utterly unscientific. Rahner sees both of these options as false. They are false because theology is a more primordial discipline than modern science. Theology's rationality is more capacious than modern science's. Thus theology's rationality is a condition for the possibility of scientific rationality, not vice versa.[37] There can be no perspicuous, scientific knowledge without an acknowledgment that reality persistently and positively evades human perspicuity.

Rahner's argument goes back to his Bonaventurian view of reason, where all of "the arts," that is, all ways toward knowledge, reduce to theology, which in turn reduces to an affective experience of God's mystery. These reductions relate to language. The danger of language is its tendency to become self-enclosed. This has happened with all discourses that derive from a modern concept of reason, because they claim subjective control of a particular area of knowledge or aspect of the world. Bonaventure presented his view of the "reduction of the arts to theology" in order to oppose an analogous creeping rationalism in his day.

Rahner argues that theology must present a different model of language from subjectivist rationalism. Theology

must understand itself not as that science which develops itself more and more in a systematic drawing of distinctions down to the last possible detail, but rather as that human activity in which man, even at the level of conscious thought, relates the multiplicity of the realities, experiences, and ideas in his life to that mystery, ineffable and obscure, which we call God.[38]

The task of theology does not consist in honing clear propositions. Such a practice would entrench a false view of language that reduces it to its purely utilitarian aspect, thereby restricting its range of function. Instead, the task of theology resides first in referring all words and propositions—clear or not—to the only true mystery: God.

37. RM 101–2.
38. RM 102.

The character of theological language lies in its "special and peculiar relativity." Theology's words cannot be disjoined from their radical reference to what infinitely transcends them.[39] This is not to say, though, that theologians must remain silent, as Ludwig Wittgenstein might have it.[40] Rahner points to the impossibility of silence in this lifetime. As we learned in our examination of angels, what makes humans human is discursiveness. One cannot avoid speech. But one can direct it properly.

For this reason, Rahner prescribes a twofold theological modesty. First, Catholic theologians must formulate theological statements keeping in mind that they should serve as mystagogical steps on the way to God's mystery.[41] They are not destinations in themselves. This first valence of theological modesty leads to a second. It relates to the Magisterium. The official teaching office of the Church must be modest in its rejection of certain theological propositions as heretical. Rahner affirms the Church's duty to reject statements that militate directly against the faith. But he entreats theologians and Church officials to exercise greater prudence and patience vis-à-vis alleged heresies than was customary in past ages.[42] Greater care for language and its proper action of *reductio in mysterium* can, perhaps, make theology more vulnerable to error, but it also opens theology to have "a little trust in the reality to which it refers."[43]

Because theology remains benighted by modernity's addiction to propositional mastery, it falls short of its appropriate task: "I believe that theology today has still very much to learn before it speaks in such a manner that men can achieve a direct, effective, and clear recognition of the special quality of this language."[44] Properly, theology is a language that dis-closes instead of closing, which opens all

---

39. RM 111–12.   40. RM 102.

41. On Rahner and mystagogy, see the classic study, James Bacik, *Apologetics and the Eclipse of Mystery: Mystagogy according to Karl Rahner* (Notre Dame, Ind.: University of Notre Dame Press, 1980).

42. RM 112–13.   43. RM 114.

44. RM 112.

realities, experiences, and ideas in this life—all things—to the full scope of their reference: the infinity of God. Rahner refounds theological language by recurring, in Bonaventurian wise, to the mystery that sustains it.

HEIDEGGER RELEASING ASSERTION

Rahner's strategies for refounding theological language have a counterpoint in Heidegger's thinking on language: its search for a primordial level of language beyond the everyday, its critique of modern uses of language, its insistence upon the relationship between language and mystery. At least in part, Rahner develops these strategies out of his encounter with Heidegger. For example, Rahner would have heard Heidegger proclaim in his lectures *Introduction to Metaphysics,* "The character of mystery belongs to the essence of the origin of language."[45] Rahner's participation in the first Hölderlin course provided him with ample opportunity to internalize Heidegger's thinking on language, as well.

Heidegger's later thinking on language springs from the implications of his earlier texts and courses.[46] This part will show how Heidegger's critique of assertion in *Being and Time* becomes a full-blown thinking of language as open to mystery. The earlier critique of assertion seems to have inspired Rahner's critical response to the ailments of modern Catholic theology, which accords strongly with Heidegger's proposal during the same period of a postmetaphysical rethinking of language. After having underscored this similarity, I

45. EM 182.
46. I do not mean to imply by the brevity of my presentation here that Heidegger's thought developed smoothly and uncomplicatedly from *Being and Time* to the later works, but instead that in principle one could argue for their continuity. An argument that stunningly takes into account the details is Mark Wrathall, "Discourse Language Saying Showing," in *Heidegger and Unconcealment: Truth, Language, and History* (New York: Cambridge University Press, 2011), 119–55. Also interesting is Bret Davis's location of the unity of Heidegger's thinking in the notion of *Gelassenheit*; see Bret Davis, *Heidegger and the Will: On the Way to Gelassenheit* (Evanston, Ill.: Northwestern University Press, 2007).

shall set up a contrast between Rahner and Heidegger that will occupy us later in the chapter.

ASSERTION AS DERIVATIVE LANGUAGE

During the dialogue that opens *On the Way to Language,* Heidegger directs his interlocutor to read *Being and Time* §34 to discover his thoughts in that text on language.[47] Over the next several paragraphs I shall take Heidegger's advice.

This section from *Being and Time* introduces language as a "phenomenon that has its roots in the existential constitution of *Dasein*'s disclosedness."[48] Heidegger reports that discourse is the state in which *Dasein* is disclosed as a phenomenon, and language is the expression of discourse. This may seem a rather muddled definition of language, since the terms used in the definition are themselves obscure. This appears, though, to be Heidegger's point. All prior attempts at a definition of language have failed.

In order for language to be defined adequately, one would have "to work out in advance the ontologico-existential whole of the structure of discourse on the basis of the analytic of *Dasein*." Grasping the "essence of language," then, would indeed involve "*Dasein*" and "discourse" as attendant ideas—and ones that would need to be defined prior to "language."[49] One cannot be satisfied with the current findings of the "science of language." He proposes that his rooting of language in *Dasein*'s appearance as a phenomenon reveals "the necessity of re-establishing the science of language on foundations which are ontologically more primordial."[50]

But why must this be done? If the "science of language" in its current form has run aground, why? In the previous section, §33, Heidegger describes the phenomenon of "assertion," which he calls a "derivative mode of interpretation," and consequently a derivative type of language. He lays out three possible senses of the word "as-

47. OWL 42.   48. BT 203.
49. BT 206.   50. BT 209.

sertion": "pointing out" (*Aufzeigung*), "predication" (*Prädikation*), and "communication" (*Mitteilung*). The second proves most important for Heidegger's analysis of "assertion." For him, language's original use allows a thing to manifest itself to an interpreter who experiences the thing in its manifestness, as it is. Language originally witnesses to a precognitive or pretheoretical apprehension of a thing. "Predication" is the action by which the content of language is narrowed and restricted. Through predication, *Dasein* makes a theoretical judgment about a thing.

Heidegger gives the example of a hammer. The original or immediate experience of a hammer comes to light in such sayings as "The hammer is too heavy!" "Too heavy!" or "Hand me the other hammer!" These exclamations of one working with a hammer do not convey theoretical or epistemological content. They express the everyday experience of a tool that impedes rather than facilitates work. A predicative assertion about the hammer would operate in a different mode. The statement "The hammer is heavy" would mean "This thing has the property of heaviness." It would point to a theoretical conclusion about the hammer.[51]

Assertion is, then, a derivative form of interpretation. It is secondary to the direct experience of a thing and the language that attends such experience. Assertion turns aesthetic experience into intellection.

Heidegger deems this significant because it has to do with one's idea of truth. Throughout the metaphysical tradition, thinkers have presumed that "the 'locus' of truth is assertion" and "that the essence of truth lies in the 'agreement' of the judgment with its object." Heidegger traces these views on truth back to Aristotle, who reduces truth to the activity of judgment.[52]

There are two problems with Aristotle's reduction. First, he does not argue for it. He simply stipulates that truth reveals itself

51. BT 196–98.
52. BT 257 (§44).

through noetic activity. Second, Heidegger believes he has found a more primal stratum of truth that belies Aristotle's reduction. Prior to intellection (*noesis*) is the "truth of *aesthesis*," the "uncovering" or "disclosure" of things that happens amid *Dasein*'s being in the world. Again, assertion is a derivative mode of interpretation—it "is not the primary 'locus' of truth. On the contrary ... assertion is grounded in *Dasein*'s uncovering."[53]

On account of Aristotle's positing of assertion as truth's primary locus, the metaphysical tradition has "covered up the primal phenomenon of truth." The default activity of thinking is assertion. The default use of language is assertion. Thus the metaphysical tradition assumes as axiomatic a definition of truth, a type of thinking, and a mode of language that rests on prior yet hidden conditions.

Heidegger does not attempt in *Being and Time* to reestablish the science of language on new foundations. He does, though, lay bare these foundations by demanding a more ontologically primordial view of truth and language. His purview in *Being and Time* remains mainly critical, but points to a constructive project that he undertakes in his later thinking.

RELEASEMENT, OPENNESS FOR MYSTERY, AND APPROPRIATION

This section treats Heidegger's later texts *Gelassenheit* and *On the Way to Language*. It may help to prepare for these texts with a quote from a text we have already read, the "Letter on Humanism":

Language still denies us its essence: that it is the house of the truth of being. Instead, language surrenders itself to our mere willing and trafficking as an instrument of domination over beings. Beings themselves appear as actualities in the interaction of cause and effect. We encounter beings as actualities in a calculative businesslike way, but also scientifically and by way of philosophy, with explanations and proofs. Even the assurance that

---

53. BT 268–69 (§44).

something is inexplicable belongs to these explanations and proofs. With such statements we believe that we confront the mystery. As if it were already decided that the truth of being lets itself at all be established in causes and explanatory grounds or, what comes to the same, in their incomprehensibility.[54]

This paragraph describes more vividly and pointedly than any paragraph in *Being and Time* the hegemony of assertion in metaphysics' view and use of language. Assertion is willing, trafficking, domination, positing causal relationships, calculation, explanation, proof, and claiming to take hold of mystery and incomprehensibility. Heidegger acknowledges that some of these functions of assertion are beneficial and even necessary for life. They help provide us things that we need, like food and shelter. Even so, language must be shown to be more than assertion, lest the life that language discloses be lost.[55]

Heidegger attempts such showing in his works of the 1950s.[56] In *Gelassenheit* and *On the Way to Language,* Heidegger sets up a twofold schema for understanding thinking and language. This bipartite schema reflects his earlier distinction between "assertion" and "primordial" language. In *Gelassenheit,* Heidegger calls the two kinds of thinking "calculative thinking" (*rechnendes Denken*) and "contemplative thinking" (*besinnliches Denken*).[57] In *On the Way to Lan-*

---

54. LH 223.

55. See, for example, a passage on technology as the product of calculative thinking and language: "It would be foolish to attack technology blindly. It would be shortsighted to condemn it as the work of the devil. We depend on technical devices; they even challenge us to ever greater advances. But suddenly and unaware we find ourselves so firmly shackled to these technical devices that we fall into bondage to them" (G 53, cf. 45–46).

56. The second part of *Gelassenheit* was originally composed in 1944–1945, but it was not set in final form until the late 1950s. For the original, see Martin Heidegger, "*Zur Erörterung der Gelassenheit: Aus einem Feldweggespräch über das Denken,*" in *Aus der Erfahrung des Denkens: Gesamtausgabe 13* (Frankfurt: Vittorio Klostermann, 1983). And for the longer version of which "*Zur Erörterung der Gelassenheit*" was only a part, see Heidegger, *Country Path Conversations,* trans. Bret Davis (Bloomington: Indiana University Press, 2010), which is a translation of Heidegger, *Feldweg-Gespräche (1944/45): Gesamtausgabe 77* (Frankfurt: Vittorio Klostermann, 1995).

57. G 46, ET modified. The translator renders "*besinnliche*" as "meditative." I prefer "contemplative." I shall forgo cross-references to the German for this work, because the

guage, Heidegger gives a similar formulation to describe thinking: "technical-scientific calculation" (*technisch-wissenschaftliche Rechnen*) and "reflective thinking" (*sinnende Denken*).[58] He also relates these two modes of thinking to language. Calculative thinking's language is "the language of framing" [*Ge-Stell*]. It works to control the world through technology. Reflective thinking's language is "the language of appropriation" [*Ereignis*].[59] This language "brings all present and absent beings each into their own, from where they show themselves in what they are, and where they abide according to their own kind."[60] The former language forces things to appear a certain way; the latter language lets things appear as they will.

The predominance of calculative, assertive language gives rise to the situation Heidegger describes in the "Letter on Humanism." He continues his diagnosis of the situation in *Gelassenheit.* In an address to people of his hometown of Meßkirch, he proclaims, "Man today is in flight from thinking."[61] He recognizes that people could easily object that planning, inquiry, and research are very much alive. Thinking seems to endure—it even seems better and more effective than in prior ages. Heidegger responds to the objection, though, pointing out that what has been lost is not thinking in general. Instead, thinking has been narrowed almost entirely to calculative thinking. People fly from contemplative thinking.[62]

Flight from thinking so vexes Heidegger because he regards contemplative thinking as constitutive of being human.[63] Were the capacity for this thinking lost, so would the essence of humanity be forfeited. His differentiation of the two types of thinking and his proclamation that one is in imminent danger of destruction bears,

---

English translation has a helpful German-to-English glossary at the end that includes any German terms I deem worthy of highlighting.

58. OWL 91, see 74–75; cf. *Unterwegs zur Sprache,* 185–86. Note that "*sinnende*" also connotes "sensing," thus giving "reflective thinking" an aesthetic cast.

59. OWL 131–32, cf. *Unterwegs zur Sprache,* 251–52.

60. OWL 127.   61. G 45.

62. G 56.   63. G 47.

for him, on "the saving of man's essential nature."[64] This "saving" can happen, Heidegger hopes, through the cultivation of two dispositions that relate to each other and to contemplative thinking. He calls them "releasement toward things" (*Gelassenheit zu den Dingen*) and "openness for mystery" (*Offenheit für das Geheimnis*).[65]

The two dispositions cooperate reciprocally. Releasement thinks in a way other than calculative thinking. In this way it witnesses to the possibility of contemplative thinking. It also acknowledges the possibility that, though calculative thinking and technology may seem to have no meaning, one may discover meaning in them. Openness for mystery, then, is remaining vigilant for the "meaning hidden in technology." Heidegger announces that these two dispositions "promise us a new ground and foundation upon which we can stand and endure in the world of technology without being imperiled by it."[66] Those who cultivate them can take comfort in the face of the looming, uncanny, dangerous mystery that confronts them.[67]

Releasement and openness for mystery have a linguistic analogue: the language of appropriation. As I already noted, this language is the more primordial counterpart to the language of framing. The language of framing orders and sets each being up in a "technical inventory." It channels all things toward calculative thinking, which categorizes them in terms of their technological usefulness. The language of appropriation is different, just as releasement and openness for mystery are different from calculative thinking.

The German word that we translate as "appropriation" is "*Ereignis*," which means "event," but carries the connotation of propriety or appropriateness. Heidegger deploys the term to name a pro-

---

64. G 56.   65. G 54–55.
66. G 55.

67. On releasement, openness to mystery, and technology, see Hubert Dreyfus, "Heidegger on Gaining a Free Relation to Technology," in *Heidegger Reexamined, Vol. 3: Art, Poetry, and Technology*, ed. Mark Wrathall and Hubert Dreyfus (New York: Routledge, 2002), 163–74.

cess by which all things become what they properly are. This process occurs by way of language. He explains, "[A]ppropriating saying brings to light all present beings in terms of their own properties— it lauds, that is, allows them into their own, their nature."[68] Calculative thinking and assertive language of framing bend things to the will of the subject who thinks and says them. Contemplative thinking and reflective language of appropriation let things be for themselves.

Releasement toward things, openness to mystery, and language of appropriation save the essential nature of humanity. They do so by pointing beyond a human rapport with reality characterized by forcible grasping of reality. It is not proper for human beings to make use of reality as they wish, and thus to claim a grasp on the incomprehensibility of being. It is proper for human beings to be "made use of for the nature of truth."[69] The truth of being comes to light as appropriation, and appropriation makes use of human saying. Language is not merely assertion. It is not primarily assertion. Primarily, language is a way of coming near to all that is. For Heidegger, the mystery of being is the nearness by which all beings relate to one another.[70] True language says this mystery.

WHAT SORT OF MYSTERY?

We have now seen how Heidegger's early critique of assertion develops into a probing thinking of language as open to mystery. In this wise, Heidegger's "later" thinking converges with Rahner's theology of mystery and his theological method of *reductio in myste-*

---

68. OWL 135.

69. G 84–85.

70. This is the idea that lies behind the enigmatic passage at the end of *Gelassenheit* on Heraclitus's Fragment 122: *"Anchibasíe."* Heidegger translates the fragment "moving-into-nearness," G 88–90. See also OWL 104, which contains a gripping passage on "nearness." For a critical take on Heidegger's thinking of "nearness," see Krzysztof Ziarek, *Inflected Language: Toward a Hermeneutics of Nearness: Heidegger, Levinas, Stevens, Celan* (Albany, N.Y.: SUNY Press, 1994), 43–64.

rium. Both Rahner and Heidegger insist that language must be refounded by locating and describing a primordial mode of language. Thinkers must oppose the modern metaphysical narrowing of language's capabilities and content. They must open language to its proper breadth. This involves indicating that language primarily expresses that which cannot be theoretically thematized: mystery.

Rahner and Heidegger also converge in their insistence that recovering a form of thinking and language that is open to mystery does not involve an esoteric turn. Rahner's *reductio in mysterium* and Heidegger's contemplative thinking are not, as Heidegger puts it, "'above' the reach of ordinary understanding." Again in Heidegger's words, "contemplative thinking need by no means be 'high-flown.'"[71] The same goes for Rahner. When he maintains, for instance, that the "devout person will either be a mystic — someone who has 'experienced' something — or else they will no longer be devout at all," he is not suggesting that Christianity must be rendered ever-more esoteric.[72] Philip Endean writes, "For Rahner, we need to lose the sense of elitism associated with talk of the mystical."[73] Rahner and Heidegger alike deem it necessary that people sensitize themselves to the mystery that subtends everyday living.

This is how one might reconcile the tie I have made between Heidegger's account of the worker's immediate language about a hammer — "Too heavy!" — and his thinking of *Gelassenheit.* An encounter with mystery might be had by a reorientation of thinking and language toward the ground of the everyday. The everyday is more mysterious than scientific-technical-metaphysical thinking and language allow us to experience. When he titles one of his books on Rahner, *Karl Rahner: The Mystic of Everyday Life,* Harvey Egan perfectly cap-

---

71. G 46–47.

72. Karl Rahner, "Christian Living Formerly and Today," in TI 7, 3–24, at 15, quoted in Philip Endean, "Introduction," in *Karl Rahner: Spiritual Writings,* ed. Philip Endean (Maryknoll, N.Y.: Orbis, 2004), 9–30, at 24.

73. Endean, "Introduction," 24.

tures Rahner's commitment to a reorientation toward the mystery of the everyday.[74]

If Rahner and Heidegger converge with respect to their recalling of thinking and language to the mystery that sustains them, they diverge over the question of what sort of mystery this is. Heidegger presents a finite mystery that actively hides itself from human apprehension. Rahner offers a view of mystery as infinite and actively self-giving.

Heidegger's perspective on mystery in *Gelassenheit* and *On the Way to Language* is twofold. First, as we read above, mystery is the hidden meaning of modern technology. Second, mystery refers to the autochthony of human existence, which has been covered over by metaphysics, particularly its late instantiation in modern technology.[75] There are two ties that bind these two definitions of mystery. I have already alluded to them. First, technology and human rootedness are utterly finite realities. Second, mystery withdraws from the human ability to think, to say, and to experience it. I shall focus on this latter point, since the first point should be rather obvious, given my discussions of Heidegger's apriorism of finitude.

In *Gelassenheit*, Heidegger discusses "the region" (*das Gegend*), the open site in and through which contemplative thinking transpires. During the "Conversation on a Country Path," the conversation partners note that the "region" withdraws, "rather than coming to meet us."[76] In *On the Way to Language*, Heidegger discusses language in similar terms: "withholding is in the very nature of language."[77] This "withdrawing" and "withholding" of the mystery is emblematic of Heidegger's thinking in these texts and others. In fact, these texts distill a quintessential problem of his thinking: the callousness of being.

It is true that human beings play a role in the misapprehension

74. Egan, *Mystic of Everyday Life*, cited above.
75. See G 48–49.   76. G 66.
77. OWL 81.

of being throughout the metaphysical tradition, especially during the modern period. But these texts reveal that, for Heidegger, being orchestrates its own misapprehension. Nowhere is this more patent than in the lecture "The Question concerning Technology" (first version 1949, revised in 1953, published 1954), which relates interestingly to *Gelassenheit*. Heidegger tells of a mystery that conceals itself, the danger of this concealment, and the destiny and fate of banishment that "contemporary man" must suffer with respect to that which reveals itself.[78] The danger that comes with the mysterious essence of technology does harbor a saving power (*das Rettende*).[79] Technology as an epoch of being may eventually provide people with a vision of unconcealed truth. So we can hope.[80] Nevertheless, Heidegger's presentation of technology as an epoch of being is troubling. Being uses technology to hide itself from humanity, thereby endangering the whole world. And to what effect? Heidegger does not answer this question. He does not even ask it. The mystery of being is callous, and Heidegger is callous in his unwillingness to address being's callousness.

With Rahner mystery is rendered differently. The absolute mystery for Rahner is God. As with the mystery in Heidegger, Rahner's mystery remains forever incomprehensible and unmanipulable by human minds and hands. But a gaping divide opens between Rahner and Heidegger on account of Rahner's belief that the proper end of the human being lies in the beatific vision, and that the finite life of the human being on earth anticipates this vision. Rahner states this teaching poetically in *Foundations of Christian Faith* (1976):

This is what is expressed in the Christian doctrine which says that in grace,

---

78. Martin Heidegger, "The Question Concerning Technology," in *Basic Writings*, 311–41, at 330, 332.

79. Heidegger, "Question Concerning Technology," 333–34. Cf. Martin Heidegger, "Die Frage nach der Technik," in *Vorträge und Aufsätze, Gesamtausgabe 7* (Frankfurt: Vittorio Klostermann, 2000), 7–36, at 29–30.

80. Heidegger, "Question Concerning Technology," 338.

that is, in the communication of God's Holy Spirit, the event of the immediacy to God as man's fulfillment is prepared for in such a way that we must say of man here and now that he participates in God's being; that he has been given the divine Spirit who fathoms the very depths of God; that he is already God's son here and now, and what he already is must become manifest.[81]

If we ask, then, what sort of mystery Rahner envisions, our answer is a mystery that gives itself, fully and with abandon. Heidegger does say that the "primal mystery of all thinking" is being's "self-giving into the open": the "*es gibt,*" or "it gives" of being.[82] But it is clear that any "giving" that Heidegger's mystery does pales in comparison to the self-communication of Rahner's God. Rahner's mystery does not abandon people to danger. Actually, the most perilous threat to human existence, the guilt of sin, is set always within the context of the active forgiving presence of God.[83] Heidegger's mystery holds back. Rahner's advances.

This all relates to Rahner and Heidegger's respective versions of the sublime. To hearken back to my terminology from chapter two, I shall relate the sublime to the home. Rahner's Catholic sublime stems from his faith in the infinite God who has come lovingly near to the world in Christ, thus opening the life of God as the proper home for human persons. Rahner's articulation of what constitutes a mystery is consonant with this depiction of the home. The mystery gives itself from its high height, and begins the process of elevation by which the human person joins in the mystery. Heidegger's version of the sublime also coheres with his view of the home, which he rearticulates in *Gelassenheit.* Technology threatens to destroy the human experience of being at home. In this way, technology is "uncanny": *unheimlich,* un-home-like. Openness to the mystery

81. Karl Rahner, *Foundations of Christian Faith,* trans. William Dych (New York: Crossroad, 1978), 120.
82. LH 238.
83. Rahner, *Foundations,* 93.

allows hope for a "new autochthony," a new experience of the home, a striking of "new roots."[84] As in the Hölderlin lectures of the 1930s, Heidegger's sublime boils down to an exaltation of the homeland, finite life on a patch of soil. If his mystery gives itself, this meager gift is all it gives. Rahner's sublime promises a share in the divine life: a higher exaltation, indeed.

MARY IN RAHNER AND THE THING IN HEIDEGGER

The many foregoing words on "saying mystery" and "releasing assertion" amount, among other things, to a statement that Rahner and Heidegger develop largely compatible accounts of language that evades the regime of objectness. This part will continue to explore the agreement between Rahner and Heidegger, while keeping in mind the dissonance to which I pointed in the last section.

I shall argue three main points: (1) that Rahner's writings on Mary, particularly the essay "Virginitas in partu: A Contribution to the Problem of the Development of Dogma and of Tradition," develop his idea that language ought not to be limited to its scientific, logical use;[85] (2) that Heidegger's lecture "The Thing" provides an interesting counterpoint to the aspect of Rahner's Marian writings that we shall consider in the first section; and (3) that taken together, Mary in Rahner and the thing in Heidegger can help us to describe the importance of nonproductive discourse in Rahner, that is, a type of language that resists the modern subjectivist bias toward "results." Nonproductive language falls outside the realm of assertion by asserting nothing. Instead, it allows openness to the mystery of God.

84. G 48–49, 52, 54, 57.
85. Karl Rahner, "*Virginitas in partu:* A Contribution to the Problem of the Development of Dogma and of Tradition," in TI 4.134–62, hereafter VIP.

THEOLOGICAL LANGUAGE AND MARY'S VIRGINITY

Rahner's works on Marian doctrine often fall within more general treatments of the development of dogma. Even so, the tendency of Rahnerian scholars to emphasize times when Rahner seems to push Mary to the margins of theology are somewhat distorted.[86] Rahner's writings on Mary allow him to perform the Catholic sublime, in that he attempts to redeem all Marian dogmas and doctrines and to keep Catholic theology and life open to the breadth of Marian things. He refuses to short-change *any* Catholic doctrine or practice in the interest of some apologetics we can "live with."[87]

Though Rahner's Marian writings are voluminous, I shall consider only one of them substantively here.[88] This section reads and interprets *"Virginias in partu,"* a text about the doctrine that, put

86. On Rahner and Marian dogmas, the best resources are Mary Hines, *The Transformation of Dogma: An Introduction to Karl Rahner on Doctrine* (Mahwah, N.J.: Paulist Press, 1989); and Hines, "Rahner on Development of Doctrine: How Relevant Is Rahner Today?" *Philosophy and Theology* 12, no. 1 (2000): 111–30. On Mary as "marginal" in Rahner, see Hines, "Rahner on Development of Doctrine," 125, but cf. Rahner, "Mary and the Christian Image of Woman," in TI 19.211–17, at 213. See also Peter Joseph Fritz, "Between Center and Periphery: Mary and the Saints in Rahner," *Philosophy and Theology*, 24, no. 2 (2012): 297–311.

87. In 1982, Rahner was invited to give a lecture answering the question, "Is there a theology we can live with?" Rahner begins by interrogating the question itself: "Really, just what kind of a life is meant? If what is meant is the life of the people of the West in their consumer-oriented society, people earning money, people at play and recreation, people in pursuit of a culture which has turned into a kind of self-important industry whose real purpose, if you take a close look at things, is to drown out lethal boredom; if it were absolutely clear that the skeptical positivist is right in forbidding us to talk about something that cannot be demonstrated experimentally; if it is absolutely clear and obvious that mystical experience of God (I dare to use this term), faith, prayer, the experience of an absolute responsibility, and so on are excluded from that life—if this is the kind of life that is meant, then of course theology is not something that one can live with, because right from the start all of those realities which theology has as the object of its reflection are excluded from this kind of life." Theology is, then, not primarily about what one "can live with." See Karl Rahner, "A Theology That We Can Live With," in TI 21.99–112, at 100.

88. For the authoritative collection of Rahner's Mariology, see Karl Rahner, *Maria, Mütter des Herrn: Studien zur Mariologie, Sämtliche Werke 9,* ed. Regina Pacis Meyer (Freiburg: Herder, 2004).

simply, Mary remained a virgin in giving birth to Christ. The essay demonstrates how to resist the dominance of assertoric predication, and thereby to allow doctrines to say what they mean to say.

The essay is largely a critique of a book on Mary by theologian Albert Mitterer, *Dogma und Biologie der Heiligen Familie* (1952).[89] Rahner begins by insinuating the illegitimacy of the book's starting point. He notes that Mitterer chooses a priori to approach the doctrine of *virginitas in partu* from the point of view of "modern science," rather than theology. Mitterer critiques the traditional theology of *virginitas in partu* by pointing out that it does not accord well with the concepts of "motherhood" and "virginity" as modern science understands them. He calls into question the doctrine of *virginitas in partu* by suggesting that it is merely a corollary of the doctrine of Mary's perpetual virginity. The theological tradition strategically posited the corollary to head off the objection that Mary's virginity was cancelled by Jesus' birth, which would have ruptured her hymen. *Virginitas in partu,* then, is a product of logic, and a logic that militates against Mary's true (i.e., physical-biological) motherhood.[90]

Rahner disagrees. For him, Mariology roots itself first in the apostolic conviction that "Mary is a person who as such is part of the history of salvation" whose "motherhood is free, completely human, not merely biological and so sub-human." Rahner draws an implication from the apostolic preaching on Mary:

that the active birth (the act of giving birth) is not simply a biological event which is merely a fractional happening within the sphere of a human being, and which could then be the same even in people who were inwardly different. It is much more rather, and must therefore be considered, an act that involves the *whole man* and will express the totality of the human person in question in the way in which it is done, suffered and experienced.

89. Albert Mitterer, *Dogma und Biologie der Heiligen Familie: Nach dem Weltbild des h. Thomas von Aquin und dem der Gegenwart* (Vienna: Herder, 1952).
90. VIP 134–36.

This implication follows from the apostolic preaching because the earliest Church's belief about Mary holds that her active birthing of Jesus "corresponds to her nature"—not that she is *only* a mother, but that her motherhood relates to all other aspects of her life. Mary's "whole reality is a unique and miraculous work of grace," and so "the same holds good *eo ipso* of her act of child-bearing."[91] These ideas, Rahner concludes, are fundamental to the theological assessment of Jesus' birth as virginal.

Rahner states that these ideas also lead to the question of "whether we have attained a correct concept of the '*virginitas in partu*' only when the content has been expressed unambiguously in material and biologically concrete terms."[92] His fundamental theological approach to Mary's virginity, that is, via his elucidation of the basic Mariological concept of the apostolic preaching, places a question mark over Mitterer's analysis of the doctrine in terms of the natural sciences.

Rahner writes, "Mitterer's mistake, formally speaking, is that he works only with a circumscribed, biological notion of birth."[93] The same goes for Mitterer's view of virginity. He feels compelled to deduce the "peculiarities" of Jesus' birth as the theological tradition describes it from an "objective notion of virginity" that he derives from modern science.[94] Mitterer's "objectivity," though he hopes it will help heuristically, becomes an obstacle to discovery. Instead of attempting to discern what *virginitas in partu* might mean theologically, Mitterer's task becomes trying to explain how biologically speaking Mary could remain a virgin in the act of birth.

Rahner hints that Mitterer would do well to abandon his starting point. He would be compelled to do so were he really to study the theological tradition: "A close analysis of the tradition reveals very soon that the train of thought is not: Mary is a virgin in the act of giving birth; but the concept of virgin obviously implies certain

---

91. VIP 154–55, emphasis original, ET slightly modified.
92. VIP 155.   93. VIP 155n96.
94. VIP 156n98.

factors; these factors must have been characteristic of the birth."[95] To posit such a train of thought would make doctrinal development into nothing but conceptual analysis, a procedure of propositional logic. Rahner suggests that this view of doctrine's development cannot be seriously maintained if one attends to the Mariologies of prior ages. Theologians of the patristic and medieval eras arrived at the "concept" of virginity through arguments about "fittingness"—reflection on what befits the mother of God. Notably, one could call these aesthetic arguments. Mary's virginity suits her, by aesthetic, as opposed to logical, necessity.

In keeping with prior tradition, Rahner considers Mary's virginity as a *theological* reality. "Virgin," when applied to Mary, refers to the entirety of her station as the woman who brings the Word of God into the world. It denotes her unique place in salvation history, an "infralapsarian" place. Mary lives within the world that bears the mark of the sin of Adam, but she is "other" than this world. The birth of the Word of God does not carry the stigma of Adam's sin that is attached to all other human births (see Gen 3:15).[96] Mary's virginity, then, signifies her singular role in effecting a new beginning in an old order. Given the difficulty of expressing this odd mix of the new and the old, Rahner warns, a theologian must be prudent in trying to depict Mary's "otherness"—that is, her virgin motherhood—in detail.[97] Prudence does not allow for a scientific explanation of Mary's "otherness," which would be inappropriately detailed.

The point is twofold. First, "virginity" as it applies to Mary cannot be reduced to a purely "biological" or supposedly "objective" analysis of birth and virginity because such analyses rest on questionable prior assumptions. For example, Rahner asks whether "the normal expansion of the genital passages in a completely healthy birth [is] to be considered a breach of 'bodily integrity.'"[98] That is, would the fact that Mary gave birth automatically make her not a

95. VIP 157.
96. VIP 157–60.
97. VIP 160.
98. VIP 161.

virgin? Clinically speaking, maybe so. But one must inquire further as to whether this clinical use of language illuminates or obscures Mary's reality. Second, then, Mary's virginity raises in a concentrated way the question of theological language. Rahner does not wish to rule out the possibility that scientific language could cooperate with theological language so that they could be mutually elucidating. However, his taking of Mitterer to task reveals that Rahner will set scientific language adrift in favor of properly theological language if scientific language attempts to overexplain a mystery of which it can hardly begin to speak.

THE THINKER'S LANGUAGE AND THE THING

Heidegger delivered his first public lecture series after World War II in 1949, in the northern German city of Bremen. He titled the series "Insight into That Which Is." It included a lecture that would eventually become "The Question Concerning Technology," which we examined briefly above. It opened with a lecture called "The Thing." Heidegger would revise this lecture the following year and redeliver it at the Bavarian Academy of Fine Arts. It would be included in his influential collection *Vorgtrage und Aufsätze*.[99]

The lecture is strange, even relative to many of Heidegger's other writings, its focus being a simple jug, and its title entirely unassuming.[100] But the stated topic of the lecture—the thing—implies a thoroughgoing critique of the metaphysical tradition, and mod-

---

99. Martin Heidegger, "The Thing," in *Bremen and Freiburg Lectures: Insight into That Which Is and Basic Principles of Thinking*, trans. Andrew Mitchell (Bloomington: Indiana University Press, 2012), 5–23; Heidegger, *Bremer und Freiburger Vorträge: 1. Einblick in Das Was Ist: Bremer Vorträge, 1949, 2. Grundsätze des Denkens: Freiburger Vorträge 1957: Gesamtausgabe 79*, ed. Petra Jaeger (Frankfurt: Vittorio Klostermann, 1994); Heidegger, "The Thing" in PLT, 163–80, hereafter T. Cf. Heidegger, "*Das Ding*" in *Vorträge und Aufsätze*, 165–84. All subsequent references to "The Thing" will be to the PLT version, largely because it is more familiar to English-speaking readers. Though there are interesting variations between the 1949 lecture and the 1950 revision, they cannot occupy us here.

100. T 164.

ern science and technology as the latest heir of metaphysics' errors. For us, the lecture should hold great interest because it coheres with Heidegger's thinking on language. In fact, it prepares for *Gelassenheit* and *On the Way to Language.* Even more significantly, though, the thing in this lecture plays a strikingly similar role for Heidegger to Mary's in Rahner's *"Virginitas in partu."* I shall prepare to defend this thesis in this section. The next defends it.

Heidegger charges the metaphysical tradition, from Plato and Aristotle through the Romans, the medievals, to Kant and other moderns, with an inability to think a "thing *qua* thing."[101] Throughout the history of metaphysics the thing has always been referred to something else: an idea, an appearance, a human concern, and finally the self-consciousness of the human ego. Heidegger describes Kant as the apex of this tendency, since for Kant even the unknowable "thing in itself" is still referred to the human subject by being "an object that is no object for us."[102] But for Heidegger, the thing is precisely *not* an object: "The thingly character of the thing does not consist in its being a represented object, nor can it be defined in any way in terms of the objectness, the over-againstness, of the object."[103]

Even more damning than his diagnosis of metaphysics are Heidegger's remarks on modern science. He contrasts modern science's "knowledge" of a jug with a proper understanding of a jug as a thing. Modern science holds that a jug is an object that can be filled with air or a liquid. Heidegger notes that this physical description of the jug proves, on the one hand, correct. On the other hand, it severely limits one's thinking and speaking about the jug. Such a limitation pervades scientific knowledge: "Science always encounters only what *its* kind of representation has admitted beforehand as an object

101. T 166.173–75. This particular point of critique arises in slightly modified form fourteen years earlier, in "The Origin of the Work of Art": "The Unpretentious Thing Evades Thought Most Stubbornly" (OWA 31).

102. T 174.

103. T 165.

possible for science."[104] Science's policing of the realm of possibility transforms a wine-filled jug into a "hollow within which liquid spreads." In other words, science destroys the jug. It makes the thing nothing.

Heidegger goes on to state that the annihilation of things effected by modern science precedes the destruction wreaked by the atomic bomb. The bombs that exploded over Hiroshima and Nagasaki are "only the grossest of all gross confirmations of the long-since-accomplished annihilation of the thing." Likewise, the atomic bomb confirms the "twofold delusion" of modern science: (1) that science is "superior to all other experience in reaching the real" and (2) that even after having undergone scientific investigation, things can remain things, that is, not be objectified. Science destroys everything it touches because it thinks and speaks of things as something they are not. Science does not allow the jug, for instance, to show itself as a jug, because science approaches it with a preconception of a receptacle for liquid.[105]

In contrast to physical science's obfuscation of the jug's character, Heidegger proposes that thinking the jug involves attending to how the jug holds what it holds. This leads to the further question of what it means to hold, and what comes of this holding. If the jug holds wine, it means that it takes in wine and gives it. Heidegger asks in what the giving consists. He finds that the giving is a "poured gift."[106] The jug's very thinghood is this "poured gift." We need not pursue this phrase further—Heidegger continues by developing his idea of the *Geviert* (usually translated "fourfold")—but we must note the importance of it. While science offers the dry description of the jug "receptacle for liquid," Heidegger arrives rather quickly and smoothly at the "poured gift," a depiction utterly inaccessible to science, and a richer one at that, even in its brevity.

Overcoming the annihilation of the thing, Heidegger concludes,

104. T 168, emphasis added.   105. T 168–69.
106. T 169–70.

involves a "step back" from the metaphysical-scientific thinking dominated by the subject who represents objects to itself. This "step back," he teaches, entails "co-responding." The thinking (and hence the language) he advocates allows itself to hear the "appeal" of the world. It answers this "appeal" by letting things in the world be themselves. True thinking opens itself to "things presencing" or "things thinging" (*Dinge dingend*).[107]

MARY, THE THING, AND NONPRODUCTIVE DISCOURSE

Rahner's "*Virginitas in partu*" and Heidegger's "The Thing" bear a striking similarity in their resistance to the strictures of modern scientific thinking and language. Though their topics vary widely, each thinker identifies in his respective topic an example of something that evades science's conceptual apparatus. The complexity of the question of Mary's virginity is too much for modern science—and for modern theology, which, we learned above, Rahner believes has been compromised by its adoption of scientific reasoning. On the other side, the simplicity of the jug outmatches modern science, also. Why? Because modern science (and other discourses dependent upon it), based as it is in the objectifying activity of the modern subject and a fundamental bias toward assertion, demands results. Every moment of thinking and every word must be ordered toward production—whether of an answer or a physical object. For Rahner and Heidegger, Mary and the thing are not best spoken of using productive thinking and language. Nonproductive thinking and language reveal them better.

Mitterer gets no nearer to understanding Mary with his scientific concepts of birth and virginity, though surely he could produce virtually endless caveats to the doctrine of "*virginitas in partu*" from a clinical point of view. The physicist gets no nearer to understanding a jug with his scientific concepts of the states of matter, though

---

107. T 179–80. Heidegger, "Das Ding" 184.

surely he could amass virtually endless data about every last atom of the jug and its contents.

Rahner gets nearer to understanding Mary by allowing her unique personhood to come to light from Scripture and tradition. That said, he circumspectly avoids saying too many details. Heidegger gets nearer to understanding the jug by allowing its pouring forth to manifest itself. That said, his description of the "poured gift" amounts ultimately to the tautology "the thing things." In comparison to the results of their scientific counterparts, Rahner and Heidegger produce virtually nothing.

But is nonproductivity a deficiency? I shall answer first with respect to Rahner. It is not, if we take Rahner's theology of mystery into account. As we observed at length above, God remains incomprehensible even in the beatific vision. This means that from the earthly beginning to the eschatological end the human person is sustained by an ineffable Mystery. The incomprehensibility of God is not a provisional deficiency but an abiding gift. In sum, reality is without a perspicuous, propositional, and productive answer. That is not to say that it is without answer—all questions point to God. Instead, it is to say that the final answer may not be had scientifically. Scientific productivity cannot attain to the sublimity of theological nonproductivity.

With Heidegger answering the question of whether nonproductivity is a deficiency proves more complicated. Heidegger castigates the metaphysical tradition and modern science for their strict drawing of limitations upon thought and language. He offers his nonproductive discourse as a means for overcoming these limitations. He champions responsiveness rather than representation. Nevertheless, the question might be posed as to whether Heidegger limits thinking and saying in a way analogous to the traditions away from which he claims to step. Again, his apriorism of finitude proves a stumbling block. Rahner allows thinking to think and saying to say that the ground of all things grounds them infinitely. Heidegger proscribes infinitude, thus limiting the reality to which he can respond to the earth, sky, divinities, and mortals that make up the world. In this, Heidegger's nonproductive discourse proves deficient.

But Rahner and Heidegger do converge, and resoundingly, in the essays this part has considered. Taken together, they attest to the possibility of a discourse that avoids overhasty predication. This discourse elucidates an aesthetic rapport with reality prior to reality's noetic determination. This discourse is a sublime discourse, in that it effects a mutual elevation of things and their apprehenders, a heightened sense of what things are in themselves. This heightened sensitivity comes with openness to mystery.

RAHNERIAN VERSUS HEIDEGGERIAN OPENNESS

From the note of convergence between Rahner and Heidegger, we must again move to their divergence. The problematic that will occupy us in this final part of the chapter can be phrased as two questions: (1) How do Rahner and Heidegger differ in their inflections of "openness to mystery"? and (2) What are the ramifications of their differences? I shall propose in this part that the difference of openness to mystery between Rahner and Heidegger relates to good and evil. Rahner's openness accedes to absolute goodness. Heidegger's openness sways toward evil.[108] Openness manifests itself through language, and for both Rahner and Heidegger, language is the medium through which we live. A difference of openness defines the difference between the Rahnerian and the Heideggerian ethos.

The Rahner-Heidegger difference might be depicted as the disjunction of two articulations of formlessness. I commented at the end of this chapter's introduction that Rahner's ethos, his version of the sublime, relates to formlessness. The issue of openness in Rahner

---

108. Bret Davis's book on Heidegger and the will deserves a second mention here. Though I will not quote him directly, his extensive, perceptive, and lucid analysis of Heidegger's thoughts on evil greatly clarified my own thought in this part. See Davis, *Heidegger and the Will*, 100–121, 276–304.

and Heidegger likewise implicates formlessness. By "formlessness," I mean that which evades circumscription by a human subject. Rahner's Catholic openness opens toward the formlessness of God, which cannot be said with the perspicacity of human terms and propositions, but to whose goodness human words and actions testify. Heidegger's openness to being upholds being, which cannot be said with the perspicacity of human terms and propositions, but to whose callousness all human words testify. In order to establish this contrast, I must first write of Heidegger, then move on to Rahner, and finally indicate how this contrast yields two competing versions of the sublime.

OPENNESS TO EVIL

Near the end of the "Letter on Humanism," Heidegger presents thinking as the ethos that lets being be. Thinking is "ek-sistence," a venturing forth into being. Heidegger characterizes the "realm" into which the thinker ek-sists as a "clearing." This clearing allows the "upsurge of healing" (*des Heilens*)—a word that Heidegger exploits for its etymological relationship to the holy (*das Heilige*). Heidegger follows these thoughts with a remark that now demands our consideration: "With healing, evil appears all the more in the clearing of being."[109] Why does evil appear "more" than healing? Heidegger does not answer this question. He does not acknowledge it as a question. But the words that follow suggest an answer.

Heidegger relates evil to the negative side of language: the "no." Evil is hidden in being, which in turn conceals "the essential provenance of nihilation." This "nihilation" Heidegger calls the "essence of the nothing." And he contends, "because it thinks being, thinking thinks the nothing."[110] Thinking centers on the nothing, negating beings so it might accede to being. The essence of the nothing is nihilation, and the occurrence of nihilation is evil.[111] At the heart of thinking, then, is evil. It seems that evil appears "more" than

---

109. LH 259–60.   110. LH 261.
111. LH 260.

healing because evil fits more properly with thinking's focus on the nothing. Evil is no longer a question of morality, but of the "malignancy" with which being clears itself.[112]

A year prior to writing the "Letter on Humanism," Heidegger composed an imagined dialogue that he titled "Evening Conversation: In a Prisoner Camp in Russia between a Younger and an Older Man" (1945). This text would not be published until its release in volume 77 of the *Gesamtausgabe* in 1995. The text is relevant to us because of its dual reference to healing and evil, and its replacement of evil from the realm of morality to the center of being.[113] The comments on evil in the "Letter on Humanism" are far surpassed in intensity and suggestiveness by some apposite comments in the "Evening Conversation."

The two interlocutors commence their conversation by referring to the younger man's experience of "something healing." Their brief dialogue on this "healing" leads quickly, as in the "Letter on Humanism," to a fervent discussion about the opposite of healing—"the devastation of the earth and the annihilation of the human essence." They describe this devastation and annihilation as "somehow evil itself." Then, being careful to differentiate this evil from "what is morally bad," they define evil as "the rage of insurgency." They trace the devastation visited upon the world by World War II to this primordial raging.[114]

The idea of evil as *primordial* raging bears great significance here. As the younger and older man present it, evil possesses a power beyond the human capacity "to grasp, much less abolish or even mitigate" it.[115] On the one hand, human actors are utterly passive with

---

112. LH 260: "The essence of evil does not consist in the mere baseness of human action, but rather in the malice of rage." On malignancy, see LH 261.

113. Heidegger, "Evening Conversation," in *Country Path Conversations*, 132–57, at 132–35, 139–40. It is also relevant in that it relates intimately to *Gelassenheit*, which took shape alongside it.

114. Heidegger, "Evening Conversation," 132–34.

115. Heidegger, "Evening Conversation," 134.

respect to evil, which rages where it may. On the other hand, though, Heidegger's conversation partners maintain that the effects of evil's raging can be exacerbated by the human drive for self-realization.[116] Thus Heidegger renders humanity doubly passive with respect to evil: (1) people cannot oppose it, (2) but it can make use of them. This line of thought culminates when the younger man suggests, "For malice, as which the devastation occurs, may very well remain a basic trait of being itself." The older man's reply crystallizes the younger man's thought: "being is in the ground of its essence malicious." The two men agree that thinking this thought constitutes "an awful demand," but they insinuate that it is a necessary step in "thinking what is essential."[117] In order to be a true and noble thinker, one must let this thought occur. But why? Why does Heidegger feel the need in this text and the "Letter on Humanism" to rehabilitate evil, and even to posit it at the center of being, as one of its basic traits — or perhaps its most constitutive trait?

Heidegger's conception of an essential thinking of evil derives from his lectures on Friedrich Schelling's 1809 treatise, *Philosophical Investigations into the Essence of Human Freedom.*[118] Heidegger lectured on the freedom treatise in the summer semester of 1936.[119] It was the last course of Heidegger's that Rahner attended.

Schelling's treatise contains a substantial reflection on evil in conjunction with his attempt to address the problem of theodicy after Kant's destruction of all prior theodicies. Though he indicates in the title of the treatise that *human* freedom will be the focus, the freedom of God, or a metaphysics of freedom proves to be the treatise's main subject. Heidegger does not take as much of an inter-

---

116. Heidegger, "Evening Conversation," 136.

117. Heidegger, "Evening Conversation," 139.

118. Friedrich Schelling, *Philosophical Investigations into the Essence of Human Freedom,* trans. Jeff Love and Johannes Schmidt (Albany, N.Y.: SUNY Press, 2006).

119. The course was later published under Heidegger's direction (1971) and then translated into English. See Martin Heidegger, *Schelling's Treatise on the Essence of Human Freedom,* trans. Joan Stambaugh (Athens: Ohio University Press, 1985), hereafter ST.

est in the question of theodicy as he does in the centrality Schelling affords to evil. According to Heidegger, Schelling raises evil as *the* metaphysical question.[120] Heidegger assigns considerable weight to Schelling's statement, "The real and vital concept [of freedom] is that [it] is the capacity for good and evil."[121] Heidegger repeats this, but elaborates: "Human freedom is not the decidedness for good or evil, but the decidedness for good and evil, or the decidedness for evil and good."[122] The emphasis falls on the *and*. The tendency in analyses of human freedom is to privilege goodness as freedom's proper telos. But human freedom comes to light, Heidegger argues with Schelling as his proxy, only when one keeps an eye on evil, too.

Heidegger goes even further than placing good and evil on par. He states, "[E]ven in the terror of evil an essential revelation occurs."[123] This remark is a direct and important predecessor to the passages we examined above. It is a short leap from saying that the terror of evil occasions an essential revelation to positing evil as a basic trait of being. If being is the mystery for which human existence must be open, and being is at its heart evil, then openness to mystery is openness to evil. Again one must ask, why would Heidegger wish to hold this position? Why does Heidegger deem the language of evil to be illuminating for his account of being? Before answering these questions, let us consider some Rahnerian texts that relate to evil, keeping in mind that Rahner witnessed Heidegger's romancing of evil in the lectures on Schelling and freedom.

OPENNESS TO GOOD

Rahner's theology of Mystery is a major crux of his divergence from Heidegger. The closer Rahner comes to the end of his life, the more he emphasizes two points: (1) the perplexity of human exis-

---

120. ST 104.
121. Schelling, *Essence of Human Freedom*, 23.
122. ST 156.
123. ST 157.

tence, particularly as it is generated by an awareness of widespread suffering; and (2) the incomprehensibility of God. In two late texts, "The Human Question of Meaning in the Face of the Absolute Mystery of God" (1977) and "Why Does God Allow Us to Suffer?" (1980), he relates both points to each other and to the question of theodicy.[124]

The "Human Question of Meaning" lecture calls into question any "apologetical theodicy of the terrible course of world events and the horror of the history of humanity" that asserts "quickly and unctuously" that the meaning of it all will become blindingly clear in heaven.[125] Given our prior consideration of Rahner's view that God remains incomprehensible in the beatific vision, we can surmise why Rahner would criticize such a theodicy. It is wrongheaded in at least three ways: first, in its view of the beatific vision; second, in its aspiration to construct an all-encompassing, perspicuous theory of everything—including horrors that evade explanation; and third, in its pretension to employ God as a term in this overarching theory. This last point bothers Rahner most. He understands the human tendency to view God as an answer to all questions of meaning, but he points out that this view of God cannot be accepted, either.[126] God is more than the glue that holds our propositions neatly together.

Rahner confronts the problem of conceiving of God as the

124. Karl Rahner, "The Human Question of Meaning in the Face of the Absolute Mystery of God," in TI 18.89–103; Rahner, "Why Does God Allow Us to Suffer?" in TI 19.194–208; cf. Rahner, "The Question of Meaning as a Question of God," in TI 21.196–207. As Johann Baptist Metz notes, Rahner only infrequently pronounces on the theodicy question. Though Metz is often seen as criticizing his teacher on this count, his most definitive statement on Rahner and theodicy in a 1994 article evaluates Rahner's reticence positively. Metz associates it with Rahner's "fundamental theological respect for the suffering and the history of suffering of humanity." It does not stem from a callous, bourgeois disregard for suffering. See Johann Baptist Metz, "Karl Rahner's Struggle for the Theological Dignity of Humankind," in *A Passion for God: The Mystical-Political Dimension of Christianity*, trans. J. Matthew Ashley (New York: Paulist Press, 1998), 107–20, at 116.

125. Rahner, "Human Question of Meaning," 95.

126. Rahner, "Human Question of Meaning," 93.

transparent answer to all questions with the classical doctrine of God's incomprehensibility. Though for some people it may be dissatisfying to avoid a theoretical theodicy, Rahner indicates that likewise one cannot be satisfied with an idea of God who fits neatly into human calculations. He uses a metaphor from business: "[God] simply cannot be regarded as the last item in our bookkeeping bringing out the meaning of the whole series of our accounts."[127] Reducing God to the final line of a balance sheet would serve merely subjective ends. Rahner rejects this possibility.

But if God remains incomprehensible, and cannot help us to make immediate sense of the problem of evil and suffering, then the danger remains that one might regard God as standing callously above the historical fray. For this reason, Rahner clarifies that a theology that emphasizes God's incomprehensibility must distinguish between God's incomprehensibility as "beatifying" or "annihilating." The theologian must pose the question of whether God's incomprehensibility "brings happiness" or expresses "the empty absurdity of existence."[128] And then, the theologian must choose. She cannot leave this point undecided. This is so because Christianity proclaims "a definitive victory of God's grace," which means salvation rather than perdition, the triumph of goodness rather than evil. God's incomprehensibility is not indistinct and undecided, because God has communicated God's decision and made it effective in Jesus Christ.

This may sound like Rahner's own theodicy, which avoids the pitfalls of traditional theoretical theodicy while succumbing to other, more subtle traps. For instance, Rahner's connection of the incomprehensibility of suffering to God's incomprehensibility in "Why Does God Allow Us to Suffer?" is, on the face of it, rather unsettling. He writes, "The incomprehensibility of suffering is part of the incomprehensibility of God."[129] Here it may sound as if Rahner

---

127. Rahner, "Human Question of Meaning," 102.
128. Rahner, "Human Question of Meaning," 101–2.
129. Rahner, "Why Does God Allow Us to Suffer?" 206.

makes a move akin to Heidegger's retrojection of evil into being. Has Rahner done this? I cannot answer this question directly, but only by way of an example from earlier in the text. Rahner contrasts his "theistic" approach to the question of evil from those of the "convinced atheist" and a "skeptical positivist": "For these, what we call 'evil' ... could not by any means arouse that protest which the theist in particular raises against suffering in the name of an infinitely good God."[130] Those who do not allow God into their thinking will allow suffering and evil. Put otherwise, they exercise a certain *Gelassenheit* toward suffering and evil. They let suffering and evil be. But thinkers like Rahner who allow God into thinking meet suffering and evil with protest. For Rahner, a great difference obtains between the person who would allow suffering and evil, and the person who would protest against them. The former person despairs. The latter hopes.

Rahner's connection of suffering's incomprehensibility with God's incomprehensibility is, in effect, a *reductio in mysterium*. Suffering, like all parts of creation, finds its proper place only when it leads back to the mystery of God. This is not to say that Rahner calls suffering good or ultimately redemptive because it relates to God. Nor is it to say that Rahner posits primordial maliciousness in God, making God into a font of suffering. Nor, finally, is it to say that Rahner dismisses suffering. As Metz argues, Rahner never relinquishes his recognition of the unmasterable negativity of suffering.[131] But it is to say that Rahner remains open to the goodness of God, even in the face of suffering.

This openness to the good is an ascetical act of thought and language. Rahner resists the temptation to primordialize suffering. He refuses to open himself to evil. Rahner opens himself to the victory of grace, whereby God dis-closes the evil of the world.

---

130. Rahner, "Why Does God Allow Us to Suffer?" 197.
131. See Metz, "Karl Rahner's Struggle," 118–19.

REPOSING THE QUESTION OF ETHOS

In chapter two I contrasted Rahner and Heidegger with respect to ethos. The reader should recall the difference we discovered between Rahner's priest and Heidegger's priest of Dionysos. It came down to the disparity between a form of life centering on God's offer of salvation to all people and a form of life centering on being's dispensation of a unique destiny on one people. I contended that the Rahnerian, Catholic sublime allows for a greater scope of thinking, and thus a greater manifestation of being, than the Heideggerian sublime. The ethos that each thinker espouses illustrates this. This divergence of ethos stems, I have continually argued, from Heidegger's apriorism of finitude and Rahner's eschewing of any such apriorism.

The present chapter brings us back to the question of ethos, and to the implications of Heidegger's apriorism of finitude. We must recall that Heidegger's apriorism of finitude has a strategic purpose: it contributes to the defeat of the omnicompetent modern subject by highlighting human existence's noetic and aesthetic limits. Now we must revise our account of the apriorism of finitude to include a radical element that we had not previously considered: Heidegger's affinity for evil.

I have already given examples of this, but I shall adduce another. In *Contributions to Philosophy* (written 1936–1938, first published 1989), a work that will command our attention in chapter five, Heidegger contends that the end of the dominance of metaphysics must come by devastation, presumably by the power of a primordial malice and rage: "Only after enormous ruinings and downfalls of beings do those beings which are already pressured into machination and live-experience and rigidified into non-beings yield to be-ing [*Seyn*] and thus to truth."[132] He heralds a new age beyond metaphys-

---

132. Heidegger, *Contributions to Philosophy*, 170.

ics, beyond the mastery of modern, subjectivist reason, and beyond the machinations of technology and late-modern business. He callously prophesies the cost of this passing to the new age. The ruin and downfall of beings are mere collateral damage, resulting from the malicious autodestruction of the technological epoch. Beings, whatever they be, mean nothing. Heidegger's thinking on language, which culminates in his advocacy of *Gelassenheit,* leads to this conclusion. This conclusion is the logical end of his apriorism of finitude.

This conclusion is a decision about ethos. Heidegger confronts the uncontrollability—the formlessness—of modern technology with a form of life that lets technology deploy itself however it may. He extricates himself from modern subjectivism's pretension to control everything by relinquishing control of anything, by submitting aimlessly to the destructive whims of metaphysics' ultimate epoch. In the absence of a loving God and in the presence of malicious and raging being, he leaves beings to fend for themselves. Sublimity lies in the thrill of standing by while being abandons beings.

Sublimity means something different for Rahner. In prior chapters I have explicated Rahner's twofold resistance of Heidegger with the *Vorgriff* and the Cross. The *Vorgriff* reaches beyond Heidegger's apriorism of finitude by going toward God in the infinite scope of the imagination. This infinite stretching toward God accords with dying to the world. The nexus of *Vorgriff* and Cross proves helpful here as we further distinguish the Rahnerian from the Heideggerian ethos. At its heart, Rahner's view of reality looks something like Heidegger's, since both thinkers attest to the formlessness or namelessness of the sustaining ground. But the *Vorgriff* and the Cross help illustrate a gap between the Rahnerian and the Heideggerian views of formlessness. If being's formlessness proves destructive in Heidegger, God's "namelessness" and "pathlessness" in Rahner proves redemptive.

Jesus models this form of life. Jesus the Son, whose life was subtended by the Holy Spirit who moved through him (cf. *Vorgriff*), and whose life ended with a death to the world on the Cross, was raised—not annihilated—by the incomprehensible and formless Mystery. Rahner exhorts his listeners in a 1976 lecture:

> If we love Jesus, quite personally and directly, if in our love we allow his life and his fate to become the internal form and entelechy of our own life, then we learn that he is the way, the truth, and the life, that he leads us to the Father, that we may and can call the incomprehensible God Father despite his namelessness, that God's namelessness and pathlessness can be our home, bringing us not to extinction, but eternal life.[133]

Instead of adopting a disposition of fascination with the malice of annihilation, Rahner's Catholic sublime follows Jesus in embracing an attitude of wonder at the power of reconciliation. Instead of condemning all things by feigning to affirm them while denying them any meaning, Rahner's Catholic sublime blesses all things by truly affirming God's merciful intention to grant them eternal significance by gathering them to God's self. The entelechy of Jesus' life is a *reductio in mysterium,* a dive into the mystery of God. So is the entelechy of the Catholic ethos, the Catholic sublime.

---

133. Karl Rahner, "What Does It Mean Today to Believe in Jesus Christ?" in TI 18.143–56, at 156.

5 RAHNER'S APOCALYPSE

THIS FIFTH and final chapter further elaborates Rahner's version of the sublime by relating it to the theology of history. Rahner's sublime has its roots in his aesthetics in *Geist in Welt*. His understanding of history reflects this aesthetic perspective. The amplification of his aesthetics yields his sublime. His theology of history, likewise amplified, is apocalyptic. These statements demand a preliminary explanation.

In *Geist in Welt*, Rahner presents the human imagination as opened from within by God, who moves through it. In his later theology of history, Rahner contends that history is propelled from within by God, who draws it toward its end in the beatific vision. The imagination in *Geist in Welt* is an occasion for the revelation of absolute being, that is, God. In Rahner's theology of history, history is a massive revelation of God, in its individual facets and as a whole. God interprets all of history, and all of history—though in halting, ineffective, and even grossly deficient ways—reveals God. Given its pronounced index of revelation, or *apocalypsis*, I argue that Rahner's theology of history is apocalyptic.

This chapter characterizes Rahner's theology of history as apocalyptic for three reasons: (1) doing so provides a more generative reading of Rahner than prior accounts of his writings in theology of history and eschatology, which file these writings under his *"anthropologische Wende"*;[1] (2) Christian apocalyptic is, I shall argue, the optimal way of defeating Heidegger's project of thinking the "history of being," which is a false apocalypse; and (3) apocalyptic is a sublime discourse, broad enough and open enough to express the Catholic ethos.

Part one of the chapter introduces Rahner's theology of history by relating his view of history to his aesthetics, with regard to God's movement through the imagination, the twofoldness of history, and the Cross as history's decisive turning point. Part two discusses in depth a topic that I have already treated, but not as concertedly as I do in this chapter: Heidegger's "history of being." I present Heidegger's rendering of ancient Greek philosophy as being's protology, and Nietzsche as being's eschatology. Then I interpret his book *Contributions to Philosophy* as a comprehensive presentation of his view of being's history. Finally, I interrogate how he casts himself as the turning point of being's history, and as an apocalyptic seer.[2] Part three is an important methodological portion of the chapter,

1. The most recent significant example is Peter Phan, "Eschatology," in *The Cambridge Companion to Karl Rahner*, 174–92; see also Phan, *Eternity in Time: A Study of Karl Rahner's Eschatology* (Cranbury, N.J.: Associate University Presses, 1988), which throughout reads Rahner as a theologian of an "anthropological" or "subjective" turn.

2. I shall argue in more detail below for the ascription of "apocalyptic" to Heidegger's thought, though this ascription has become so commonplace in the literature that one need not necessarily argue for it. This is largely because of Jacques Derrida's work on Heidegger. See, among other texts, Jacques Derrida, "On a Newly Arisen Apocalyptic Tone in Philosophy," in *Raising the Tone of Philosophy: Late Essays by Immanuel Kant and Transformative Critique by Jacques Derrida,* trans. John Leavey Jr., ed. Peter Fenves (Baltimore, Md.: Johns Hopkins University Press, 1993), 117–72, at 145–46, 149, 165–66; and Derrida, *Of Spirit: Heidegger and the Question*, trans. Geoffrey Bennington and Rachel Bowlby (Chicago: University of Chicago Press, 1991), passim. Now that *Contributions to Philosophy* has been named as a focal text, I can preface my argument with another commentator's estimation of that text, and thus of Heidegger. Richard Polt observes of *Contributions,* "It is a book saturated with emergency, drunk on apocalypse"; see Polt, *The Emergency of Being: On Heidegger's* Contributions to Philosophy (Ithaca, N.Y.: Cornell University Press, 2006), 254. The difference between Polt and me is that he regards *Contributions* negatively because of its apocalyptic quotient, while I deem this to be the book's positive feature—even if Heidegger's apocalyptic ends up being insufficient in comparison with Rahner's.

because it makes the case for Rahner as an apocalyptic theologian. I do so even though Rahner has been interpreted as being theologically allergic to apocalyptic. Thus, in the face of difficulty, I work to set up hermeneutical conditions for calling Rahner an apocalyptic theologian. Part four concludes the chapter, and this book-length treatment of Rahner's dual resistance of modern subjectivism and Heidegger, by indicating how Rahner overcomes both apocalyptically. He defeats the limits and strictures of both by holding open a universal field of revelation, which concerts with the ethos of Catholicism.

RAHNER'S THEOLOGY OF HISTORY

Of all the ideas that Rahner and Heidegger share, perhaps one proves paramount: history is revelatory.[3] For Heidegger, history reveals being (or conceals it, with concealment as a modality of revealing). For Rahner, the same might be said, if one understands being as we have throughout this book, at the intersection of philosophy and theology. Absolute being, when it fully and freely manifests itself, does so as God. From the philosophical point of view expounded in *Geist in Welt,* which discusses "world" as an arena for God's manifestation, one could infer that history reveals God as the sustaining ground of history. And from a theological point of view that coheres with and yet elaborates the philosophical viewpoint, the sustaining ground of history manifests itself not just as an empty possibility for history in general, but as the ground of an actual history that culminates in the self-revelation of being as the God of Jesus Christ. This part of the chapter aims to make sense of this last sentence.

---

3. Thomas O'Meara makes a suggestion to this effect: "If truth is a disclosure process of aspects of Being, salvation history could be understood as an expanded form of the history of Being in the realm of grace"; see O'Meara, *God in the World,* 33n40. That said, most treatments of the Rahner-Heidegger relationship regarding history stop at a brief comparison of the two on the topic of death. While this is by no means a specious comparison, it is only a preliminary one.

Toward this end, we must read and interpret some of Rahner's extensive writings on history.[4] I commence by making explicit a connection between Rahner's aesthetics and his view of history. This orients a discussion of "salvation/sacred" and "world/profane" history in Rahner's thinking from the early 1960s through the early 1980s, and of his location of the turning point of history in the Cross of Jesus Christ. Since this latter point has been insufficiently treated in prior Rahner scholarship, here I discuss it at length.

HISTORY AND RAHNER'S AESTHETICS

This section contends that the aesthetic contribution that we identified in Rahner's metaphysics of knowledge from *Geist in Welt* can help us to make sense in a fresh way of Rahner's later theology of history. Rahner's aesthetics in *Geist in Welt* specifies the philosophical view of God in two ways. First, God is figured as the sustaining ground (*tragende Grund*) of the world. Second, this sustaining ground comes exemplarily to light in the human imagination, via the *Vorgriff*, which is an anticipatory sense of God. This view of God applies first and foremost to human knowledge, since in *Geist in Welt* Rahner offers a metaphysics of knowledge. The idea of God may be extended to relate to history, if one concedes the point that history is discovered primarily (perhaps exclusively) by human apprehension of it. This section will have, then, to establish how Rahner expands his metaphysical account of human knowledge to a metalevel reflection on history.

4. On history specifically, see especially Rahner, "The History of the World and Salvation History," in TI 5, 97–114, hereafter HWSH; Rahner, "The Theological Problems Entailed in the Idea of a 'New Earth,'" in TI 10, 260–72, hereafter "New Earth"; Rahner, "Immanent and Transcendent Consummation of the World," in TI 10, 273–89; Rahner, "Theological Observations on the Concept of Time," in TI 11, 288–308; Rahner, "Profane History and Salvation History," in TI 21, 3–15. On the future, see especially Rahner, "A Fragmentary Aspect of a Theological Evaluation of the Concept of the Future," in TI 10, 235–41; Rahner, "On the Theology of Hope," in TI 10, 242–59; Rahner, "The Question of the Future," in TI 12, 181–201; and Rahner, "The Inexhaustible Transcendence of God and Our Concern for the Future," in TI 20, 173–86. To these writings I shall add some more below.

Rahner's contribution to theological aesthetics consists in a nuanced description of the openness of human subjectivity—an openness to which the modern subject cannot attain, and short of which Heidegger's revision of subjectivity falls. Openness in Rahner's case has at least five meanings: (1) the openness of sensibility to the intellect; (2) the openness of the intellect to sensibility; (3) the openness of the imagination as the vertex at which sensibility and intellect meet; (4) the openness of human subjectivity toward "another," be it a particular sensible object, the world in general, or intelligible objects that can be apprehended by analogy with sensible apprehension (this includes intersubjectivity); and (5) the paradigmatic openness of human subjectivity beyond itself to the God who sustains it. In short, openness is the key to Rahner's aesthetics.

Two of Rahner's essays lie at the point of convergence between his "early" metaphysics of knowledge and his theology of history: "The Unity of Spirit and Matter in the Christian Understanding of Faith" (1963) and "The Body in the Order of Salvation" (1967).[5] Both of these essays are commonly regarded as treating mainly of theological anthropology. This is a limited reading of the essays. The following reflections should enrich the interpretation of these texts, and should support my claim that Rahner's "early" aesthetics bears out in his "later" theology of history. Aesthetics and theology of history converge because they both center on openness.

The "Unity" essay answers a provocation from contemporary "world-wide materialism, which disputes the foundation of the Christian faith."[6] Rahner takes it that the main concern of materialists is that Christianity, with its devotion to spirit, axiomatically denigrates matter and rejects the world. Hence Rahner's strategy of answering materialism's provocation with an insistence upon the *unity* of spirit and matter in Christian faith. He supposes early in

---

5. Karl Rahner, "The Unity of Spirit and Matter in the Christian Understanding of Faith," in TI 6, 153–77; Rahner, "The Body in the Order of Salvation," in TI 17, 71–89.
6. Rahner, "Unity," 153.

the essay that skittish Christians will regard his careful resistance of materialism as an untoward "concession to the opponent."[7] Indeed, this would eventually happen, but not in the way Rahner assumed it would. While he fears being misunderstood as a materialist, recent commentators, especially Burke, suspect Rahner of a creeping "philosophical monism,"[8] where spirit takes all. If one reads Rahner carefully, though, one finds a nuanced perspective on spirit and matter that refuses to relinquish either—and that grows fruitfully out of his aesthetics in *Geist in Welt.*

In this way, Rahner contributes vitally to Christian theology of history. He devotes several pages to this topic.[9] He observes that Christianity is gravely misapprehended if one believes that it espouses a dualism of spirit and matter. Christianity does not, for instance, regard the world as the purely material stage on which the history of human spirit transpires. Rahner admits that "the basic Christian assessment regarding the unity of the history of matter and spirit has not yet been thought through in all its aspects," but even so he deems it a commonplace that Christians agree that there is a historical unity of matter and spirit.[10]

He adduces two major dogmatic examples to defend this claim. First, even at its most speculative limit, where Christian doctrine seems to envision a spirit world free from matter, that is, with angels, still Christianity affirms a relationship between spirit and matter. As we saw in chapter 3, Rahner disallows that Christianity discount any relation between angels and the material world. Here again he insists that angels be regarded as "cosmic powers of the order of nature and its history."[11] Second, the Christian doctrine of salvation remains rooted in the Old Testament writings, where no dualism obtains between matter and spirit. Old Testament nondualism guides the Christian understanding of salvation history, which

---

7. Rahner, "Unity," 154.
9. Rahner, "Unity," 157–61.
11. Rahner, "Unity," 159.

8. Burke, RR 110.
10. Rahner, "Unity," 158.

never at any point includes an exit of spirit from history. Rahner adds to this a reminder that "the climax of salvation history is not the detachment from the world of man as a spirit in order to come to God, but the descending and irreversible entrance of God into the world, the coming of the divine Logos in the flesh."[12]

This statement recalls the closing page of *Geist in Welt,* which I have flagged as the most hermeneutically determinative page of the entire text. There Rahner indicates that the metaphysics of knowledge he has set forth means to suggest that spirit's openness to world and world's openness to spirit point to the definitive event of this twofold openness in the person of Jesus of Nazareth. Rahner's entire aesthetic perspective begins and ends with Jesus Christ. So too with his theology of history, which is subtended by his thinking of the unity of spirit and matter, which stems from Jesus Christ.

One more paragraph from the "Unity" essay demands our attention. It comes from the second half of the essay, where Rahner reflects systematically on the data of faith he presented in the first half. I shall quote Rahner at length, and then expose his words:

Matter is, therefore, the openness and the bringing-itself-to-appear of the personal spirit in the finite world and hence is from its very origin related to the spirit, is a moment in the spirit.... This is not meant in any way to turn matter idealistically into spirit, for by the same statements the spirit is equally originally "materialized." It comes to be seen, rather, that spirit and matter cannot, like any two objects of our individual experience, be thought of as existing side by side in alien disparateness from one another.[13]

We can detect echoes here of *Geist in Welt.* Matter is figured as openness to spirit's self-realization, and indeed matter is called an "inner moment" of spirit. This hearkens back to the theory of the emanation of matter from spirit that we examined earlier in the book. Lest Rahner be misread, though, as "spiritualizing" matter,

12. Rahner, "Unity," 160.
13. Rahner, "Unity," 170–71.

he clarifies that matter's openness to spirit likewise conditions spirit, which is "materialized." Spirit is depicted as opened from within to encounter matter. Finally, taking a swipe at modern subjectivist-objectivism, Rahner rejects any view of spirit and matter as discrete objects. Spirit and matter are not alien to one another. They always coinhere.

Interestingly, Rahner makes these remarks as part of a detailed discussion of the Incarnation of the Logos. He cites a maxim from Augustine: "the creation of what is . . . 'assumed' is only a movement in the 'coming-to-appear' of the Logos in his own being, a moment in his self-expression projected into the dimension of the finite."[14] This maxim indicates that the Incarnation ought not to be conceived of as the unification of two preexisting, disparate—objective—elements. Instead, the Incarnation occurs as coinherence: the entrance into history of the Logos (spirit) *as* the appearance of the flesh (matter) the Logos assumes. This proves instructive for the Christian understanding of created spirit and matter. If the Incarnation, as the perfection of creation, happens as an event of spiritual-material coinherence, then creation generally ought to be seen as likewise coinherent.

"The Body in the Order of Salvation" continues the line of thought prosecuted in "Unity," while sharpening the focus to soteriology. This essay bears distinct mention because of Rahner's observations on the world and history on the essay's final pages. These pages comprise a section called "Our Reality as Open System."[15] This section proves striking because of a significant, if slight, advance that Rahner makes on his thinking of spirit and matter. He enlists the help of modern physics to approach the question of where one body ends and another begins. Modern physics helpfully obscures the boundaries between bodies. Having observed this, Rah-

---

14. Rahner, "Unity," 170.
15. Rahner, "Body," 87–89. The next two quotes are from this section. Also noteworthy given my argument in the current section is Rahner's footnote to *Geist in Welt* earlier in the essay: 82n19.

ner proposes that the world be conceived of as "one total physical existence," which is "the common space which makes intercommunication between spiritual subjects possible from the start." Seeing materiality as a common space highlights the passivity of the human subject, as a counterweight to a view that holds the world out to be a stage on which discrete actors play out their individual roles. Rahner writes, "Since everyone, as a spiritual person, lives essentially in the space of existence that is common to all, into which he continually acts—and acts into the whole—and from which he continually receives, he is continually active and continually passive."[16] This insight has an important theological upshot. It relates to the theology of history. Christian theologies of history must, in keeping with scriptural evidence, conclude with an end-time transfiguration: a new earth and a new heaven.[17] This transfiguration is a transformation of the common space. Individual subjects who live within this common space are saved or damned based on their disposition toward it. Christianity demands a choice with respect to the whole of history.

Rahner adds in a footnote: "This one, all-embracing history is one of Christianity's essential features. To use a traditional term, it may be described as 'catholic.'"[18] The aesthetic interplay of human passivity (matter) and activity (spirit) is not just of noetic concern, but is of import for the theology of history. And this theology of history raises the question of catholicity—the breadth of the Christian ethos. Thus I have established how Rahner's aesthetics and his theology of history, like matter and spirit, coinhere; and how this coinherence angles toward the Catholic sublime.

16. Rahner, "Body," 88.
17. As I shall point out again later on, one ought not to ignore that this phrase, "new earth and new heaven," derives from New Testament apocalyptic literature.
18. Rahner, "Body," 88n21.

TWOFOLD HISTORY

While the last section narrated how Rahner defines history as spirit and matter working in unity, this section must describe the distinction that Rahner draws between two types of history: world history and salvation history. One might be tempted to deem the former as more nearly material and the latter more nearly spiritual, due to the relative distance of the former from God and the relative proximity of the latter to God. Rahner does not condone this, though. The distinction is a complex one, because Rahner refuses to reinscribe the sharp differention between the profane and the sacred that he learned in his neo-Scholastic theological training.[19] But also he does not wish to elide the generality of world history and the particularity of salvation history. The subtle distinctions he articulates flow from his conviction that God reveals Godself as both the sustainer of the whole creation, thus all of history, *and* the savior and sanctifier who heals and elevates creation in a particular way.

Rahner's chief text on the theology of history is "The History of the World and Salvation History" (1962). The text prosecutes three main theses: (1) "Salvation history takes place within the history of this world"; (2) "Salvation history is distinct from profane history"; (3) "Salvation history explains profane history."[20] The first two theses are inseparable reciprocals. The third thesis explicates the second.

The first thesis indicates the unity of salvation history and world-profane history. Concrete history with which people are normally faced shows itself primarily as profane history, that is,, a world history that "cannot of its nature be interpreted with absolute certainty in questions regarding what part of it is salvation and what damnation."[21] It is not clear, then, what aspect of world-profane history can be called salvation history. But at the same time, the Chris-

---

19. Most famous with regard to this topic is the 1950 essay, Karl Rahner, "Concerning the Relationship between Nature and Grace," in TI 1, 297–317.

20. HWSH 97, 100, 109.   21. HWSH 99, cf. 101.

tian faith embraces world history as salvific, since the "history of this world has become transparent in regard to salvation (in a way which cannot be surpassed in this world) through the Christ-event in Jesus of Nazareth."[22] Thus, on the one hand, Rahner emphasizes the indistinctness of world-profane history and salvation history in the normal human perception of them.

But on the other hand, Rahner never reneges on the Christian conviction that world-profane history and salvation history are not precisely the same. In fact, they are vastly different. The difference lies in God's judgment. Salvation history is world-profane history that has been judged by God.[23] Rahner explains further,

Salvation history and profane history are distinct because God has interpreted part of this profane and otherwise ambiguous history by his word (which is a constitutive element of salvation history itself), by giving it a saving or damning character. Thus he has distinguished this particular part of the one history from the rest of history and has made it the actual, official, and explicit history of salvation.[24]

He follows this quote by laying out a complex conceptual apparatus that includes two major aspects: (1) the necessity of an event of revelation to be interpreted by words, and (2) the division of salvation history into two types: general and official-special. Despite the significance of these ideas, the main idea here—and the one that perhaps has been entirely ignored by prior commentators—is God's initiative in distinguishing between the sacred and the profane. This idea is so important because Rahner is often misread, by his supporters and critics alike, of unduly collapsing the distinction between the sacred and the profane, and proclaiming all the world sacred. If Rahner's less-than-precise précis of his theology of history in the fifth chapter of *Foundations* has contributed to this,[25] a close reading of the closing pages of the essay we have been examining should set the record right.

22. HWSH 100. 23. HWSH 101.
24. HWSH 106. 25. Rahner, *Foundations*, 138–75.

The third thesis, "salvation history explains profane history," means three things. All of them express something negative about profane history. First, salvation history's explanation reveals the history of the world as "undeified": "History is not the history of God himself—a theogony—and so does not find its ultimate basis in itself and is not self-explanatory."[26] World history stands in need of a salvation that comes from elsewhere—Rahner maintains this position even though he takes care to avoid an extrinsicist view of salvation and revelation as divine intervention.[27] Salvation history reveals profane history as insufficient.

Second, "[s]alvation history interprets the history of the world as something antagonistic and veiled. Precisely because salvation is not simply the immanent fruit of profane history, Christianity is skeptical towards divine history." Profane history proceeds in a series of conflicts and antitheses that will never yield a perpetual peace. Instead, the world "will always be a land of death and darkness."[28] Salvation history unveils profane history as disastrous.

Third, the Christian interpretation "depotentiates" (*depotenzierte*) profane history. Salvation history relativizes profane history, takes from it its power. Rahner clarifies that he is not advocating a flight from the world, in the sense of a private pursuit of salvation somehow separate from profane history. He remains consistent with texts we have already examined. He regards such a flight as impossible. He likewise remains consistent, though, in maintaining that Christians have to look at profane history as relativized by Christ: "Neither death nor life, neither things present nor future possibilities are the ultimate, the finally significant, that which is salvation." Christ outmodes history and all its possibilities. Salvation history unmasks profane history as ultimately valueless.[29]

---

26. HWSH 110.
27. Cf. Karl Rahner, "Revelation," in *Encyclopedia of Theology*, 1460–66, at 1461.
28. HWSH 111–12.
29. HWSH 112.

These statements from Rahner do not cohere well with the conventional reading of him as the profligate baptizer of all history. But these statements are Rahner's. They must be taken into account in order for more recognizable Rahnerian teachings to be understood properly. For example:

the religious element is everywhere the meaning and root of history and is never merely the most sublime flower of a merely human culture which is the word of men; it is already propelled from within by God-effected grace and co-determined from within by the proper, general salvation history.[30]

In light of the passages we have just observed, we cannot understand this proclamation of the omnipresence of the "religious element" as a philosophical monist's celebration of the disappearance of history's distinctions. It is not an idealist's baptism of all history with absolute spirit. It is a faithful theologian's recognition of profane history's need to be baptized, and of God's gracious and merciful baptism of it.

And when we read in a later article (1982) that "the meaning of history lies in a peculiarly dialectic way beyond history, yet at the same time in history,"[31] we need not worry that Rahner has fallen prey to idealism yet again. Instead, he is expressing the theological aesthetic that I have been presenting since chapter 1 of this book, where the Spirit of God moves concretely through the world, and where the world—when judged by God—is the arena for Christ's effecting of salvation.

HISTORY AND THE CROSS

With this invocation of Christ effecting the world's salvation, we come to the Cross. At several points in this book I have emphasized the importance of the Cross of Christ for Rahner, often in conjunction with my discussions of Rahner's retrievals of Ignatius

30. HWSH 108.
31. Rahner, "Profane History and Salvation History," 9.

Loyola. I have drawn a connection between two ways that Rahner insists that human persons encounter the "beyond" of history: the Spirit's movement in the *Vorgriff*, and a death to self modeled on the death of Christ on the Cross. This may seem like an artificial exercise designed to oppose Rahner's critics, who so often paint him as a theologian unconcerned with the Cross, and solely concerned with an idealism centering on the *Vorgriff*. Instead, I have insisted on the import of the Cross for Rahner because, simply, *it is actually important for him*. Furthermore, Rahner's thoughts on the Cross differentiate him from modern subjectivism and from Heidegger.

This section argues that Rahner views the Cross as the center of history. Jesus' death is not an unfortunate accessory to the triumph of the Incarnation.[32] Instead, the Cross makes history what it is, and opens history beyond what it is. The Cross accomplishes this inside history: tangibly, palpably, dramatically—historically.

In a vitally important passage in his much-discussed yet often misread text, *On the Theology of Death* (1961), Rahner makes a series of statements that may strike his critics as very un-Rahnerian. He contends that the Cross of Christ is the center of history and the axis of the world. Rahner remarks, "[T]he world as a whole and as the scene of personal human actions has become different from what it would have been had Christ not died." In fact, Christ's death reorders the whole cosmos. Rahner acknowledges the apparent peculiarity of this claim, and that it might even make committed Christians uncomfortable. But he stipulates that this would not be so were people to view history and the cosmos differently:

32. Rahner, "Body in the Order of Salvation," 76: "When we say that we have been redeemed through the blood of Christ, through Christ's death, through his sufferings on the cross, then we must not mean by this that a spiritual event of love and obedience was unfortunately or strangely accompanied by rather unpleasant circumstances.... The statement that we have been redeemed through the death of this Son of God, and through the shedding of his blood (i.e., a bodily event) is the concrete, bodily form of what we express in abstract and formalized terms, as it were, when we merely say that we have been redeemed through the Son's obedience and love, and his readiness to sacrifice himself."

The thought that Christ, in his life and death, belongs to the innermost reality of the world, would be less alien to us if we were not so prone to identify the world with the handful of crude and superficial data gathered from everyday sense-experience, or if we were better able to realize how profound, mysterious and filled with spiritual realities this world is, and how everyone draws life from the whole of the universe, which extends to such measureless depths. When the vessel of his body was shattered in death, Christ was poured out over all the cosmos; he became actually, in his very humanity, what he had always been by his dignity, the heart of the universe, the innermost center of creation.[33]

This way of thinking about the Cross of Christ breaks with any type of thinking (namely, modern subjectivism or Heideggerianism) that would interpret world history as merely finite, and thus as admitting of merely finite transformation. The Cross of Christ alters the very constitution of world-historical reality. We can specify how with reference to a few more of Rahner's essays.

Rahner is, quite rightly, regarded as a great influence on and champion of the Second Vatican Council. Commentators tend to ignore, though, the multiple ways in which Rahner attempted in the postconciliar years to address theological questions that were not answered with requisite clarity by the council's documents. The 1975 lecture, "The Death of Jesus and the Closure of Revelation," provides such a supplement to Vatican II's Constitution on Divine Revelation, *Dei Verbum*.[34]

Rahner clarifies the council's teaching on the "closure of revelation," its marking of the end-point of God's definitive self-revelation, beyond which there is nothing new revealed. He notes that this Catholic belief presents a problem to modern historical consciousness. The Church holds that revelation properly ended with the

---

33. Rahner, *On the Theology of Death*, 65–66.

34. Karl Rahner, "The Death of Jesus and the Closure of Revelation," in TI 18, 132–42, hereafter DJCR. For a related article on *Dei Verbum*, see Rahner, "On the 'History of Salvation' according to the Second Vatican Council," in TI 16, 191–98.

Christ event, or at the latest with the death of the last apostle—thus many centuries ago. Modern, historically conscious people, then, ask whether our time has any value vis-à-vis this closed revelation. The modern mind prefers to view history as open to the future, rather than hearkening back to a closed past. Rahner, along with the council, remains steadfast in not budging on the idea of revelation's closure, but he writes this 1975 lecture to show how modern people might be swayed to espouse the doctrine of revelation's closure. The Cross is his lecture's anchor point.

Rahner argues for the following thesis: "It is only by the cross of Jesus as such that the unsurpassability of Christian revelation can be and is established; the theology of the cross is an internal constituent of the doctrine of the unsurpassability of the Christian revelation as a whole."[35] Notably, Rahner's thesis transposes the idea of revelation's closure into language of "unsurpassability." This latter word does not have the immediately negative connotation of closure, even if in this case the two words mean roughly the same thing. Rahner uses this word, though, to indicate that that Christian revelation closes with an event of disclosure, whose force and effectiveness cannot be outshone.

The Cross is, for Rahner, doubly disclosive—and necessarily so. The Cross discloses God's unbounded self-offer to the world. It reveals in history the world's opportunity to respond to God's self-giving love. But also, the Cross does not disclose merely an open possibility, an opportunity that the world may or may not take. It reveals in history the world's actual acceptance of the opportunity to respond to God's self-giving love. With his death, a free act of accepting God's promise that coincides with supreme powerlessness, Christ accepts God's self-offer definitively and effectively.[36] Rahner underscores the *efficacy* of God's self-offer as accepted by Christ. Thus the second aspect of the Cross's disclosure proves determinative of the

35. DJCR 136.
36. DJCR 137, 139, 140.

Cross as it relates to the history of revelation. The Cross is the historical event of the actualization of God's self-promise to the world, in the world's affirmative response to this promise. Because of this, the Cross is unsurpassable, as the "disclosing closure of revelation."[37]

Rahner indicates that he aims to persuade modern people to accept the idea of revelation's closure. Conventional readers would assume this to mean that he would portray this teaching as somehow palatable to modern tastes. But he takes the opposite tack. He concludes the article with a paragraph attacking the modern mind's distaste for a closed revelation. Modern people have an "absolute will for boundless freedom," which leads them to believe that they can surpass their ancestors and create an absolutely new future. Rahner points out that "this will of man today is nevertheless continually repudiated and foiled by death." Death defeats any human claim to accede to the pinnacle of history. Rahner sternly reminds modern people of this. But with this admonition he pairs a positive theological statement: the death of *Christ* shows that even though death foils all human projects, one death—which happened long ago—actualized the possibility latent in every human death, that history can be (and has been) "dissolved by God's own act into God's infinite freedom."[38] Christ's Cross closes revelation history, thus all history, because all history after it lives under its sign.

Rahner continues this thought in the late essay, "Profane History and Salvation History" (1982). He explicitly contrasts his view of history with the Enlightenment view, in which history goes on endlessly, becoming more meaningful because more reasonable and autonomous. Against the progressive vision of modernity, Rahner reaffirms that history's highest development has arrived already: "Due to the influence of this Christ-event the theology of history can no longer be seen with the pattern of an ascending development. Rath-

37. DJCR 140.
38. DJCR 142.

er will history present ever new but ultimately equivalent ways for the realization of human development and for the relationship to God."[39] Surely history goes on, but never in the sense that it evolves beyond the definitive closure of revelation in Jesus Christ. As we saw in chapter 3 with Rahner's essay "Christian Humanism," God's revelation in Jesus Christ relativizes all human projects. Here Rahner adds historical backing to this idea. All historical events and "ways" are relativized in the face of the Way.

This relates to subjectivity. The Way of Christ leads the subject outside of herself, into the realm of that which she cannot control. Rahner discusses this divine "leading outside the subject" in a lecture from 1967, "On the Theology of Hope." He frames the discussion in traditional Scholastic terms, presenting faith, hope, and love as the constitutive acts of human subjectivity. He adds that hope is the "original and unifying medium" between faith and love.[40] Hope is the basic modality by which human persons (individually, but more importantly collectively) accept their "orientation toward the incalculability and uncontrollability of God."[41] "Hope" names the act of recognizing and accepting that time opens into eternity, and this world opens to its "beyond." This hope grounds itself, Rahner reports, in the highest historical manifestation of hope in God as the "absolute future": "Christ precisely as *crucified*, and thereby as surrendering himself in the most radical sense to the disposing hand of God." The grace that subtends and enables human subjectivity establishes itself definitively in Christ's death on the Cross, because this death is "the most radical act of hope (into *thy* hands I deliver up my life)."[42]

The definitive moment of history is the definitive moment of human subjectivity being drawn "outwards from self." This mo-

---

39. Rahner, "Profane History and Salvation History," 12.

40. Rahner, "Theology of Hope," 248.

41. Rahner, "Theology of Hope," 256.

42. Rahner, Theology of Hope," 255. Cf. similar remarks in Rahner, "The Body in the Order of Salvation," 75–76.

ment occurs on the Cross. This is the quintessential revelatory moment for Rahner. The Cross sets the standard for human ethos,
because the Cross unveils that all history finds its end in the unfathomable Mystery of God. The Cross of Christ opens history to its
fullest breadth, its catholicity.

HEIDEGGER'S HISTORY OF BEING

The introduction to this book suggested that eventually I would
make understandable how an encounter with Heidegger at Freiburg
helped to initiate Rahner's life-long work of presenting the ethos of
Catholicism. I preliminarily indicated that Rahner's mode of thinking, which at once positively and critically takes into account both
the full breadth and the individual details of Catholic tradition, reflects strikingly Heidegger's wide-ranging and detailed interpretation of the metaphysical tradition. I proposed that Heidegger's diagnosis of the closure of the metaphysical tradition, and his prediction
of a new opening of this tradition beyond itself, likely contributed to
Rahner's attitude toward Catholic tradition.

Heidegger aims to reinvigorate philosophy's stagnant thinking by recurring to the basic question of being. This recurrence involves a review of metaphysics' history, wherein Heidegger discovers being's own history. Rahner enacts a similar strategy, in that
he devotes his career to revitalizing Catholic theology, which had
stagnated under the aegis of Neo-Scholasticism, by rethinking theology's principal questions—history being a major one. This inquiry leads him not so much into a review of Catholic history, but into
an overview of history in the Christian understanding of the faith.
This is what we examined in the last part.

This part presents Heidegger's reinvigoration of the thinking
of being. To understand this, we must understand his conception of
the limits of metaphysics—both in terms of time (early Greeks/late
modernity) and of proximity to being (how thinkers at the extreme
temporal limits of metaphysics lay bare or conceal being). With this

understanding, we can come to recognize why Heidegger is rightly viewed as an apocalypticist.

PROTOLOGY AND ESCHATOLOGY IN HEIDEGGER

Christian theology of history proceeds between two temporal bounds: the beginning of creation, when God made the heavens and the earth (Gen 1:1), and the end of time, when Jesus Christ will come again to judge the living and the dead (Mt 24:31; 1 Thes 4:16–17; 1 Pet 4:17–19; Rev 20:12–15, 22:12). Thus the theology of history has a protology and an eschatology.

There are many ways that Heidegger deforms Christian theology in order to serve his own thinking, yielding not a little danger. For instance, his *Gelassenheit* is a distortion of Christian mystical theology, in particular Meister Eckhart's.[43] Rahner saw this distortion coming decades before *Gelassenheit*, when he characterized Heidegger's thinking as a "secularist negative theology."[44] But more significant—and damning—is Heidegger's history of being, which is a parody of Christian theology of history. It offers an alternative protology, an alternative eschatology, and, I shall contend below, an alternative apocalypse, with Heidegger as an alternative Daniel or John of Patmos. For Heidegger the dawn of the thinking of being in the "early Greeks" replaces the Christian moment of creation, and the last gasp of metaphysics in Nietzsche replaces the end of time and Christ's Second Coming.

Heidegger expresses unequivocally in *Introduction to Metaphysics* his antagonism toward the Christian doctrine of creation. This doctrine proposes an answer to the question of "why there are beings rather than nothing" before the question has even been asked.[45]

---

43. The classic text on the Eckhart-Heidegger relationship is John Caputo, *The Mystical Element in Heidegger's Thought*, rev. ed. (New York: Fordham University Press, 1986); see especially the section "The Danger of Heidegger's Path," 245–54.

44. See my introduction for a short commentary. For this quote, see Rahner, "Unveröffentliche Manuskripte," 446.

45. EM 7–8.

It involves a pernicious entrenchment of the Platonic "chasm" between merely apparent beings and real, supersensuous being. Creatures exist "below" and the Creator abides "above."[46] Thus the doctrine of creation posits two worlds. Heidegger condemns this as an illicit move, because being is finite, and refers to rootedness in *this* world. Furthermore, the Christian belief in creation paves the way for modern calculative thinking. The doctrine of creation reduces being to "being-created." When the Enlightenment calls into question faith in a Creator, "being-created" loses its meaning as an expression for being, so being becomes "being-calculable."[47] Heidegger makes Christianity responsible, then, for making the world vulnerable to the ills of modern technocracy. On these grounds, he rejects Christian protology, and in its stead he constructs his own.

Hans-Georg Gadamer avers that everything the "later" Heidegger says about being points back to a "Greek origin."[48] The early Greek philosophers Anaximander, Parmenides, and Heraclitus are centrally important for him. This is true of *Introduction to Metaphysics,* but his most notable forays into early Greek philosophy come post-1940. Here I shall discuss one such text: "Anaximander's Saying" (1946). I select it because Heidegger indicates that Anaximander, Parmenides, and Heraclitus must be thought together, with Anaximander, the earliest, being the one who clarifies the thinking of the other two.[49] Moreover, the Anaximander essay contains a few general remarks on the history of being that prove quite helpful for my

46. EM 111.   47. EM 207.

48. Hans-Georg Gadamer, "The Beginning and the End of Philosophy," in *Martin Heidegger: Critical Assessments, Volume 1: Philosophy,* ed. Christopher E. Macann (New York: Routledge, 1992), 16–28, at 28: "If one has not come to terms with the meaning of this Greek origin for Heidegger, it becomes virtually impossible to understand the late Heidegger." For a rich and varied set of reflections on Heidegger's relationship to the ancient Greeks, see the volume of essays, Drew Hyland and John Panteleimon Manoussakis, eds., *Heidegger and the Greeks: Interpretive Essays* (Bloomington: Indiana University Press, 2006).

49. Martin Heidegger, "Anaximander's Saying (1946)," in *Off the Beaten Track,* trans. Julian Young and Kenneth Haynes (New York: Cambridge University Press, 2002), 242–80, at 279.

brief consideration of this topic. The essay is worthy representative of Heidegger's early Greek protology.[50]

Anaximander's philosophy survives mainly in a fragmentary and obscure statement about the genesis of beings. Heidegger calls it the "oldest saying of Western thinking." In it he finds a primal unveiling of being as withdrawing in the revelation of a being. Anaximander's words present being's dawning, the opening moment of its history, and a preliminary glimpse of its destiny. In this way, Anaximander lays bare the constitutive character of the Greeks: "What is Greek is that dawn of destiny as that which being itself lights up in beings and lays claim to an essence of humanity, a humanity which, as destined, receives its historical path, a path sometimes preserved in, sometimes released from, but never separated from being."[51] The historical path into which the Greeks initiate humanity is the path of being's oblivion.[52] The Greeks, with Anaximander at their forefront, commence the "event of metaphysics," by discovering being's concealment of its difference from beings.

Anaximander discloses that the whole of world history dawns in the concealment of being. All of history centers on being, and "being keeps to itself." History proceeds in epochs. Each epoch is an epoch of errancy. This means that throughout history, which is the history of being, human beings are unable to see themselves for what they truly are. Being sends them into its own self-concealment.[53]

Anaximander's fragment also suggests that this self-concealment characterizes not only the dawn of history, but its latest point: "The history of being gathers itself in this departure. The gathering in this departure, as the gathering [logos] of the utmost [escha-

50. For Heidegger's three other major essays on the early Greeks, see Martin Heidegger, *Early Greek Thinking,* trans. David Farrell Krell and Frank Capuzzi (New York: Harper and Row, 1975); and for further reading, see the 1942–43 seminar, Heidegger, *Parmenides*; and the 1966–67 seminar with Eugen Fink, *Heraclitus Seminar,* trans. Charles Siebert (Evanston, Ill.: Northwestern University Press, 1993).

51. Heidegger, "Anaximander's Saying," 253.

52. Heidegger, "Anaximander's Saying," 275.

53. Heidegger, "Anaximander's Saying," 254.

ton] of its hitherto prevailing essence, is the eschatology of being. As destining, being itself is inherently eschatological."[54] Heidegger will contend elsewhere that this eschatology of being comes most clearly to light in Nietzsche.

It is well known that Heidegger characterizes Nietzsche's thought as "the most extreme completion of metaphysics."[55] Heidegger develops this characterization out of Nietzsche's own words, where he claims to reverse Platonism. Platonist philosophy inaugurates metaphysics by codifying the self-concealment of being in beings that Anaximander first reveals in a dichotomy between supersensuous and sensuous worlds: "beings and being are in different places."[56] That is, Platonism deals with the self-concealment of being by positing another "place" where being abides and grounds beings. This supersensuous "place" is the true world, and the sensuous "place" is merely apparent and untrue. Nietzsche's reversal consists in rejecting the truth of the supersensuous world and placing truth in the sensuous world.[57] Nietzsche's declaration, "God is dead!" illustrates this reversal by proclaiming the "absence of a supersensory, binding world."[58] Nietzsche

54. Heidegger, "Anaximander's Saying," 246.

55. Martin Heidegger, "Sketches for a History of Being as Metaphysics," in *The End of Philosophy*, trans. Joan Stambaugh (Chicago: University of Chicago Press, 2003), 57. Two things are true vis-à-vis Heidegger's reading of Nietzsche as the consummate metaphysician: (1) the details of this reading change over the course of the Nietzsche lectures (1937–1939) and beyond, when Heidegger shifts positions slightly on Nietzsche's significance during the 1940s; and (2) the thesis of Nietzsche as "last metaphysician" has been widely debated among Heidegger commentators and disputed among scholars of Nietzsche and continental philosophy in general. I have two remarks with respect to this: (1) though the details change, Heidegger's diagnosis of Nietzsche as standing at the end of metaphysics stays largely the same, and I shall treat it here as such; (2) I am not arguing for the validity of Heidegger's interpretation of Nietzsche, but only for its important place in his history of being. For an apt treatment of the range of issues surrounding the Heideggerian Nietzsche, and a new, balanced contribution to the discussion, see Louis Blond, *Heidegger and Nietzsche: Overcoming Metaphysics* (New York: Continuum, 2010).

56. Martin Heidegger, *What Is Called Thinking*, trans. J. Glenn Gray (New York: HarperCollins, 1968), 227.

57. Martin Heidegger, "Overcoming Metaphysics," in *The End of Philosophy*, 92.

58. Martin Heidegger, "Nietzsche's Word: 'God is Dead,'" in *Off the Beaten Track*, 157–99, at 163.

believes Platonism (with which he conflates Christianity) to have been an evaluation of beings in light of the supersensuous world. In the absence of this otherworldly realm, he takes it as his charge to revaluate beings in terms of the will to power.[59]

If Anaximander's fragment expresses the departure of being's history, which contains its eschatological end, Nietzsche's thinking of the will to power presents the eschatological end of being's history, which contains its beginning. While Heidegger locates in Anaximander an initial statement of being's self-concealment in beings, he finds Nietzsche fixing being's self-hiding into a panoramic viewpoint.[60]

The Heideggerian Nietzsche calls this viewpoint "justice."[61] For Heidegger, this is Nietzsche's name for the "essence of truth" and the "fundamental character of thinking."[62] Truth, if viewed from the standpoint of the will to power, is the opening of an all-embracing horizon of representative, calculative thinking. Justice is this opening. As calculative, justice implements the power of modern subjectivity. As all-embracing, justice deploys this power consummately. Since for Heidegger the final epoch of metaphysics is the epoch reigned by subjectivity, and since Nietzsche's justice represents subjectivity stretched to its widest extent, Nietzsche articulates metaphysics' eschatology.

These protological and eschatological claims about Anaximander and Nietzsche are two major pillars of Heidegger's replacement of the Christian narrative of salvation history with his own narrative of being's history. The next section tells how his alternative narrative comes most radically to life in his idiosyncratic volume, *Contributions to Philosophy.*[63]

59. Heidegger, "Nietzsche's Word," 193.

60. Martin Heidegger, *Nietzsche: Volume III: The Will to Power as Knowledge and Metaphysics,* trans. David Farrell Krell (New York: HarperOne, 1991), 147–48.

61. Heidegger, *Nietzsche III,* 137–48, see also 244–45.

62. Heidegger, *Nietzsche III,* 141, 143.

63. It is worth noting here that Heidegger in *Contributions* speaks of the history of metaphysics as "the long history between Anaximander and Nietzsche" (CP 299).

CONTRIBUTIONS TO PHILOSOPHY: HEIDEGGER'S TEXT ON HISTORY

1989 marked a watershed year for the interpretation of Heidegger's thinking. That year, *Contributions to Philosophy*, a manuscript that he wrote during the years 1936–1938, was published as volume 65 of the *Gesamtausgabe*. Since then, there has been an active and often heated debate over the standing of this work among Heidegger's others. To my mind, those who argue for this work's high standing—indeed as second only to *Being and Time*—judge it rightly.[64] This is so because those who recognize the importance of *Contributions* do so on the grounds that it is a revelatory or disclosive text.

Contributions discloses being, as opposed to thematizing it in assertions. In light of the last chapter's analysis of Heidegger's opposition toward assertoric predication, and Rahner's appropriation of this opposition, we should take great interest in a text that, *in toto*, resists assertion. Furthermore, this text discloses being historically. It presents the history of being as revelatory. And it is significant for us that Heidegger wrote this text immediately after the time Rahner studied with him. Heidegger insists that the historical lectures, many of which Rahner attended, are the main impetus for his writing of the book.[65] Let us briefly trace the main lines of this revelatory, historical text.

Like Heidegger's other works, *Contributions* articulates his protology and eschatology. These two limits relate to the current situ-

64. For a tremendously helpful commentary on the conflict of interpretation surrounding *Contributions,* see George Kovacs, "The Impact of Heidegger's *Beiträge zur Philosophie* on Understanding His Lifework," *Heidegger Studies* 27 (2011): 155–76. Kovacs comes down strongly on the side of those who esteem *Contributions* as Heidegger's second major work. The main champions of *Contributions* in English-speaking scholarship are, perhaps unsurprisingly, its first translators into English, Parvis Emad and Kenneth Maly. For their commentaries on the text, see Parvis Emad, *On the Way to Heidegger's* Contributions to Philosophy (Madison: University of Wisconsin Press, 2007); and Kenneth Maly, *Heidegger's Possibility: Language, Emergence—Saying Be-ing* (Toronto: University of Toronto Press, 2008).

65. CP 123–24.

ation in which philosophy finds itself: it has come to an end. Heidegger avers that philosophy has come to an end because it has been overtaken by the dominance of the "worldview." Philosophy is no longer an inquiry into being. Instead it has become a cultured way of looking at the world, of categorizing and controlling everything, of marshaling beings into a coherent picture.[66] Having come to this endpoint, "Philosophy is wanting to go back to the beginning of history and thus wanting to go beyond itself."[67] Heidegger adds, "Philosophy must return to the beginning, in order to bring into the free-space of its mindfulness the cleavage and the beyond-itself, the estranging and always unfamiliar."[68] Philosophy has reached its eschaton in the all-too-clear mastery of modern metaphysics and technology. The only option, as Heidegger sees it, is a new beginning in philosophy, based in the impending—in other words, eschatological—manifestation of be-ing (*Seyn*).

The hallmark of *Contributions* is Heidegger's thinking on "beginnings." Rahner would have heard some of Heidegger's preliminary reflections on the question of "the beginning" during the first Hölderlin course.[69] But nowhere else than in *Contributions* does Heidegger write at such length and with such resolve about the crossroads to which philosophy has come: between the "first beginning" and the "other beginning." He characterizes the current age as lying at the crossing of "the no-longer of the first beginning and its history *and* the not-yet of the fulfillment of the other beginning."[70] The age of the first beginning, which has come to an end, is "*the epoch of the total lack of questioning.*" Heidegger proclaims the dawn of another beginning: "*an epoch of simple solitude,* in which preparedness for the truth of be-ing [*Seyn*] itself is being prepared."[71] This new epoch will not be merely counter to the epoch that is ending. Instead, it will be the beginning of "something entirely other," incomparable with that which came before.[72]

66. CP 26–29.
68. CP 29.
70. CP 17, emphasis original.
72. CP 130–31.

67. CP 26.
69. HGR 3–4.
71. CP 76–77, emphasis original.

We have, then, a twofold history, and thus a structural parallel to Rahner. But this twofold history is specifically and actively hostile toward the Christian God, whose grace, in Rahner's account, propels history. Early in the text Heidegger evokes his reading of the "flight of the gods" in Hölderlin, a theme I have discussed at length above. As in other texts that we have read, Heidegger associates the flight of the gods with the concealment of being, and the advent of the gods with being's manifestness. He removes the question of God from theology, replacing it within the history of being, which he takes to be a higher question. He demotes the Christian view of God to one among many worldviews, all of which obscure the truth of being in its history.[73] History will be misapprehended, Heidegger contends, until people experience "the distress of the abandonment by being," that is, until they awaken to the gods' flight and to the unknown time of the gods' return—though this time may be imminent, as we shall see. With this, Heidegger supplants, despite all his protests to the contrary, the Christian view of life as a pilgrim state between birth into a sinful creation (the profane) and rising to new life in Christ (the sacred). And he substitutes the "en-ownment" (*Ereignis*) of human *Dasein* by "be-ing" (*Seyn*) for God's outpouring of grace on creation.[74]

Rahner argues that the religious dimension is the meaning and root of history that remains hidden and mysterious until God reveals its salvific (or damning) character. Heidegger's *Contributions* teaches that history's meaning and root remains hidden until the event (*Ereignis*) that sustains history should manifest itself in "the last god."[75] Heidegger again takes pains to dissociate "the last god"

73. CP 17–18.
74. CP 19.
75. See CP 49: "That essential truth ... sways in its ground, which we experience as en-ownment. The nearing and flight, arrival and departure, or the simple staying away of gods; for us in being master, i.e., as the beginning and being master over this happening, this inceptual mastery of the end will show itself as the last god. In its hinting, being itself, enowning as such, first lights up; and this lighting-up needs the grounding of the essential sway of truth as clearing and sheltering-concealing and [needs] their *final*

from any "theism" (even atheism), and refers it to the abyss of being that will come to light with the dawn of the other beginning. But even so, Heidegger explicitly opposes the "last god" to any other theism. Consider the epigraph to his chapter, "The Last God": "The totally other over against gods who have been, especially over against the Christian God."[76] Heidegger's history of being, and its eschatology, runs counter to Christian theology of history and eschatology.

The summary of his eschatology of the last god can complete this section: "The last god is not the end but the other beginning of immeasurable possibilities for our history. For its sake history up to now should not terminate but rather must be brought to its end. We must bring about the transfiguration of its essential and basic positions in crossing and in preparedness."[77] Several points are noteworthy here.

First, Heidegger distinguishes between "to end" and "to terminate." Though both denote a real and substantial final point, Heidegger avails himself of the differing connotations of each. He indicates that the history of the first beginning is ending, but in the sense that it has neared a point of transformation ("crossing"), not its breaking point (*terminus*). It has not reached its destination, but is pulling into a way station from which it will set off on a new path. Second, this new path will bring "immeasurable possibilities." This follows from the end/terminate distinction. "Termination" would mean the exhaustion of possibilities. "Ending" suggests an opening toward new ones. Third, Heidegger refers to a "we" who will effect and usher in the new possibilities of the other beginning. This "we" will prepare for, welcome, and perhaps even generate (Heidegger is slightly equivocal here, since the *Ereignis* usually does all the work), the transfiguration of the first beginning. This "we," especially Hei-

---

sheltering in the altered shapes of beings" (emphasis original, brackets added by translators).

76. CP 287.
77. CP 289.

degger's placement of himself at its forefront, brings us to the argument of the next section.

HEIDEGGER'S APOCALYPSE

Mark Wrathall asks in a chapter on Heidegger and the history of being, "[H]ow does Heidegger conceive of his place in this history?" He answers that Heidegger regards himself as a "preparatory thinker—that is, as being concerned with preparing us for a transformation of the current age of being, rather than himself participating in changing the understanding of being."[78] He then supports this contention with a quote from Heidegger about the "unassuming" character of his thinking. This is certainly a viable way of reading Heidegger, but this section advocates a different one. For every Heideggerian comment pointing away from himself or insisting upon the modesty of his venture, one could find a remark to the contrary. Usually these remarks are allusive—Heidegger dissimulates his high self-esteem— but nevertheless their upshot remains clear. If Heidegger is a "preparatory thinker," this is no modest claim. He casts himself as the one who stands at the turning point of history, as the interpreter who records the revelatory words he hears from being. In doing so, he assumes a role analogous to John of Patmos, who witnesses to the revelation of Jesus Christ by reporting what an angel allows him to see (Rev 1:1–2). Hölderlin proves pivotal for this aspect of Heidegger's thinking, because he makes Hölderlin out to be the herald of the revelation of *Seyn*.

We have already seen how Heidegger, evidently without recognizing it, twists Christian theology of creation and eschatology to arrive at his own thinking. Now we glimpse him parodying Christian apocalyptic, with respect to the points I have just enumerated,

78. Mark Wrathall, "Philosophy, Thinkers, and Heidegger's Place in the History of Being," in *Appropriating Heidegger,* ed. James Faulconer and Mark Wrathall (New York: Cambridge University Press, 2000), 9–29, at 23.

and with regard to two major apocalyptic themes: vision and catastrophe.

I shall restrict my scope to the *Contributions,* because within
this text Heidegger sets an apocalyptic trajectory for the remainder
of his career. Surely a fuller treatment of Heidegger's apocalyptic
would have to consider in detail his readings of Hölderlin in *Elucidations* and, of course, in the lectures. But these would only corrob-
orate my perspective. Heidegger casts himself as the unique witness
to history's turning from the first to the other beginning. He pretends to clearer vision than all other thinkers.

This becomes most clear in his statements on Hölderlin in *Contributions.* These statements center on the following one: "The historical destiny of philosophy culminates in the recognition of the
necessity of making Hölderlin's word be heard."[79] We know from
our prior reading of the first Hölderlin course that Heidegger criticizes virtually all other interpreters of Hölderlin for their reading of
the poet from literary and/or historical (in the sense of modern, scientific history) points of view. Heidegger repeats these criticisms in
Contributions.[80] He claims to recognize in Hölderlin something that
no one else can: his poetizing of the "experience" of en-ownment
by be-ing.[81] Only if Hölderlin is heard as the poet of the *Ereignis des
Seyns* is he actually heard. Only Heidegger hears him as such. Only
Heidegger can see the history of being turning.

Hölderlin must be heard—through Heidegger—because he is
chief among the "ones to come."[82] He makes the first inroads toward
the transfiguration of history from the first to the other beginning.
That is, he is the first of the "we" with which I ended the last section. This "we" consists of people who are "attuned" to the "shock"
of being's abandonment and the "awe" of the coming *Ereignis.* When
Heidegger explains this "attunement," he directs his reader to the

79. CP 297.   80. CP 297, 326.
81. CP 326.   82. CP 277–81.

Hölderlin lectures to learn "what is essential about attunement."[83] To this less direct reference to Hölderlin, Heidegger adds another: "Hölderlin [is] the poet who comes from afar and therefore the poet most futural of the ones to come. Hölderlin is the most futural of the ones to come because he comes from the farthest away; and coming from so far away, he *traverses* and transforms what is the greatest."[84] Though the odd diction and syntax here are remarkable enough, more so are the implications of these statements vis-à-vis Heidegger's standing.

We have, then, that Hölderlin "comes from afar" and "transforms the greatest." Heidegger is the one who spies Hölderlin on the horizon and who understands the transformation. Thus Heidegger proves extraordinary by association, even if he does not transcend the poet in historical significance. Hölderlin is the herald for the ones to come. Heidegger is the prophet who can decode the herald's words. Heidegger becomes an apocalyptic seer who recognizes what no other seer can.

Heidegger's elevated self-estimation is not the most unsightly aspect of his invented apocalypse, though. As is the case with the rest of his thought, he is at his worst when he writes of evil, or as I shall call it here, catastrophe. He believes that the event of being, the enownment of history, the revelation of the other beginning must be preceded and accompanied by devastation.

It is true that Heidegger converges in some sense with Christian apocalyptic in this respect. In fact, his affinity for catastrophe contributes to me describing his thought as apocalyptic. But while one could object that Heidegger is no worse than Christian apocalypticists, particularly John of Patmos, who envision catastrophic happenings as necessary precursors to Christ's end-time return, this objection is unfounded. Catastrophes in Christian apocalyptic result from the negativity of sin, which Christians reject. Catastrophes in Hei-

---

83. CP 278.   84. CP 281.

degger's apocalyptic derive from the callousness of being, which cannot be rejected, but has to be affirmed. The disparity between Christian and Heideggerian apocalyptic is wide, and Heidegger wants it this way, in that he turns explicitly against the Christian God.

Three texts from *Contributions* can illustrate Heidegger's disposition toward catastrophe. First, he states, "In the first beginning: deep wonder. / In another beginning: deep foreboding."[85] The beginning of metaphysics, particularly in Greeks like Anaximander, Heraclitus, and Parmenides, attests the shining of being, meeting it with awe—even if this awe also means incomprehension. The other beginning, beyond metaphysics, comes with foreboding. The incomprehension of being that typifies the metaphysical tradition leads eventually to the destructiveness of modern technology, which threatens all beings. The other beginning arises from this threat.

Second, since the other beginning will develop out of a threat, Heidegger identifies "distress" as the feeling that befalls those who live at the time of the turning from the first to the other beginning.[86] As he describes this "distress," he dismisses the possible objection that this distress is an "evil," implying that those who differentiate between good and evil are benighted by calculative thinking. I have already elucidated this problematic in Heidegger. His unwillingness to recognize evil as evil is, I argued in chapter 4, indicative of a deep and abiding pathology in his thinking.

Third, Heidegger writes, "Only after enormous ruinings and downfalls of beings do those beings which are already pressured into machination and lived-experience and rigidified into non-beings yield to be-ing and thus to its truth."[87] This statement—though, admittedly, very difficult to understand—epitomizes his belief that something horrible must happen in order for the truth of be-ing (*Seyn*) to emerge.[88] Again Heidegger shows the callousness toward suffering,

---

85. CP 15.   86. CP 79.
87. CP 170.
88. Cf. Heidegger, *The End of Philosophy*, 86: "Before being can occur in its primal

death, and destruction—that is, evil—that he claims to learn from being itself. But to my mind we must protest that Heidegger's callousness arises not out of a description of being and its history, but out of an a priori decision: that *Seyn* does not care about beings, but abandons them to annihilation.

Where, then, does Heidegger place himself in the history of being? He positions himself at a point where he can see, largely through the optic provided by the poet Hölderlin, a new beginning coming after a time of catastrophe. He casts himself in the role of an apocalyptic seer. This is all to say, he places himself above history—a sick irony, since he rejects Christianity because it constructs an alter-history above the history of this world.

RAHNER'S APOCALYPTIC "BETWEEN"

This part has one aim: to establish hermeneutical conditions for calling Rahner an apocalyptic theologian. In prior chapters, the third part described a convergence between Rahner and Heidegger. This part does so only marginally, insofar as I have just shown how Heidegger implies his own apocalyptic credentials. I am breaking protocol so as to set up a final conflict between Rahner and Heidegger. It cannot be properly portrayed if we have not understood how Rahner's theology of history is an apocalyptic theology of history.

The difficulty lies in the fact that Rahner is not commonly deemed to be an apocalyptic theologian. I commence this part by giving evidence for the nonapocalyptic reading of Rahner. Then I identify a hermeneutical framework for characterizing theologians as apocalyptic. Finally, using the framework acquired in the second section, I solve this part's hermeneutical problem by describing Rahner's distinctive brand of apocalyptic.

---

truth, being as the will must be broken, the world must be forced to collapse and the earth must be driven to desolation, and man to mere labor. Only after this decline does the abrupt dwelling of the Origin take place for a long span of time. In the decline, everything, that is, beings in the whole of the truth of metaphysics, approaches its end."

THE PROBLEM: RAHNER'S EVIDENT
NONAPOCALYPTICISM

In 1960, Rahner published an essay (originally given as a lecture) called "Theological Principles of the Hermeneutics of Eschatological Assertions."[89] This essay is widely regarded as Rahner's chief contribution to Catholic eschatology. Perhaps the most frequently discussed portion of the essay concerns apocalyptic, or more specifically, Rahner's apparent demotion of it. At several points in the essay, Rahner associates apocalyptic with a false form of eschatology that grasps after a perspicuous preview of the end of the world.[90] And in his article on eschatology in *Sacramentum Mundi,* to which he refers the reader in the first footnote of the "Hermeneutics" essay, Rahner tenders a similar disparaging comment to apocalyptic.[91] His apparent understanding of apocalyptic, then, is both tightly circumscribed and manifestly negative.

This has led Peter Phan to—very influentially—raise serious questions about Rahner's understanding of apocalyptic, and thus about Rahner's authority regarding the distinction between apocalyptic and eschatology.[92] In more recent studies of Rahner's eschatology, though the authors call Phan's dismissal of Rahner on apocalyptic somewhat into question, they also suggest that Rahner's remarks on apocalyptic prove confusing and that they leave him unnecessarily open to critique.[93]

89. Karl Rahner, "Theologische Prinzipien der Hermeneutik eschatologischer Aussagen," *Zeitschrift für katholische Theologie* 82 (1960): 137–58; published the same year in Rahner, *Schriften zur Theologie 4,* 401–28; translated as Rahner, "The Hermeneutics of Eschatological Assertions," in TI 4, 323–46.

90. Rahner, "Hermeneutics of Eschatological Assertions," 330, 334, 336, 337, 343.

91. Karl Rahner, "Eschatology," in *Encyclopedia of Theology,* 434–39, at 436.

92. See Phan, *Eternity in Time,* 70–72, 76, 206–7. It is notable that Phan's questions were anticipated—and rejected—almost a decade before he articulated them, in William M. Thompson, "The Hope for Humanity: Rahner's Eschatology," in *A World of Grace,* 153–68, at 157.

93. Cf. Harald Fritsch, *Vollendende Selbstmitteilung Gottes an seine Schöpfung: Die Eschatologie Karl Rahners* (Würzburg: Echter Verlag, 2006), 110–14; Morwenna Ludlow,

In Rahner's most prominent invocations of the term "apocalyptic," then, he does not demonstrate a solid knowledge of or interest in it. Furthermore, in Rahner's many writings on eschatology and the theology of history, the word "apocalyptic" and references to biblical apocalyptic texts are conspicuously absent, and content related to those texts goes unidentified as apocalyptic. It could be said, then, that he marginalizes apocalyptic.

We have established, then, *that* Rahner comports himself negatively toward apocalyptic. We have not thereby demonstrated *why* he does this. Such a demonstration must involve analysis of the closely argued opening pages of the "Hermeneutics" essay.

Rahner begins by justifying his project of developing hermeneutical rules specifically for eschatological statements. He admits that the objection could be made that such specific rules are not needed. The objection would be twofold. First, preachers and theologians have always used implicit hermeneutics to adapt the eschatological statements from Scripture and the early apostolic tradition. Thus the rules must already be set. And second, if the first point does not necessarily hold, nevertheless there exists in general theological hermeneutics a set of rules that can be applied just as easily and rightly to eschatological statements as to any other theological statement.[94] Rahner responds to the twofold objection by insisting that the de facto operation of an implicit hermeneutic does not render explicit reflection upon this hermeneutic superfluous, and that the presumption that a general theological hermeneutic can be applied to eschatology assumes wrongly that eschatology speaks of a world like any other. Rahner stands convinced that eschatology speaks precisely of that which exceeds our world—eternity, which we do not know, given that our knowing is bound by time.

Having dispatched these objections, Rahner indicates more

Universal Salvation: Eschatology in the Thought of Gregory of Nyssa and Karl Rahner (New York: Oxford University Press, 2000), 140.

94. Rahner, "Hermeneutics of Eschatological Assertions," 323–24.

pointedly the reason for his development of a special eschatological hermeneutic. He notes that the change in cosmology between premodern and modern times proves to be an obstacle to understanding eschatological statements. This is so because the conditions of modern knowledge tempt theologians to take eschatological statements as objective descriptions of the last things, which then in turn can be compared with present-day views of the universe and its future.[95] This temptation to eschatological objectivism is the main rub that Rahner addresses in his essay. Instead of allowing theologians to continue assuming that eschatological statements provide an objective encounter with the end times, Rahner prompts them explicitly to ask the question of what kind of knowledge eschatological statements convey.

It is no coincidence that the essay we are currently considering appears in the same volume of *Theological Investigations* as "The Concept of Mystery in Catholic Theology." We learned in chapter four that this set of lectures attacks the idea that knowledge's ideal form is perspicuous subjective grasping of an object. Rahner argues that the paradigm for all knowledge reveals itself when the human subject encounters the Mystery of God. Instead of subjective-objective perspicuity, human knowledge is more properly a "being overwhelmed by light inaccessible."[96] Rahner's seven theses in the "Hermeneutics" essay revolve around a similar idea. Eschatological statements testify in a special way to the incomprehensibility, uncontrollability, and hiddenness of God, since they treat of the hidden future of salvation. It is true that God reveals this future in scriptural and apostolic eschatological statements, but here "more than ever, revelation is not the bringing of what was once unknown into the region of what is known, perspicuous, and manageable: it is the dawn and approach of the mystery as such."[97] The knowledge that eschatological state-

---

95. Rahner, "Hermeneutics of Eschatological Assertions," 324.
96. CM 56.
97. Rahner, "Hermeneutics of Eschatological Assertions," 330.

ments provide consists in a positive encounter with God's Mystery, so an unknowing. Immediately after the sentence I have just quoted, Rahner invokes apocalyptic for the first time in the essay. He states that a true eschatological statement upholds the mystery of the future, while an apocalyptic utterance "presents its contents as the anticipated report of a spectator of the future event." Apocalyptic, then, denotes a statement that succumbs to the temptation of objectivism. Rahner is not entirely incorrect to liken apocalypticism to objectivism. He knows, of course, that *apocalypsis* means unveiling. If one understands this unveiling as an unveiling of information, it could sound like objectivism. Take, for instance, Daniel 9:22: "Daniel, I have now come to give you an understanding"; or Revelation 1:22: "The revelation of Jesus Christ, which God gave to him, to show his servants what must happen soon"; or Revelation 22:6: "And he said to me, 'These words are trustworthy and true, and the Lord, the God of prophetic spirits, sent his angel to show his servants what must happen soon.'" In such scriptural passages, Rahner would have recognized the apocalyptic seer (Daniel or John of Patmos) as a spectator of the future. Doubtless Rahner is also aware of the various millenarian strands of apocalypticism that took such scriptural statements as warrant for perspicuously predicting the future. While it may be wrong to reduce apocalypticism to simple prediction of the future, it does make sense in light of these points that he would do so.

I have attempted to establish that Rahner's evident nonapocalypticism has less to do with the literary-biblical genre or the theological traditions that come out of it, and more to do with his opposition to modern subjectivist-objectivism. I should note here that this interpretation of Rahner diverges sharply from Phan's, in that Phan attributes Rahner's resistance to apocalypticism to his "anthropological turn,"[98] while I credit it to his turn away from the anthropo-

98. In addition to the relevant pages in Phan's *Eternity in Time*, see Phan, "Eschatology," 178, 190, 191. For more on my disagreement with Phan's reading of Rahner, see

subject and toward the divine Mystery. We can now ask whether Rahner might have been persuaded to recognize how his concern with preserving the mysteries of faith from the dominance of subjectivist-objectivism actually coheres with apocalyptic theology. Even further, we can ask how affinities with apocalypticism might be coaxed out of Rahner's apparently nonapocalyptic eschatology. In the next section I shall identify some criteria for such coaxing.

A MODEL FOR DISCOVERING RAHNER'S APOCALYPTIC

Cyril O'Regan's Père Marquette Lecture in Theology, *Theology and the Spaces of Apocalyptic* (2009), constructs a model for classifying twentieth-century apocalyptic discourses in theology and philosophy.[99] Rahner does not appear among the many and varied theologians he examines. Nevertheless, given Rahner's close relationship (both personally and theologically) with some of these theologians, it is worthwhile to ask whether, and if so how, Rahner might fit into O'Regan's model. I shall now trace the main lines of O'Regan's classificatory schema, which he calls "the spaces of apocalyptic." In the next section I shall propose a way of envisioning Rahner's theology of history and eschatology as fitting into O'Regan's schema.

O'Regan sets out to classify twentieth-century apocalyptic discourses because he believes that a contemporary "turn to apocalyptic" demands serious attention and close analysis.[100] A model for classification would serve to make sense of the diverse discourses that assume the name "apocalyptic." He chooses a "metaphorics of space" as the means for classification. He explains that "space" admits of connotations that are helpful for describing the interaction between discourses. For example, the way "space" is used in mechanics relates

---

Peter Joseph Fritz, "'I Am, of Course, No Prophet': Rahner's Modest Eschatological Remark," *Philosophy and Theology* 23, no. 2 (2011): 317–32.

99. Cyril O'Regan, *Theology and the Spaces of Apocalyptic* (Milwaukee, Wis.: Marquette University Press, 2009).

100. O'Regan, *Spaces of Apocalyptic*, 23–24.

to "fields of force," that is, repulsion and attraction. Thus apocalyptic discourses that belong within one space will hang together by a force of mutual attraction, while these discourses will repel those of other spaces.[101]

To this O'Regan adds that the spaces of apocalyptic "arrange themselves along two different axes: an epistemic and an ethical axis." These express concerns with Christian identity and justice, respectively. O'Regan focuses in the lecture on the epistemic, or "eidetic," axis. He writes that the issue with this axis is "how full is the disclosure of divine reality and its relation to the world and history and how directive is it of specifically Christian practices and forms of life."[102] Given my emphasis throughout this book on Rahner as a thinker of God's manifestation and disclosure, and of the Catholic ethos, one may already sense how we might find a space for Rahner.

The next and final step in O'Regan's initial sketch of the model consists in naming the spaces of apocalyptic. He identifies three. He calls them "pleromatic," "kenomatic," and "metaxic," so as to indicate the "fullness" and "emptiness" of divine disclosure and other eidetic content in the first two spaces, and to denote that the third space stands in tension between the others.[103] He expresses a clear preference for the pleromatic space. It is preferable on two major counts: (1) with respect to theological breadth and depth: theologians representing the pleromatic space can account for a greater span of scriptural and doctrinal material, along with a wider range of Christian practice than can theologians of other spaces; and (2) theologians in this space encourage commitment to Christian identity to a greater extent than theologians of other spaces. This is to say that theologians of the pleromatic space provide for a maximal apocalyptic vision that theologians of other spaces eschew, either actively (*kenomatic*) or passively (*metaxic*).

O'Regan names three theological features that tie together theo-

---

101. O'Regan, *Spaces of Apocalyptic*, 26.   102. O'Regan, *Spaces of Apocalyptic*, 27.
103. O'Regan, *Spaces of Apocalyptic*, 29.

logians of the pleromatic space: (1) "commitment to Christian vision that has an absolutely comprehensive content, where this commitment can be further parsed into a conviction that Christianity is characterized by a Trinitarian metanarrative," (2) "a clear perception that the axis upon which history swings is cross and resurrection," and (3) "a sense that human participation in the divine life is incompatible only with a binary construction of transcendence which crucially misunderstands Christianity."[104] Hans Urs von Balthasar is O'Regan's favored pleromatic theologian, due to the comprehensiveness of his vision, which is governed by the Trinity, his foregrounding of the Paschal Mystery of Christ, and his rejection of Kantian, Hegelian, Heideggerian, and other critiques of the Christian view of transcendence.[105] Indeed, Balthasar is a concertedly and comprehensively apocalyptic theologian, as the fourth and fifth volumes of his *Theo-Drama* (1980–1983) attest, along with the earlier texts, *A Theology of History* (1952) and, before it, the three-volume *Apocalypse of the German Soul* (1937–1939).[106] His privileging of the Paschal Mystery is patent, most remarkably in *Mysterium Paschale* (1970).[107] And across his corpus he prosecutes his resistance to modern philosophy along apocalyptic lines, often within an exegesis of the biblical apocalypses, particularly John's. Balthasar provides a narrative of the apocalypse with a fullness of eidetic content unparalleled by any other twentieth-century theologian, from the inner-workings of the Trinity, to the historical moment of Christ's crucifixion, to the passive-action of Christ in hell on Holy Saturday.

His championing of the pleromatic space in general and Baltha-

104. O'Regan, *Spaces of Apocalyptic*, 102.

105. For O'Regan's reading of Balthasar, see especially *Spaces of Apocalyptic*, 44–53.

106. Hans Urs von Balthasar, *Theo-Drama: Theological Dramatic Theory IV: The Action and V: The Last Act*, trans. Graham Harrison (San Francisco: Ignatius Press, 1994–1998), see especially TD IV 15–67, the part entitled "Under the Sign of the Apocalypse"; Balthasar, *A Theology of History*, trans. not noted (San Francisco: Ignatius Press, 1994); Balthasar, *Apokalypse der deutschen Seele*, 3 vols. (Einsiedeln: Johannes Verlag, 1998).

107. Hans Urs von Balthasar, *Mysterium Paschale: The Mystery of Easter*, trans. Aidan Nichols (New York: T. and T. Clark, 1990).

sar in particular sets the criteria for O'Regan's readings of thinkers in the other spaces. The philosophers representing the kenomatic space, Walter Benjamin and Jacques Derrida, do not occupy much of O'Regan's attention—nor should they—largely because they invoke the label apocalypse but leave it as little more than a label.[108] Derrida's "apocalypse *sans* apocalypse" is emblematic of his apocalyptic emptiness, which derives at least in part from a similar emptiness in Benjamin. O'Regan calls this apocalyptic space, then, a "pseudo-space."[109] More interesting to him is the metaxic space, represented by Rahner's protégé Johann Baptist Metz and the American theologian Catherine Keller.[110] O'Regan's treatment of Metz can close this section.

I shall summarize what O'Regan says about Metz by referring Metz to the constitutive features of the pleromatic space: comprehensive Trinitarian metanarrative, focus on the Paschal Mystery, and resistance of modern misreadings of the Christian view of transcendence. Metz belongs to the metaxic space because he synthesizes "noneidetic" and "eidetic" forms of apocalyptic.[111] By this O'Regan means that, on the noneidetic side, Metz avoids articulating a comprehensive, symbol-filled narrative of the Trinity; but, on the eidetic side, he pays sustained and intensive attention to the mystery of the Passion, Cross, and Resurrection of Christ;[112] and back on the noneidetic side, he tends toward an apophatic reading of Christianity that outmatches its critics by demonstrating Christianity's own critical force.

Metz compares well with Balthasar, then, only with regard to his narration of the memory of Christ's passion and death. Otherwise, his theology contrasts with Balthasar's. Whereas Balthasar fills a stage with a panoply of characters (biblical and otherwise, di-

---

108. O'Regan, *Spaces of Apocalyptic*, 61–74.

109. O'Regan, *Spaces of Apocalyptic*, 115.

110. O'Regan, *Spaces of Apocalyptic*, 74–88.

111. O'Regan, *Spaces of Apocalyptic*, 78.

112. See especially Metz's late set of essays, *Memoria passionis: Ein provozierendes Gedächtnis in pluralistischer Gesellschaft* (Freiburg: Herder, 2006).

vine and human) acting in an elaborate apocalyptic drama, Metz's apocalyptic keys in on the interruptive moments when God breaks into history—the paradigmatic one, of course, being the end of history for which Christians should wait with imminent expectation. Metz does not empty apocalyptic of content, like Derrida and Benjamin, but he does limit and call into question grand, symphonic narratives like Balthasar's.[113]

My claim at the beginning of this section was that O'Regan's apocalyptic "spaces" could provide a hermeneutical structure for identifying Rahner's theology of history as apocalyptic. The schema of "pleromatic," "metaxic," and "kenomatic" spaces is helpful, but even more so is the set of criteria O'Regan uses to classify a theology as pleromatic, thus setting the norm against which other apocalyptic theologies are compared or contrasted. To repeat once more, these are: (1) comprehensive vision and Trinitarian metanarrative, (2) setting the cross and resurrection as the axis of history, and (3) resisting modern critiques of the Christian conception of transcendence. In the next section I shall use this schema and these criteria to propose a new reading of Rahner as an apocalyptic theologian.

HERMENEUTICAL SOLUTION: THE "BETWEEN"

Balthasar appends a note to beginning of *Theo-Drama V*. A portion of the note reads as follows: "Karl Rahner has dubbed our theology 'gnostic'; in all probability he will find this verdict even more strongly confirmed when he reads the chapter on the 'pain of God.'" A paragraph later, Balthasar continues,

As this final volume of *Theo-Drama* comes to an end, it broadens out into what Karl Rahner rightly and emphatically refers to as the "mystery of God." Anything we say, by way of a conclusion, regarding the "last act" of the play that involves earth and heaven is nothing more than an astonished stammering as we circle around this mystery on the basis of particular lu-

---

113. O'Regan, *Spaces of Apocalyptic*, 117.

minous words and suggestions of Holy Scripture. We have tried to go as far as revelation permits—some may feel we have gone one step too far.[114]

This note proves significant for three reasons. First, it shows Rahner's overt opposition to Balthasar's theology, in particular its most apocalyptic moments, since Rahner's charge seems to be directed at the fourth volume of *Theo-Drama,* which I highlighted above as an apocalyptic text. Second, the word Rahner uses, "gnostic," is one that he uses as a synonym for "false apocalyptic" in his "Hermeneutics of Eschatological Assertions" essay. He seems to associate Balthasar, then, with a false form of apocalyptic. Third, given Balthasar's self-description in the latter part of the quote, the problem between him and Rahner appears to be a difference of strategy with respect to the eidetic content of apocalyptic discourse. Balthasar suggests that apocalyptic should proceed, stammering, to the outer limits of revelation. Evidently Rahner disagrees.

Balthasar's note provides an opportunity to reassess Rahner's disposition toward apocalyptic. According to the view of Rahner as a nonapocalypticist, it would be unsurprising that Rahner would reject Balthasar's apocalypticism as gnostic. But it is worth entertaining the hypothesis that the Balthasar-Rahner argument transpires not between a nonapocalypticist and an apocalypticist, but between apocalyptic theologians of different spaces. O'Regan's metaphorics of space allows for repulsion and attraction between apocalyptic theologies occupying different spaces. If this holds true, then we could speak of a Rahnerian apocalyptic that is repelled by Balthasarian apocalyptic. This relationship of repulsion would not render Rahner's theology nonapocalyptic. Instead, it would suggest that Rahner's apocalypticism is not pleromatic.

I have already suggested that Rahner and Balthasar diverge with respect to the level of eidetic content that each theologian deems appropriate. Balthasar evidently deems it licit and even neces-

114. Balthasar, *Theo-Drama V,* 13.

sary for an apocalyptic theology to "go as far as revelation permits," and thus to utilize every possible bit of scriptural (and traditional) language to stammer out an account of God's self-unveiling. This perspective further cements Balthasar's pleromatic credentials. Even a surface comparison of Balthasar's texts with Rahner's would show that Rahner exercises much more eidetic reserve. In this respect, Rahner resembles his student, Metz. With the moniker "gnostic," Rahner calls into question Balthasar's metanarrative, thus placing himself outside the pleromatic space. But Rahner does not empty his theology of apocalyptic content. My section earlier in this chapter on "History and the Cross" should indicate that he regards the Cross as the axis of history. And the other sections on Rahner's theology of history should imply that Rahner adheres tenaciously to Christian faith in the human capacity for participation in the divine life. So Rahner, like Metz, stands between a Balthasarian pleroma and a nonapocalyptic (or, as with Derrida and Benjamin, apocalyptic) kenoma. Rahner's apocalyptic theology belongs to the metaxic space.

I shall support this claim with reference to one of Rahner's postconciliar essays: "On the Theological Problems Entailed in the Idea of the 'New Earth'" (1967). This essay can serve as an hermeneutical aid for reading other Rahnerian texts on history and eschatology, thus revealing him as an apocalyptic theologian, if a reticent one. It is most obviously associable with apocalyptic because its title includes an apocalyptic topos: the new earth (see Rev 21:1; 2 Pet 3:13). Rahner discusses this apocalyptic topos as it is employed by *Gaudium et spes,* Vatican II's "Pastoral Constitution on the Church in the Modern World." The Vatican Council's use of this term raises, for Rahner, fundamental questions about the Christian view of history—questions that press upon contemporary Christians with special urgency.

Gaudium et spes contains several injunctions to Christians that they work "to achieve a 'better world.'" Rahner points out that these injunctions carry the implication that Christians "must impress the framework of *secular* life with the stamp of [specifically Christian] *eschatological hope*."[115] But the Constitution also explicitly exhorts Christians to collaborate with people of other faiths and no faith. Thus the Constitution appears to envisage two tasks: a Christian one, and a secular, merely human one. This compels Rahner to ask how Vatican II conceives of the relationship between these two tasks. This brings him to interrogate the Council's invocation of the term "new earth."

The phrase "new earth" refers both to "the eschatological gift of God himself and is, therefore, not simply the outcome of the *progressus terrenus*," and to "a transformation of the world as it has existed hitherto."[116] The Constitution does not reflect specifically on this dual meaning of "new earth," leading to a problem of interpretation. Rahner summarizes the problem in a series of questions: "Does the 'new earth' come down from heaven? ... Or alternatively will this world be constructed here in time by man himself? Are we to read the relevant phrase as 'new earth' or 'renewed earth' (admittedly taking this as applying to the final consummation of God who is eternally new)?"[117] Why does Rahner insist on the importance of clarifying this "or" between the "new earth" or "renewed earth"? The answer to this question can disclose for us why and how Rahner is an apocalyptic theologian.

When Rahner writes of a "new earth" "constructed here in time by man himself," he is thinking of Marxism, or as he refers to it in this essay, "the present-day ideology of the future or of the future utopia."[118] Marxism confronts Christianity with the question of whether Christians take the world with "due seriousness." Marxists take the world and history seriously in that they believe history can achieve a utopia ("renewed earth") by its own self-transcendence.

115. Rahner, "New Earth," 260–61, emphasis original.
116. Rahner, "New Earth," 265.
117. Rahner, "New Earth," 266.
118. Rahner, "New Earth," 267. Cf. Rahner, "Marxist Utopia and the Christian Future of Man," in TI 6, 59–68.

Rahner argues that Christians can be understood to take the world and its history with similar seriousness — Christians believe in a substantial way in history's self-transcendence — but always with the proviso that the finality of history "will be the deed of God."[119] One does not have to believe that history's final commitment has to come by human effort alone in order to take history seriously.

The breaking point between the Marxist and the Christian "renewed earth," then, is that Christians, as they work in the world, await the divinely bestowed "new earth" — the "new earth" of which the Book of Revelation speaks (Rev 21:1–3). Thus Rahner clarifies the theological position of *Gaudium et spes,* and by extension his own theology of history, while opposing it to an ideology that, particularly during his time, was directly hostile to the Christian view of history's transcendence. And he does so with reference to apocalyptic.

What is interesting here with respect to O'Regan's schema is that Rahner uses apocalyptic strategically against Marxism, much like his student, Metz.[120] Unlike a pleromatic thinker like Balthasar, Rahner does not provide a detailed vision of the "new earth." In fact, in keeping with his comments in the "Hermeneutics" essay, Rahner disallows any "actual *conception* of history in its enduring finality."[121] Instead, he uses an apocalyptic *eidos* ("new earth") noneidetically (without extensive description). He resides in the space between eidetic and noneidetic apocalyptic. This may make it seem like Rahner fulfills only minimal apocalyptic criteria, and in an isolated instance. But the situation need not be read in this way. Instead, this

---

119. Rahner, "New Earth," 268–69.

120. See, for instance, Johann Baptist Metz, *Faith in History and Society: Toward a Practical Fundamental Theology,* trans. J. Matthew Ashley (New York: Herder & Herder, 2007), especially "Hope as Imminent Expectation — or, The Struggle for Lost Time: Untimely Theses on Apocalyptic," 156–65, which deploys apocalyptic against Marxist ideas of utopia (162).

121. Rahner, "New Earth," 269: "The actual *conception* of history as it will exist in its enduring finality is impossible. Any attempt at depicting it (and in a real sense we are actually warned against this in Mt 22:30) would be a pseudo-Christian apocalyptic and no true Christian eschatology" (emphasis original).

essay about *Gaudium et spes*'s theology of history can serve as a heuristic device, with which one might discover an apocalyptic undercurrent in Rahner's theology of history.

If, for instance, we understand Rahner's statements about God as absolute future[122] as referring also to the God of the Book of Revelation, who does away with the "former heaven and the former earth" (Rev 21:1) and who "makes all things new" (Rev 21:5), then a different Rahner is disclosed. We shall see in the next part that this apocalyptically understood Rahner is well-equipped to grapple with modern subjectivism (of which Marxism is a late instantiation) and Heideggerian apocalypticism. To the subjectivist and Heideggerian misunderstandings of human life, work, and being, Rahner opposes a theological thinking enlightened by the glory of God (cf. Rev 21:23–24).

RAHNER'S OVERCOMING

The entire book has been building toward this final part, which serves as the denouement of the book's three major argumentative threads. I have been arguing that Rahner turns away from the modern subject, not toward it; that he converges with Heidegger on certain points, but then diverges sharply from his teacher; and that he presents a distinctive theological sublime-aesthetic that testifies to the breadth of the Catholic ethos. This part both summarizes and supplements these arguments, bringing them and this chapter to a close. It contends that Rahner's late writings on theology of history offer nothing less than an eschatological surpassing of the modern subject, an apocalyptic overcoming of Heidegger, and an apocalyptic amplification of his sublime-aesthetic.

Each of this thesis's phrases demands explication. But even prior to this it should be clear that Rahner's theology of history (under which I file his eschatology) is a privileged site that reveals the aes-

---

122. See especially Rahner, "Marxist Utopia," 61–66.

thetic and intellectual force of his thinking in general. The title of this part, "Rahner's Overcoming," suggests not only his overcoming of modern subjectivism and Heideggerianism, but also an outstripping of prior portrayals of him.

SURPASSING THE MODERN SUBJECT ESCHATOLOGICALLY

In 1978 Rahner delivered a radio lecture in Austria in conjunction with the Salzburg Conference on Humanism. In this lecture, "The Inexhaustible Transcendence of God and Our Concern for the Future," he continues the type of critical commentary on humanism that we encountered near the end of chapter 3. Rahner calls this lecture a "kind of burlesque sermon."[123] We may call it a rebuke directed toward humanists for limiting the scope of their concern for the future. Rahner accuses humanism of being, ultimately, a return to the self, an egoism masquerading as concern for others.[124] He describes Christianity as "utterly different from a humanism," and "absolutely incomparable" with humanism.[125] The absolute difference between Christianity and humanism hinges on the eschatological orientation of the former, and the merely intramundane direction of the latter.

Humanism, as I argued in chapter 3, is a variety of modern subjectivism. Rahner contends that Christianity's eschatological (we might substitute "apocalyptic" here) index allows it to outmatch humanism. Thus Rahner proposes Christian resistance of the strictures of modern subjectivism, along eschatological lines. The following passage illustrates this resistance:

Christianity is aware of the apparently excessive and even absurd demands it makes on man and in the course of its history there have been enough attempts—deliberate or not deliberate—to reinterpret the inexorability of

123. Rahner, "Inexhaustible Transcendence," 174.
124. Rahner, "Inexhaustible Transcendence," 179.
125. Rahner, "Inexhaustible Transcendence," 179.

that love for God which tears man away from himself and thrusts him into God's incomprehensibility as into an unfathomable, dark abyss: new interpretations which turn all this into a sublime form of self-assertion in which a holy egoism can also be put—fortunately—at the service of God and thus be able to assert itself forever. Christianity knows and expressly states that this love for God, in which man must lose itself, is possible only by God's love approaching man and being itself offered from its innermost center as the power of *that* love in which man has the courage to get away from himself, to abandon himself, as the only obvious thing to do: to allow himself to fall, to regard mystery as the true light illuminating everything, to know that death is the gate to life and that the love which seeks, not itself, but the God who is loved as such, means true life and eternity.[126]

The eschatological dimension of this lengthy quote comes out at its end, when Rahner evokes the theme of death, correlating it to a dive into mystery. The resistance of modern subjectivism occurs throughout the passage. Rahner censures those who attempt to reinterpret the excessive demands of Christianity as a "holy egoism," characterized by a "sublime form of self-assertion." By describing the turn away from oneself toward God as courageous, he implies that the egoism that turns toward the self is cowardly. Self-assertion and egoism, two constitutive features of modern subjectivism, thus humanism, attempt to avoid the inevitable: love for God, which asks for nothing other than an abandonment of self. Self-assertion and egoism, then, are exercises in futility. They set undue limits on human transcendence, by rejecting any true absolute to which human persons can surrender, and by which—in the end—they may be elevated.

The futility of modern subjectivism manifests itself most perniciously, Rahner argues, in the widespread idolatry of the contemporary world. He notes a contemporary trend toward absolutizing individual realities, and he explains that this trend derives from the desire for control. Such a desire is, of course, a chief feature of modern subjectivism. As a replacement for this idolatrous desire, Rah-

126. Rahner, "Inexhaustible Transcendence," 177–78.

ner proposes a course of action directly opposed to control: "we must be able to set ourselves free without any guarantee, tested in advance, of getting anywhere and yet hope to do so … with childish simplicity; we must venture out into the pathless incomprehensibility without fear of losing the way; we must really get away from ourselves."[127] Rahner follows these words with some eschatological reflections. His proposed praxis of relinquishing control will break people's idolatrous attempts to control the future. It will open them to the God who is above all names, but nevertheless is "for us eternal light, eternal life, ineffable glory, peace without end." This God, who is the absolute future, relativizes all humanisms, all egoisms, all subjectivisms.

The radio address I have just been examining is a prime example of how Rahner's late writings on the future, on the end of history, and how God breaks through history to relativize human projects, show definitively his theological turn away from the subject. Rahner is not a theologian who makes Christianity palatable to modern people. In fact, the participants at the Salzburg conference likely regarded him as an unwelcome guest, since he declares that "the Christian message cuts right across the tasks and concerns of the kind of humanism seeking expression at this conference," and he proceeds to accuse his humanist colleagues of an insincere "harmonizing of egoisms."[128] Rahner does not submit to humanism and subjectivism. He combats them. At one point in his remarks he asks, "Where today are the prophets who cry aloud: 'Seek first the kingdom of God'?"[129] Rahner himself was such a prophet.

OVERCOMING HEIDEGGER APOCALYPTICALLY

Rahner's overcoming of modern subjectivism could be read as an apocalyptic announcement: the old ways of modern subjectivism

127. Rahner, "Inexhaustible Transcendence," 185–86.
128. Rahner, "Inexhaustible Transcendence," 179.
129. Rahner, "Inexhaustible Transcendence," 180.

and its attendant humanism are passing away; things will be made new again when human persons enact their "inexhaustible transcendence," a "movement towards God that does not spring back on man and does not again find its endpoint in man himself."[130] From our prior consideration of Heidegger's *Contributions to Philosophy*, we know that he too announces apocalyptically that the first beginning, which culminates in modern subjectivism implemented as machine technology, has arrived at its end. Heidegger proclaims a time of preparation for the other beginning, during which human *Dasein* must relinquish its claim to subjectivity and recognize itself as "the one blown upon by history [*enowning*] and pulled along into be-ing," the one "who no longer returns from the ab-ground and who in this foreign land *keeps* the remote neighboring to be-ing."[131] Rahner and Heidegger converge, then, in that they aim to defeat modern subjectivism by contending that the truth of being human comes to light not through a return to self, but through a dive into the abyss. And the abyss is, for Rahner and Heidegger, the consummate site of disclosure, revelation, or *apocalypsis.*

Of course, Rahner and Heidegger differ over the meaning they assign to "abyss." For Rahner, the abyss is the incomprehensibility of God's love, which is attested in Scripture and the Christian theological tradition. For Heidegger, the abyss is the region where the ground of beings withdraws, making way for the advent of the gods; to this abyss, Hölderlin's revelatory poetic saying attests.[132] These diverse ways of defining "abyss" constitute the main breaking point between Rahner and Heidegger. Ultimately, everything in Rahner's theology reduces to the self-revealing, loving Mystery of God, and everything in Heidegger's philosophy reduces to the self-concealing, callous

---

130. Rahner, "Inexhaustible Transcendence," 181.
131. CP 346.
132. See Martin Heidegger, "The Poem," in *Elucidations of Hölderlin's Poetry,* 218. After citing a line from Hölderlin's poetry that envisions the "step" of poets "toward the abyss," Heidegger says this: "The poet's saying is needed — showing, veiling-unveiling — to allow the appearance of the advent of the gods."

mystery of *Seyn*. As I have already noted, for each thinker, the human person reduces to the mysterious abyss. Thus when they differ over the meaning of "abyss," they disagree over the nature and end (or in Heidegger's words, destiny) of the human person. An explicit conflict arises between Rahner and Heidegger over Heidegger's phrase "the shepherd of being." This specific conflict can teach us a general lesson about Rahner's apocalyptic resistance of Heidegger.

In key places in *Contributions* and other texts, including ones that have figured into my reading of Heidegger in this book, like "Anaximander's Saying" and the "Letter on Humanism," Heidegger refers to human *Dasein* as "guardian" of being or, more famously, "the shepherd of being."[133] By this he means that it belongs to the human essence to preserve being's truth. If the modern subject was the "lord of beings," the human person figured as "guardian" or "shepherd" is "poor" by comparison (i.e., in power).[134] But as the custodian over the truth of being, the "shepherd" does what the subject could not: let be-ing come, let it become manifest, let it be newly revealed, unconcealed, unveiled. Heidegger conveys this idea when he describes *Dasein* as "the guardian of the stillness of the passing of the last god."[135] For Heidegger, the other beginning marks a new age in which be-ing will disclose itself through simplicity, particularly the simple words of the poet, Hölderlin. The shepherd-guardian ushers in be-ing's apocalypse.

Volume 7 of *Theological Investigations* includes a collection of brief meditations on the mysteries of the life of Christ. One of them, entitled "Encounters with the Risen Christ" (1955), includes a passage that I deem extraordinary because of its explicit reference to and disagreement with Heidegger:

---

133. For "guardian," see CP 13, 17, 163, 171, 208, 211, 215, 326, 350. On "shepherd," see "Anaximander's Saying," 262; and LH 234, 245.

134. See LH 245, CP 171.

135. CP 208.

The great thinker of our times has called man a "shepherd of being," and summed up in this phrase the whole destiny and value of man, which, by our own resources, we recognize in ourselves. But the truth which Jesus is uttering to us here is still more basic and primary, and when we let it speak to us in a spirit of faith this truth reveals itself to us as an experience of ours that is more basic and more primary: the fact that we are those over whom the shepherd of men watches, and whom he gathers and guides.[136]

Heidegger remains unnamed here, but the fact that he is target of praise and blame is clear. Rahner situates the passage I have just quoted within a larger discussion of Jesus Christ as "shepherd."[137] He gives numerous references to scriptural descriptions of Jesus as shepherd, from all four gospels, Hebrews, and First Peter, and he even sets these descriptions on the background of Ezekiel 34. But most remarkably, Rahner cites several places in the Book of Revelation. He argues that Jesus' role as shepherd cannot be understood correctly unless one notices that this shepherd is the divine "author and maker" of all things. When this shepherd gathers all things together, he does so as the one to whom all things belong, as "the unity of their common beginning." The shepherd is the guardian *and* origin of all things.[138] This "shepherd of being" is, then, markedly different from Heidegger's.

His shepherd, though he guards be-ing's truth, is not be-ing itself. His shepherd, though he ushers in be-ing's revelation, does little more than this, other than being "blown over" by history. His shepherd is merely a man, with merely his own resources, who is radically subject to the whims of being—and given that the first beginning brought an age that must end in destruction, it is unclear how hopeful the other beginning might be.

Rahner's shepherd is, also, a man. But this man is the "Alpha and the Omega, the first and the last, the beginning and the end" (Rev 22:13). This shepherd is the

---

136. Karl Rahner, "Encounters with the Risen Christ," in TI 7, 169–76, at 175–76.

137. Rahner, "Encounters with the Risen Christ," 173–76.

138. Rahner, "Encounters with the Risen Christ," 175.

one to whom all the scattered and lost ones belong, one who knows all things, however scattered and confused they may be in a dark and meaningless void; one whom the ultimate instinct of reality, still cohering in its confusion, yet recognizes; one who, by entering into this confusion and offering himself up in sacrifice there, ventures into the desolation of death and so achieves the gathering of the scattered; one, in short, who can unite all things.[139]

The true shepherd is not the one who ushers in the apocalypse, but one who is himself the apocalypse — the revelation of God in the sacrifice on the Cross that gathers the scattered sheep to God. The true shepherd is not the one who leaves all things to fall into the abyss of destruction, but the one who unites all things in the abyss of God's love. This true shepherd, into whom Christians are baptized, and who is present at the Eucharist,[140] is the one Heidegger denies, whom he deems an impossibility, by an illicit and a priori philosophical decision.

The escalating conflict I have narrated throughout this book reaches its pinnacle over the idea of the "shepherd of being." Rahner's rejection of this phrase from Heidegger proves to be the best entry point for a Rahnerian critique of Heidegger's whole philosophical project. This critique would predicate itself upon Rahner's unveiling, which I have detailed in previous chapters, of the disastrous consequences of Heidegger's apriorism of finitude.

THE CATHOLIC SUBLIME AND APOCALYPTIC

All that remains is to make a few closing remarks on the relationship between the Catholic sublime and apocalyptic. At the beginning of this chapter, I pointed to an affinity between apocalyptic and the Catholic sublime, in that the former, qua discourse, holds open a universal field of revelation, while the latter, qua ethos, holds life open so that it might receive and cooperate with God's self-

---

139. Rahner, "Encounters with the Risen Christ," 175.
140. See Rahner, "Encounters with the Risen Christ," 176.

communication. Since that point, I have built a case that Rahner's
theology of history merits apocalyptic ascription, particularly with
regard to its making the Cross the axis of history, and its intensive
description of human transcendence as having its completion in a *reductio in mysterium*. I have added that Rahner's theology of history
shows itself to be apocalyptic through its direct confrontation with
the modern subjectivist-humanist view of evolutionary time, with
the intraworldly utopianism of Marxism, and with the ersatz apocalypse of Heidegger.

I would like to return to the Rahner-Balthasar quarrel over
apocalyptic. I proposed that Rahner's labeling of Balthasar's apocalyptic theology as "gnostic" is indicative of a disagreement between
apocalypticists of different spaces, and that this disagreement arises over Balthasar's Trinitarian metanarration. Since Rahner calls
this into question, and since Balthasar is undeniably a pleromatic theologian, I suggested that Rahner likely belongs to O'Regan's
metaxic space. Rahner would be, then, a theologian suspicious of
metanarratives, yet unwilling to release completely a wide-ranging
historical-eschatological vision.

This latter idea is vitally important to the reading of Rahner
I have set forth in this book. If, indeed, Rahner's chief contribution consists in presenting the Catholic ethos, this means that as a
whole Rahner's theology witnesses to and performs the virtually unbounded breadth of Catholicism, whose name—again—means according to the whole. Given this description, it sounds as if Rahner
would be sympathetic with and prone to metanarrative. But Rahner's criticism of Balthasar's apocalyptic, along with Rahner's praxis of writing—essays, lectures, and fragments were the norm, with
monographs being the exception—reveal that Rahner is suspicious
of metanarratives. At once, then, Rahner needs metanarrative range
yet chooses an episodic approach to this range.

Philip Endean's book on Rahner ends with this statement: "Seen
in themselves, our efforts are only fragments: mere attempts to clear

space so that God's grace can be disclosed."[141] Endean's words can assist us in making sense of Rahner as an apocalyptic theologian and a theologian of the sublime. "Apocalyptic" can be understood in two different ways when applied to Rahner's theology: as clearing the way for full disclosure, and as interrupting, relativizing, and rendering fragmentary any manifestations of God in the world. The same goes for the "sublime": it can mean a word that refers to great magnitude, a wide range of manifestation, but also the short-circuiting, and shattering of any beautiful—that is, positively and simply pleasurable—vision of the whole. Rahner's theology of history is, in some sense, a grand vision, a birds-eye view, maybe even a "hedgehog trick,"[142] but given a closer examination, it shows up as a series of fragments that attempt to give word to God's multifaceted drawing of all things to God's self, and to the exalted task to which God calls people: to say yes to being so drawn.

---

141. Endean, KRIS 260.

142. This phrase represents the early Metz's accusation of the ahistoricality of Rahner's theology. See Metz, *Faith in History and Society*, 151–52.

CONCLUSION

THIS BOOK'S introduction outlined three main contributions
that the chapters to follow would make: they would reveal Rahner as (1) a theologian of a turn away from the modern subject, (2) a
theological aesthetician, and (3) resistant theologically and philosophically to Heidegger. Each chapter has worked toward all three. I argued that the three can be pursued successfully only if one pursues
them together. From the start, in chapter one, I showed how Rahner
resists modern subjectivism (contribution 1) by developing an aesthetic (sensibility-oriented) account of subjectivity (2) modeled largely on, while critically reshaping, Heidegger's re-vision of Kant's doctrine of the schematism (3). And by the end, in chapter 5, I indicated
that Rahner continues resisting modern subjectivism, even in his "later" works. He constructs a wide-ranging description of history not
as centering on the subject (1), but on the sublime judgment of God
(2), thereby providing a Catholic alternative to Heidegger's history of
being, where being decides everything in its "missions" (3). The chapters in between prosecute similar lines of argument.

I have demonstrated three things. First, Rahner studies can
no longer be satisfied with the commonplace reading of Rahner
as a theologian of the turn to the subject, or of an anthropological turn. Second, Catholic theological aestheticians should revisit Rahner to learn from him a model for theological aesthetics that

differs from and thus could supplement other ones, especially the dominant paradigm of Hans Urs von Balthasar. Third, it no longer suffices simply to remark that Rahner "once studied with Heidegger," or that Rahner "attended Heidegger's seminars"; the Rahner-Heidegger relationship is a complex and generative one. Furthermore, on this count, the Rahner-Heidegger relationship as I have explicated here surely has further implications for what Rahner might offer for Catholic theology's encounter (or confrontation) with post-Heideggerian philosophies. I have already begun to entertain the idea of a positive relationship between Rahner and Jean-Luc Marion, who is a devoutly Catholic philosopher and theologian, but no less a post-Heideggerian.[1] The question of how Rahner's theology might interact with post-Heideggerian philosophies of a deconstructionist stripe, like those of Jacques Derrida and Jean-Luc Nancy, also merits sustained inquiry.

A fourth contribution should be added as this book concludes. This contribution is inscribed in the book's thesis. And in fact, it concerns the idea with which this book began: the ethos of Catholicism. My thesis states that Rahner's major achievement is his performance and presentation of the Catholic sublime, which is my name for Catholicism's constitutive ethos. I initially described the Catholic ethos as a radical openness to God's self-manifestation in the world. In the book's chapters, I augmented this description with details from Rahner's investigations of Christian theology, history, and life.

I foregrounded certain investigations of Rahner's that bear on what one might call the outer limits of Catholicism: flight from the world spirituality, the priest being entirely overtaken by Christ's word, angels as created cosmic powers, the doctrine of Mary's virginity *in partu*, and apocalyptic. In focusing on such Rahnerian topoi, I contest the conventional reading of Rahner as the theologian

1. See Peter Joseph Fritz, "Karl Rahner Repeated in Jean-Luc Marion?" *Theological Studies* 73 (June 2012): 318–38.

who makes Catholicism palatable to modern tastes — who constructs a theology we can "live with." If one reads his theology closely, comprehensively, and well, one will recognize the vision of Rahner I have unveiled. This Rahner is a theologian who confronts his students, listeners, and readers with the fundamental difficulty of Catholicism at its best: its absolutely unrelenting unrestrictedness of scope vis-à-vis God's self-revelation.

Thoughts about angels and a virgin who remains virgin even through the process of birth are not "normal" ones, especially by modern standards. Were Rahner the theologian many believe him to be, he would avoid such thoughts. But he approaches them directly, sympathetically, and constructively. He shows himself to be truly, unreservedly catholic. He thinks the whole of God's self-offering. Thereby he encourages a life shaped by the whole of God's self-offering. Since this self-offering is so boundless and demands such a boundlessness of life, I call it sublime — a word that carries rich connotations of negotiating thresholds, limits, and boundaries.

But sublime also suggests indeterminacy, plurality, heterogeneity, formlessness. There are two ways one can understand catholicity. According to one, catholicity entails a determinate form of life — a holiness directly patterned on this life of Christ, or the Christ form. This proposal inclines more or less toward uniformity. According to another, catholicity consists in following Christ without repeating Christ. This definition of catholicity allows for pluriformity.

Certain things I have written in this book about Rahner and ethos may suggest that he espouses the former way, either occasionally or completely, since I call ethos a "form of life." But the overall thrust of the text, particularly the discussion of formlessness in chapter 4our, should indicate that Rahner more nearly follows the second way. I was barely able to scratch the surface of Rahner's writings in this book, even if I treated many of them. But a comprehensive reading of Rahner reveals that he views the Christian life as inextricably heterogeneous — a collection of seemingly disparate devotional practices, prayers, social actions, utopian visions, political leanings, ecclesial happenings, and dogmatic teachings, all of which center on Christ, but from varied angles. The Catholic ethos demands not symphony, but polyphony, which allows God to be heard in numerous, even discordant tones. As Rahner once said, we cannot make this world's pluralism into a symphony; only God can hear it as such.[2]

Heidegger proves helpful at this point, though somewhat against his will. His narrative of the history of being tells of a grand betrayal. Being should be manifest and it should be recognized, but throughout the history of metaphysics it is not. Heidegger makes it clear that he does not chalk up this hiddenness and misrecognition to a primal "fall" or to subjective inadequacy on the part of human knowers. In fact, he asserts the opposite, as we have seen: being remains hidden and misapprehended because being withdraws from view and keeps to itself. Even so, Heidegger's critical descriptions of Aristotle's reduction of language to apophansis, of Descartes's reduction of thinking to calculation, and late modernity's reduction of beings to a technocratic standing reserve are more nearly critical than descriptive. His view of the metaphysical is that it betrays the essence of thinking. The new dawn of thinking he announces in *Contributions to Philosophy* will involve a renunciation of this betrayal, and an appropriation of thinking to and by being.

From Heidegger, then, we can learn how to narrate a history of betrayal. We can draw an analogy between being, figured as the ethos proper to yet denied by the West, and the Catholic sublime, the ethos proper to yet denied by Catholicism. Being proves too sublime a thought for metaphysics. The Catholic ethos proves too sublime, too expansive and pluriform, for most adherents of the Church.

2. See Philip Endean's remarks on Rahner's pluralism, including this quote from Rahner: KRIS 258–60.

It would be an interesting—and daunting—exercise to demonstrate how modern Catholicism, from the time of the Reformation forward, betrayed the Catholic sublime. Obviously such a demonstration lies outside the bounds of this book, though I might preliminarily indicate that the Council of Trent's program for Church uniformity could be a starting point. I shall keep my claims more modest, focusing on how Rahner's readers have betrayed his presentation of the Catholic sublime.

Many of Rahner's supporters betrayed the Catholic sublime as soon as he presented it. Rahner's theological vision was too comprehensive to take in, so they fled to practicality to simplify and to make digestible his contribution—to make his theology one that people could live with. They ignored his devotion to Mary, the saints, and the Sacred Heart. They smoothed over the difficulties of his theoretical proposals, especially his theory of symbol and his theology of history. They sloganized him, bandying about "supernatural existential" and "anonymous Christians" without understanding or expounding their content. Though they claimed to appreciate the political dimension of his theology, they failed to plumb its depth or consider its breadth. They evacuated his richly textured theology of Mystery of its dogmatic substance, making it into an excuse not to study dogma or Christian history. This led to many popular appropriations of Rahner that fled not only from him, but often also from Catholicism, into vapid spiritualities that were wrongly called "mysticism" because no mystery remained.

Likewise, Rahner's detractors betray the Catholic sublime by setting limits on it, by asking that it be shackled to a "form." Those most likely to find fault with Rahner's thinking, it has turned out, have been those most likely to set prohibitions, to be moralists, or scrupulously to attempt to shore up "the sacred." Such persons achieve less Catholic openness even than the atheist Heidegger. Rahner's detractors seek a lost clarity, they utilize Catholic doctrines like bricks in a bastion, they treat church discipline as military training, and they regard liturgy as a paean to divinely withheld secrets (rendered all the more secret in a return to the Latin language). They hunger for closure. Such is the atmosphere of a growing majority of today's Catholic Church. The history of Rahner-interpretation, from his first supporters through his most recent detractors, is largely a history of betrayal. And it is not just a betrayal of Rahner, but of the Catholicism to which he dedicated his life.

Every ethos inscribes both temptations and promises. I have briefly, sketchily rehearsed how people have succumbed to temptation. The question now, as regards Catholic thought and life is this: do we recover the ethos Rahner presented? That is, do we recover it, cover it over again with betrayal, consider it a nightmare that we can repress? Or, do we recover the Catholic sublime, bring it forward to assist us along our way? It may seem, in light of the betrayals I have described, that the choice has been definitively and irrevocably made for the first option. Yet the choice remains, if barely, open.

SELECTED BIBLIOGRAPHY

WORKS BY KARL RAHNER

"'Behold This Heart!': Preliminaries to a Theology of Devotion to the Sacred Heart." In *Theological Investigations 3: The Theology of the Spiritual Life*, translated by Karl H. and Boniface Kruger, 321–30. New York: Crossroad, 1982.

"Being Open to God as Ever Greater: On the Significance of the Aphorism '*Ad Majorem Dei Gloriam*.'" In *Theological Investigations 7: Further Theology of the Spiritual Life 1*, translated by David Bourke, 25–46. New York: Seabury Press, 1971.

"The Body in the Order of Salvation." In *Theological Investigations 17: Jesus, Man, and the Church*, translated by Margaret Kohl, 71–89. New York: Crossroad, 1981.

"Christian Humanism." In *Theological Investigations 9: Writings of 1965–67, 1*, translated by Graham Harrison, 187–204. New York: Herder and Herder, 1972. Original: "Christlicher Humanismus." In *Schriften zur Theologie VIII*, 239–59. Einsiedeln: Benziger, 1967.

"Christianity and the 'New Man.'" In *Theological Investigations 5: Later Writings*, translated by Karl–H. Kruger, 135–53. Baltimore: Helicon Press, 1966.

"Christmas in the Light of the Ignatian Exercises." In TI 7.3–7.

"The Concept of Existential Philosophy in Heidegger." *Philosophy Today* 13, no. 2 (Summer 1969): 126–37.

"The Concept of Mystery in Catholic Theology." In *Theological Investigations 4: More Recent Writings*, translated by Kevin Smyth, 36–73. Baltimore: Helicon Press, 1966. Original: "Über den Begriff des Geheimnisses in der katholischen Theologie." In *Schriften zur Theologie IV: Neuere Schriften*, 51–99. Einsiedeln: Benziger, 1964.

"Concerning the Relationship between Nature and Grace." In *Theological Investigations 1: God, Christ, Mary, and Grace,* translated by Cornelius Ernst, 297–317. Baltimore: Helicon Press, 1961.

"Courage for Devotion to Mary." In *Theological Investigations 23: Final Writings,* translated by Joseph Donceel and Hugh M. Riley, 129–39. New York: Crossroad, 1992.

"The Death of Jesus and the Closure of Revelation." In *Theological Investigations 18: God and Revelation,* translated by Edward Quinn, 132–42. New York: Crossroad, 1983.

"The Doctrine of the Spiritual Senses in the Middle Ages." In *Theological Investigations 16: Experience of the Spirit: Source of Theology, 104–34.* New York: Crossroad, 1983. Original: "La doctrine des 'sens spirituels' au Moyen-Age en particulier chez Saint Bonaventure." *Revue d'Ascétique et de Mystique* 14 (1933): 263–99.

"Encounters with the Risen Christ." In TI 7, 169–76.

Encounters with Silence. Translated by James M. Demske, SJ. Westminster, Md.: Newman Press, 1965.

Encyclopedia of Theology: A Concise Sacramentum Mundi, ed. New York: Continuum, 1975.

Foundations of Christian Faith: An Introduction to the Idea of Christianity. Translated by William V. Dych. New York: Crossroad, 1978.

"A Fragmentary Aspect of a Theological Evaluation of the Concept of the Future." In *Theological Investigations 10: Writings of 1965–1967, 2,* translated by David Bourke, 235–41. New York: Seabury Press, 1977.

Hearer of the Word: Laying the Foundation for a Philosophy of Religion. Translated by Joseph Donceel, edited by Andrew Tallon. New York: Continuum, 1994. Original: *Hörer des Wortes: Schriften zur Religionsphilosophie und zur Grundlegung der Theologie. Sämtliche Werke: Band 4.* Edited by Albert Raffelt. Freiburg im Breisgau: Herder, 1997.

"The Hermeneutics of Eschatological Assertions." In TI 4.323–46. Original: "Theologische Prinzipien der Hermeneutik eschatologischer Aussagen." *Zeitschrift für katholische Theologie* 82 (1960): 137–58.

"The Hiddenness of God." In TI 16.227–43.

"The History of the World and Salvation History." In TI 5.97–114.

"The Human Question of Meaning in the Face of the Absolute Mystery of God." In TI 18.89–103.

"The Ignatian Mysticism of Joy in the World." In TI 3.277–93.

"Ignatian Spirituality and Devotion to the Sacred Heart." In *Christian in the Market Place,* translated by Cecily Hastings, 119–46. New York: Sheed and Ward, 1966.

Ignatianischer Geist: Schriften zu den Exerzitien und zur Spiritualität des Ordens-gründers, Sämtliche Werke 13. Edited by Andreas Batlogg, Johannes Her-zgsell, and Stefan Kiechle. Freiburg: Herder, 2006.

"Ignatius Speaks to a Jesuit Today." In *Ignatius of Loyola,* introduction by Paul Imhof, translated by Rosaleen Ockenden, 11–38. London: Collins, 1979. Original: "Rede des Ignatius von Loyola an einen Jesuiten von heute." In *Wissenschaft und christlicher Glaube: Schriften zur Theologie XV,* edited by Paul Imhof, 373–408. Zurich: Benziger, 1983.

"Immanent and Transcendent Consummation of the World." In TI 10. 273–89.

"The Inexhaustible Transcendence of God and Our Concern for the Future." In TI 20.173–86.

"An Investigation of the Incomprehensibility of God in St. Thomas Aquinas." In TI 16.244–54.

Karl Rahner: Spiritual Writings. Edited by Philip Endean. Maryknoll, N.Y.: Orbis, 2004.

"The Logic of Concrete Individual Knowledge in Ignatius Loyola." In *The Dynamic Element in the Church,* translated by W. J. O'Hara, 84–170. New York: Herder and Herder, 1964. Original: "Die Logik der existentiellen Erkenntnis bei Ignatius v. Loyola." In *Das Dynamische in der Kirche,* 74–148. Freiburg: Herder, 1958.

"The Man of Today and Religion." In TI 6.3–20.

Maria, Mutter des Herrn: Studien zur Mariologie. Sämtliche Werke: Band 9. Edited by Regina Pacis Meyer. Freiburg im Breisgau: Herder, 2004.

Mary, Mother of the Lord: Theological Meditations. Translated by W. J. O'Hara. New York: Herder and Herder, 1963.

"Modern Piety and the Experience of Retreats." In TI 16. 135–55.

"On Angels." In *Theological Investigations 19: Faith and Ministry,* translated by Edward Quinn, 235–74. New York: Crossroad, 1983.

On the Theology of Death. Translated by C. H. Henkey. Revised by W. J. O'Hara. New York: Herder and Herder, 1965.

"On the Theology of Hope," In TI 10.242–59.

"Poetry and the Christian." In TI 4.357–67.

"Priest and Poet." In TI 3.294–317. Original: "Priester und Dichter." In *Schriften zur Theologie, Band III: Zur Theologie des Geistlichen Lebens,* 349–75. Einsiedeln: Benziger Verlag, 1956.

"Profane History and Salvation History." In *Theological Investigations 21: Science and Christian Faith,* translated by Hugh M. Riley, 3–15. New York: Crossroad, 1988.

"The Question of the Future." In *Theological Investigations 12: Confrontations 2,* translated by David Bourke, 181–201. New York: Seabury Press, 1974.

"The Question of Meaning as a Question of God." In TI 21.196–207.

"Reflections on Methodology in Theology." In TI 11.68–114. Original: "Überlegungen zur Methode der Theologie." In *Schriften zur Theologie IX*, 79–126.

"Some Implications of the Scholastic Concept of Uncreated Grace." In TI 1.319–46.

"Some Theses for a Theology of Devotion to the Sacred Heart." In TI 3.331–54.

Spirit in the World. Translated by William Dych, foreword by Johannes B. Metz. New York: Continuum, 1969. Original: *Geist in Welt: Philosophische Schriften. Sämtliche Werke: Band 2*. Edited by Albert Raffelt. Freiburg i.B.: Herder, 1996.

"The 'Spiritual Senses' according to Origen," in TI 16.81–103.

"The Theological Meaning of the Veneration of the Sacred Heart." In TI 8.217–28.

"Theological Observations on the Concept of Time." In TI 11.288–308.

"Theological Problems Entailed in the Idea of the 'New Earth.'" In TI 10.260–72.

"The Theology of the Symbol." In TI 4.221–52.

"A Theology That We Can Live With." In TI 21.99–112.

The Trinity. Translated by Joseph Donceel; introduction, index, and glossary by Catherine Mowry LaCugna. New York: Crossroad, 1997.

"Unity–Love–Mystery." In TI 8.229–47.

"The Unity of Spirit and Matter in the Christian Understanding of Faith." In TI 6.153–77.

"Utopia and Reality: The Shape of Christian Existence Caught between the Ideal and the Real." In *Theological Investigations 22: Humane Society and the Church of Tomorrow*, translated by Joseph Donceel, edited by Paul Imhof, 26–37. New York: Crossroad, 1991.

"*Virginitas in Partu*. A Contribution to the Problem of the Development of Dogma and of Tradition." In TI 4.134–62.

"What Does It Mean Today to Believe in Jesus Christ?" In TI 18.143–56.

"Why Does God Allow Us to Suffer?" In TI 19.194–208.

WORKS BY MARTIN HEIDEGGER

"Anaximander's Saying (1946)." In *Off the Beaten Track*, translated by Julian Young and Kenneth Haynes, 242–80. New York: Cambridge University Press, 2002.

Being and Time. Translated by John Macquarrie and Edward Robinson. San Francisco: HarperSanFrancisco, 1962.

Contributions to Philosophy (From Enowning). Translated by Parvis Emad and Kenneth Maly. Bloomington: Indiana University Press, 1999.

Country Path Conversations. Translated by Bret Davis. Bloomington: Indiana University Press, 2010. Original: *Feldweg-Gespräche (1944/45): Gesamtausgabe 77.* Frankfurt: Vittorio Klostermann, 1995.

Discourse on Thinking. Translated by John M. Anderson and E. Hans Freund. New York: Harper and Row, 1966. Original: *Gelassenheit.* Pfullingen: Neske, 1959.

Elucidations of Hölderlin's Poetry. Translated by Keith Hoeller. Amherst, N.Y.: Humanity Books, 2000. Original: *Erläuterungen zu Hölderlins Dichtung: Gesamtausgabe, Band 4.* Frankfurt am Main: Vittorio Klostermann, 1981.

The End of Philosophy. Translated by Joan Stambaugh. Chicago: University of Chicago Press, 2003.

Hölderlin's Hymn "The Ister." Translated by William McNeill and Julia Davis. Bloomington: Indiana University Press, 1996.

Hölderlin's Hymnen 'Germanien' und 'Der Rhein.' Frankfurt: Vittorio Klostermann, 1999.

Introduction to Metaphysics. Translated by Gregory Fried and Richard Polt. New Haven, Conn.: Yale University Press, 2000.

Kant and the Problem of Metaphysics. 5th ed. Translated by Richard Taft. Bloomington: Indiana University Press, 1997. Original: *Kant und das Problem der Metaphysik.* Frankfurt: Vittorio Klostermann, 1998.

"Letter on Humanism." In *Basic Writings,* edited by David Farrell Krell, 217–65. New York: HarperCollins, 2008.

Nietzsche: Volume I. The Will to Power as Art and Volume II. The Eternal Recurrence of the Same. Translated by David Farrell Krell. New York: HarperOne, 1991.

Nietzsche: Volume III. The Will to Power as Knowledge and Metaphysics and Volume IV. Nihilism. Translated by David Farrell Krell. New York: HarperOne, 1991.

On the Way to Language. Translated by Peter D. Hertz and Joan Stambaugh. New York: Harper and Row, 1971. Original: *Unterwegs zur Sprache: Gesamtausgabe 12.* Frankfurt: Vittorio Klostermann, 1985.

"The Origin of the Work of Art." In *Poetry, Language, Thought,* translated by Albert Hofstadter, 17–86. New York: Harper Perennial Modern Classics, 2001. Original: *"Der Ursprung des Kunstwerkes."* In *Holzwege, Gesamtausgabe Band 5,* 1–74. Frankfurt: Vittorio Klostermann, 1977.

Parmenides. Translated by André Schuwer and Richard Rojcewicz. Bloomington: Indiana University Press, 1992.

"Phenomenology and Theology." In *The Religious,* edited by John D. Caputo, 49–66. Malden, Mass.: Blackwell Publishers, 2002.

The Question concerning Technology. Translated by William Lovitt. New York: Harper and Row, 1977.

Schelling's Treatise on the Essence of Human Freedom. Translated by Joan Stambaugh. Athens: Ohio University Press, 1985.

"The Thing." In *Bremen and Freiburg Lectures: Insight into That Which Is and Basic Principles of Thinking,* translated by Andrew Mitchell, 5–23. Bloomington: Indiana University Press, 2012.

"The Thing." In *Poetry, Language, Thought,* 161–84.

Vorträge und Aufsätze, Gesamtausgabe 7. Frankfurt: Vittorio Klostermann, 2000.

"What Are Poets For?" In *Poetry, Language, Thought,* 89–139. Original: "Wozu Dichter." In *Holzwege,* 269–320.

What Is Metaphysics?" In *Basic Writings,* 89–110.

"Who Is Nietzsche's Zarathustra?" In *Nietzsche: Volume Two,* translated by David Farrell Krell, 211–33. New York: Harper and Row, 1984.

"*Zur Erörterung der Gelassenheit: Aus einem Feldweggespräch über das Denken.*" In *Aus der Erfahrung des Denkens: Gesamtausgabe 13.* Frankfurt: Vittorio Klostermann, 1983.

OTHER SOURCES

Aquinas, Thomas. *Summa theologiae.* Latin text and English translation, various translators. Cambridge: Blackfriars, 1964ff.

Bacik, James. *Apologetics and the Eclipse of Mystery: Mystagogy according to Karl Rahner.* Notre Dame, Ind.: University of Notre Dame Press, 1980.

Balthasar, Hans Urs von. "Rezension: Karl Rahner, *Geist in Welt,* und J. B. Lotz, *Sein und Welt.*" *Zeitschrift für katholische Theologie* 63 (1939): 371–79.

———. *The Glory of the Lord 1: Seeing the Form.* Translated by Erasmo Leiva-Merikakis. San Francisco: Ignatius Press, 1982.

———. *The Moment of Christian Witness.* Translated by Richard Beckley. San Francisco: Ignatius Press, 1994.

———. *Theo-Drama: Theological Dramatic Theory V: The Last Act,* Translated by Graham Harrison. San Francisco: Ignatius Press, 1998.

Bambach, Charles. *Heidegger's Roots: Nietzsche, National Socialism, and the Greeks.* Ithaca, N.Y.: Cornell University Press, 2003.

Batlogg, Andreas. *Die Mysterien des Lebens Jesu bei Karl Rahner: Zugang zum Christusglauben.* Innsbruck: Tyrolia, 2001.

Batlogg, Andreas R., and Melvin E. Michalski, ed. and trans. *Encounters with*

Karl Rahner: Remembrances of Rahner by Those Who Knew Him. Milwaukee, Wis.: Marquette University Press, 2009.

Bauerschmidt, Frederick. "Aesthetics: The Theological Sublime." In *Radical Orthodoxy: A New Theology,* edited by John Milbank, Catherine Pickstock, and Graham Ward, 201–19. New York: Routledge, 1999.

Betz, John. "Beyond the Sublime: The Aesthetics of the Analogy of Being." *Modern Theology* 21, no. 3 (2005): 367–411 and 22, no. 1 (2006): 1–50.

Blond, Louis. *Heidegger and Nietzsche: Overcoming Metaphysics.* New York: Continuum, 2010.

Blond, Phillip. "Introduction: Theology before Philosophy." In *Post-Secular Philosophy: Between Philosophy and Theology,* edited by Phillip Blond, 1–33. New York: Routledge, 1998.

Bonaventure. *De reductione artium ad theologiam.* In *Saint Bonaventure's De Reductione Artium ad Theologiam: A Commentary with an Introduction and Translation, 20–41,* by Emma Thérèse Healy. St. Bonaventure, N.Y.: Franciscan Institute, St. Bonaventure University, 1955.

Bonsor, Jack Arthur. *Rahner, Heidegger, and Truth: Karl Rahner's Notion of Christian Truth, the Influence of Heidegger.* Lanham, Md.: University Press of America, 1987.

Börsig-Hover, Lina, ed. *Unterwegs zur Heimat: Martin Heidegger zum 100. Geburtstag.* Fridingen: Börsig-Verlag, 1989.

Bradley, Denis J. M. "Rahner's *Spirit in the World*: Aquinas or Hegel?" *The Thomist* 41, no.2 (1977): 167–99.

Burke, Patrick. *Reinterpreting Rahner: A Critical Study of His Major Themes.* New York: Fordham University Press, 2002.

Capobianco, Richard. "Heidegger's Turn toward Home: On Dasein's Primordial Relation to Being. *Epoché* 10, no. 1 (2005): 155–73.

Caponi, Francis J. "A Speechless Grace: Karl Rahner on Religious Language." *International Journal of Systematic Theology* 9, no. 2 (April 2007): 200–221.

Caputo, John. *The Mystical Element of Heidegger's Thought.* New York: Fordham University Press, 1986.

Conway, Pádraic, and Fáinche Ryan, eds. *Karl Rahner: Theologian for the Twenty-First Century.* New York: Peter Lang, 2010.

Crowley, Paul. "Encountering the Religious Other: Challenges to Rahner's Transcendental Project." *Theological Studies* 71 (2010): 567–85.

Davis, Bret. *Heidegger and the Will: On the Way to Gelassenheit.* Evanston, Ill.: Northwestern University Press, 2007.

Derrida, Jacques. *Of Spirit: Heidegger and the Question.* Translated by Geoffrey

Bennington and Rachel Bowlby. Chicago: University of Chicago Press, 1991.

———. "On a Newly Arisen Apocalyptic Tone in Philosophy." In *Raising the Tone of Philosophy: Late Essays by Immanuel Kant and Transformative Critique by Jacques Derrida,* translated by John Leavey Jr., edited by Peter Fenves, 117–72. Baltimore: Johns Hopkins University Press, 1993.

Dreyfus, Hubert. "Heidegger on Gaining a Free Relation to Technology." In *Heidegger Reexamined, Volume 3: Art, Poetry, and Technology,* edited by Mark Wrathall and Hubert Dreyfus, 163–74. New York: Routledge, 2002.

Dupré, Louis. *Passage to Modernity: An Essay in the Hermeneutics of Nature and Culture.* New Haven, Conn.: Yale University Press, 1993.

Egan, Harvey. *Karl Rahner: Mystic of Everyday Life.* New York: Crossroad, 1998.

Eicher, Peter. *Die anthropologische Wende: Karl Rahners philosophischer Weg vom Wesen des Menschen zur personalen Existenz.* Freiburg: Universitätsverlag, 1970.

Emad, Parvis. *On the Way to Heidegger's Contributions to Philosophy.* Madison, Wis.: University of Wisconsin Press, 2007.

Endean, Philip. "Introduction," in *Karl Rahner: Spiritual Writings.*

———. *Karl Rahner and Ignatian Spirituality.* New York: Oxford University Press, 2004.

———. "Has Rahnerian Theology a Future?" In *The Cambridge Companion to Karl Rahner,* edited by Declan Marmion and Mary Hines, 281–96. New York: Cambridge University Press, 2005.

Ernst, Cornelius. "Introduction." In TI 1.v–xix.

Falque, Emmanuel. "The Phenomenological Act of *Persucratio* in the *Proemium* of St. Bonaventure's *Commentary on the Sentences.*" Translated by Elisa Mangina. *Medieval Philosophy and Theology* 10 (2001): 1–22.

Faye, Emmanuel. *Heidegger: The Introduction of Nazism into Philosophy.* Translated by Michael Smith. New Haven, Conn.: Yale University Press, 2009.

Fields, Stephen. "Balthasar and Rahner on the Spiritual Senses." *Theological Studies* 57 (1996): 224–41.

———. *Being as Symbol: On the Origins and Development of Karl Rahner's Metaphysics.* Washington, D.C.: Georgetown University Press, 2000.

———. "Rahner and the Symbolism of Language." *Philosophy and Theology* 15, no. 1 (2003): 165–89.

Fiorenza, Francis P. "Karl Rahner and the Kantian Problematic." In *Spirit in the World,* xix–lv.

Fritsch, Harald. *Vollendende Selbstmitteilung Gottes an seine Schöpfung: Die Eschatologie Karl Rahners.* Würzburg: Echter Verlag, 2006.

Fritz, Peter Joseph. "I Am, of Course, No Prophet: Rahner's Modest Eschatological Remark." *Philosophy and Theology* 23 (2011): 317–32.

———. "Between Center and Periphery: Mary and the Saints in Rahner." *Philosophy and Theology* 24, no. 2 (2012): 297–311.

———. "Karl Rahner Repeated in Jean-Luc Marion?" *Theological Studies* 73 (2012): 318–38.

Gadamer, Hans-Georg. "The Beginning and the End of Philosophy." In *Martin Heidegger: Critical Assessments, Volume 1: Philosophy,* edited by Christopher E. Macann, 16–28. New York: Routledge, 1992.

Gosetti-Ferencei, Jennifer Anna. *Heidegger, Hölderlin, and the Subject of Poetic Language: Toward a New Poetics of Dasein.* New York: Fordham University Press, 2004.

Guardini, Romano. *The End of the Modern World.* Introduction by Frederick Wilhelmsen, foreword by Richard John Neuhaus, translated by Joseph Theman et al. Wilmington, Del.: ISI Books, 1998.

Hart, David Bentley. *The Beauty of the Infinite: The Aesthetics of Christian Truth.* Grand Rapids, Mich.: Eerdmans, 2003.

Hemming, Laurence Paul. *Heidegger's Atheism: The Refusal of a Theological Voice.* Notre Dame, Ind.: University of Notre Dame Press, 2002.

———. "Introduction." In *The Movement of Nihilism: Heidegger's Thinking after Nietzsche,* edited by Laurence Paul Hemming, Bogdan Costea, and Kostas Amiridis. New York: Continuum, 2011.

Hines, Mary E. *The Transformation of Dogma: An Introduction to Karl Rahner on Doctrine.* New York: Paulist Press, 1989.

———. "Rahner on Development of Doctrine: How Relevant is Rahner Today?" *Philosophy and Theology* 12, no. 1 (2000): 111–30.

Hogan, Kevin. "Entering into Otherness: The Postmodern Critique of the Subject and Karl Rahner's Theological Anthropology." *Horizons* 25, no. 2 (1998): 181–202.

Hölderlin, Friedrich. *Selected Poems and Fragments.* Translated by Michael Hamburger. New York: Penguin Books, 2007.

Hurd, Robert. "Heidegger and Aquinas: A Rahnerian Bridge." *Philosophy Today* 28 (1984): 105–37.

Hyland, Drew, and John Panteleimon Manoussakis, eds. *Heidegger and the Greeks: Interpretive Essays.* Bloomington, Ind.: Indiana University Press, 2006.

Imhof, Paul, and Harvey Egan. *Karl Rahner in Dialogue: Conversations and Interviews, 1965–1982.* New York: Crossroad, 1986.

Kant, Immanuel. *The Critique of the Power of Judgment.* Translated by Paul

Guyer and Eric Matthews. New York: Cambridge University Press, 2000.

———. *Critique of Pure Reason.* Translated by Paul Guyer and Allen Wood. New York: Cambridge University Press, 1998.

Kilby, Karen. "Balthasar and Karl Rahner." In *The Cambridge Companion to Hans Urs von Balthasar,* edited by Edward T. Oakes and David Moss, 256–68. New York: Cambridge University Press, 2004.

———. *Karl Rahner: Theology and Philosophy.* London: Routledge, 2004.

Klein, Terrance W. "The Forge of Language." *Philosophy and Theology* 15, no. 1 (2003): 143–63.

Kovacs, George. "The Impact of Heidegger's *Beiträge zur Philosophie* on Understanding His Lifework." *Heidegger Studies* 27 (2011): 155–76.

LaSalle-Klein, Robert. "Rethinking Rahner on Grace and Symbol: New Proposals from the Americas." In *Rahner beyond Rahner: A Great Theologian Encounters the Pacific Rim,* edited by Paul Crowley, 87–99. Lanham, Md.: Rowman and Littlefield, 2005.

Little, Brent. "Anthropology and Art in the Theology of Karl Rahner." *The Heythrop Journal* 52 (November 2011): 939–51.

Losinger, Anton. *The Anthropological Turn: The Human Orientation of the Theology of Karl Rahner.* Translated by Daniel O. Dahlstrom. New York: Fordham University Press, 2000.

Ludlow, Morwenna. *Universal Salvation: Eschatology in the Thought of Gregory of Nyssa and Karl Rahner.* New York: Oxford University Press, 2000.

Lyotard, Jean-François. *Lessons on the Analytic of the Sublime.* Translated by Elizabeth Rottenberg. Stanford, Calif.: Stanford University Press, 1994.

Maly, Kenneth. *Heidegger's Possibility: Language, Emergence—Saying Be-ing.* Toronto: University of Toronto Press, 2008.

Marion, Jean-Luc. *The Idol and Distance: Five Studies.* Translated by Thomas A. Carlson. New York: Fordham University Press, 2001.

Maritain, Jacques. *Integral Humanism.* Translated by Joseph Evans. New York: Charles Scribner's Sons, 1968.

Marmion, Declan. *A Spirituality of Everyday Faith: A Theological Investigation of the Notion of Spirituality in Karl Rahner.* Grand Rapids, Mich.: Eerdmans, 1998.

Marmion, Declan, and Mary Hines. "Introduction." In *The Cambridge Companion to Karl Rahner,* edited by Declan Marmion and Mary Hines, 3–10. New York: Cambridge University Press, 2005.

Masson, Robert. "Rahner and Heidegger: Being, Hearing, and God." *The Thomist* 37, no. 3 (1973): 455–88.

———. "Interpreting Rahner's Metaphoric Logic." *Theological Studies* 71 (June 2010): 380–409.

McDermott, John M. "The Analogy of Knowing in Karl Rahner." *International Philosophical Quarterly* 36, no. 2 (June 1996): 201–16.

McGrath, S. J. *The Early Heidegger and Medieval Philosophy*. (Washington, D.C.: Catholic University of America Press, 2006.

Metz, Johann Baptist. *A Passion for God: The Mystical-Political Dimension of Christianity*. Translated by J. Matthew Ashley. Mahwah, N.J.: Paulist Press, 1997.

———. *Faith in History and Society: Toward a Practical Fundamental Theology*. Translated by J. Matthew Ashley. New York: Crossroad, 2007.

Milbank, John. "The Sublime in Kierkegaard." *The Heythrop Journal* 37, no 3 (1996): 298–321.

———. "Sublimity: The Modern Transcendent." In *Transcendence: Philosophy, Literature, and Theology Approach the Beyond*, edited by Regina Schwartz, 207–29. New York: Routledge, 2004.

———. *Theology and Social Theory*. Malden, Mass.: Blackwell, 2006.

Mugerauer, Robert. *Heidegger and Homecoming: The Leitmotif in the Later Writings*. Toronto: University of Toronto Press, 2008.

Nietzsche, Friedrich. *Ecce Homo*. In *The Anti-Christ, Ecce Homo, Twilight of the Idols, and Other Writings*, translated by Aaron Ridley and Judith Norman. New York: Cambridge University, 2005.

O'Donovan, Leo, ed. *A World of Grace: An Introduction to the Themes and Foundations of Karl Rahner's Theology*. Washington, D.C.: Georgetown University Press, 1995.

O'Meara, Thomas. *God in the World: A Guide to Karl Rahner's Theology*. Collegeville, Minn.: Liturgical Press, 2007.

———. "Johannes B. Lotz, SJ, and Martin Heidegger in Conversation: A Translation of Lotz's *Im Gespräch*." *American Catholic Philosophical Quarterly* 84, no. 1 (2010): 125–31.

O'Regan, Cyril. *Theology and the Spaces of Apocalyptic*. Milwaukee, Wis.: Marquette University Press, 2009.

Phan, Peter. *Eternity in Time: A Study of Karl Rahner's Eschatology*. Cranbury, N.J.: Associate University Presses, 1988.

Polt, Richard. *The Emergency of Being: On Heidegger's Contributions to Philosophy*. Ithaca, N.Y.: Cornell University Press, 2006.

Pseudo-Dionysius. *The Complete Works*. Translated by Colm Luibheid and Paul Rorem. Mahwah, N. J.: Paulist Press, 1987.

Purcell, Michael. "Rahner Amid Modernity and Post-Modernity." In *The Cambridge Companion to Karl Rahner,* edited by Declan Marmion and Mary Hines, 195–210. New York: Cambridge University Press, 2005.

Raffelt, Albert. "Geist in Welt: Einige Anmerkungen zur Interpretation." In *Die philosophische Quellen der Theologie Karl Rahners,* edited by Harald Schöndorf. Freiburg, i.b.: Herder, 2005.

Richardson, William J. *Heidegger: Through Phenomenology to Thought.* The Hague: M. Nijhoff, 1963.

Rilke, Rainer Maria. *The Duino Elegies and Sonnets to Orpheus* (bilingual edition). Translated by A Poulin Jr. New York: Houghton Mifflin Books, 2005.

Risser, James, ed. *Heidegger toward the Turn: Essays on the Work of the 1930s.* Albany, N.Y.: SUNY Press, 1999.

Rosiek, Jan. *Maintaining the Sublime: Heidegger and Adorno.* New York: Peter Lang, 2000.

Ross, Alison. *The Aesthetic Paths of Philosophy: Presentation in Kant, Heidegger, Lacoue-Labarthe, and Nancy.* Stanford, Calif.: Stanford University Press, 2007.

Sartre, Jean-Paul. *Existentialism Is a Humanism.* Translated by Carol Macomber; introduction by Annie Cohen-Solal; notes and preface by Arlette Elkaïm-Sartre; edited by John Kulka. New Haven, Conn.: Yale University Press, 2007.

Schelling, Friedrich. *Philosophical Investigations into the Essence of Human Freedom.* Translated by Jeff Love and Johannes Schmidt. Albany, N.Y.: SUNY Press, 2006.

Sheehan, Thomas. *Karl Rahner: The Philosophical Foundations.* Athens: Ohio University Press, 1987.

———. "Rahner's Transcendental Project." In *The Cambridge Companion to Karl Rahner,* edited by Declan Marmion and Mary Hines, 29–42. New York: Cambridge University Press, 2005.

Thiessen, Gesa Elsbeth. "Karl Rahner: Toward a Theological Aesthetics." In *The Cambridge Companion to Karl Rahner,* edited by Declan Marmion and Mary Hines, 225–34. New York: Cambridge University Press, 2005.

Viladesau, Richard. *Theological Aesthetics: God in Imagination, Beauty, and Art.* New York: Oxford University Press, 1999.

———. *Theology and the Arts: Encountering God through Music, Art and Rhetoric.* New York: Paulist Press, 2000.

Voiss, James. "Rahner, von Balthasar and the Question of Theological Aesthetics." In *Finding God in All Things: Celebrating Bernard Lonergan, John Court-*

ney Murray, and Karl Rahner, ed. Mark Bosco and David Stagaman, 167–81. New York: Fordham University Press, 2007.

Vorgrimler, Herbert. *Understanding Karl Rahner: An Introduction to His Life and Thought.* Translated by John Bowden. New York: Crossroad, 1986.

Wrathall, Mark. "Philosophy, Thinkers, and Heidegger's Place in the History of Being." In *Appropriating Heidegger,* edited by James Faulconer and Mark Wrathall, 9–29. New York: Cambridge University Press, 2000.

——. "Discourse Language Saying Showing." In *Heidegger and Unconcealment: Truth, Language, and History* by Mark A. Wrathall, 119–55. New York: Cambridge University Press, 2011.

Young, Julian. *Heidegger's Philosophy of Art.* New York: Cambridge University Press, 2001.

Ziarek, Krzysztof. *Inflected Language: Toward a Hermeneutics of Nearness: Heidegger, Levinas, Stevens, Celan.* Albany, N.Y.: SUNY Press, 1994.

INDEX

281

Karl Rahner's Theological Aesthetics was designed in Agmena and Garda Titling No. 2
and composed by Kachergis Book Design of Pittsboro, North Carolina. It was printed
on 60-pound Sebago IV B18 Cream and bound by Maple Press of York, Pennsylvania.